TANIA LEÓN'S STRIDE

A POLYRHYTHMIC LIFE

ALEJANDRO L. MADRID

**UNIVERSITY OF
ILLINOIS PRESS**
Urbana, Chicago, and Springfield

Grant from the General Fund of the American
Musicological Society,
supported in part by the National Endowment for the
Humanities and
the Andrew W. Mellon Foundation

Library of Congress Cataloging-in-Publication Data
Names: Madrid, Alejandro L., author.
Title: Tania León's Stride: a polyrhythmic life / Alejandro
    L. Madrid.
Description: Urbana: University of Illinois Press,
    2021. | Series: Music in American life | Includes
    bibliographical references and index.
Identifiers: LCCN 2021028011 (print) | LCCN 2021028012
    (ebook) | ISBN 9780252043949 (hardcover) | ISBN
    9780252086014 (paperback) | ISBN 9780252052873
    (ebook)
Subjects: LCSH: León, Tania. | Composers—United
    States—Biography.
Classification: LCC ML410.L514 M33 2021 (print) | LCC
    ML410.L514 (ebook) | DDC 780.92 [B]—dc23
LC record available at https://lccn.loc.gov/2021028011
LC ebook record available at https://lccn.loc.gov/
    2021028012

Dlya moikh russkikh zhenshchin,
Marina Alejandrovna i Ekaterina Petrovna

Contents

List of Figures   ix

List of Music Examples   xi

Acknowledgments   xiii

Introduction   Notes on a Biographical Counterpoint   1

Chapter 1   Tonic: The House on Salud Street   11

Chapter 2   Modulation and Displacement:
cubana de adentro . . . cubana de afuera   33

Chapter 3   Syncopation and Color:
Adapting to New Life Rhythms   59

Chapter 4   Direction: Leading in Music, Leading in Life   93

Chapter 5   Voice: Style and Idea in the Music of Tania León   126

Chapter 6   Canon: Representation, Identity, and Legacy   166

Epilogue   Tania León's *Stride*: An Echo that Reaches Our Ears   181

Appendix A   List of Works   185

Appendix B   Tania León's Life   193

Notes   203

Bibliography   229

Index   241

List of Figures

Figure 1.1   Tania León and the National Symphony Orchestra of Cuba.   12

Figure 1.2   Marta Valdés, Juan Piñera, Tania León, and Alfredo Diez Nieto; Oscar Jr. observes the scene in the background.   13

Figure 1.3   Dora "Mima" Ferrán and Oscar León.   15

Figure 1.4   Tania León's paternal grandparents, José León and Rosa Julia de los Mederos "Mamota."   16

Figure 1.5   Two-year-old Tania León wearing a Carmen Miranda–inspired dress made by her grandmother, Mamota.   17

Figure 1.6   Eight-year-old Tania León practicing piano at home.   21

Figure 1.7   Tania León at the time of her secondary school graduation.   23

Figure 1.8   Postcard of the Eiffel Tower sent to Tania Léon in 1952.   24

Figure 2.1   Tania León, Mima, and Oscar José León during one of the composer's first trips back to Cuba.   43

Figure 2.2   Pre-concert talk during Sonidos de las Américas-Cuba. From left to right, Ileana Pérez-Velázquez, José Loyola, Keyla Orozco, Tania León, Juan Piñera, and Orlando Jacinto García.   48

Figure 2.3   Conversation between Harold Gramatges, Alfredo Diez
              Nieto, and Aurelio de la Vega.   50
Figure 2.4   Tania León conducting a rehearsal of *Indígena* with Cuba's
              National Symphony Orchestra.   54
Figure 3.1   The first Dance Theatre of Harlem company at Church of
              the Master.   66
Figure 3.2   The Dance Theatre of Harlem Orchestra.   67
Figure 3.3   Arthur Mitchell and Tania León during the recording of
              Tones.   69
Figure 3.4   Karel Shook, Tania León, and Arthur Mitchell. Two pictures
              that tell a story.   73
Figure 3.5   Tania León and Marian Anderson discussing *Spiritual
              Suite.*   77
Figure 3.6   Arthur Mitchell, Tania León, Nelson Rockefeller, and
              Nelson Mandela during the Dance Theatre of Harlem South
              African Tour.   84
Figure 3.7   Wole Soyinka, Tania León, and Henry Louis Gates Jr.   86
Figure 3.8   A picture of Tania León's integrated class in elementary
              school. León is fourth from the right, second row.   89
Figure 4.1   Tania León conducting Joaquín Rodrigo's *Concierto de
              Aranjuez* with the Concert Orchestra of Long Island and
              Manuel Barrueco as soloist.   96
Figure 4.2   Tania León and Leonard Bernstein in Tanglewood.   97
Figure 4.3   Tania León conducting.   100
Figure 4.4   Gathering at Noel Da Costa's apartment. Standing: Talib
              Rasul Hakim, Hale Smith, Oliver Lake, and Carman Moore.
              Seated: Arthur Cunningham, Noel Da Costa, Tania León,
              Julius Eastman, and Dorothy Rudd Moore, 1977.   102
Figure 4.5   Tania León and John Duffy, founder of Meet the
              Composer.   106
Figure 5.1   Programmatic Chart of *Indígena.*   154
Figure 5.2   Programmatic Chart of *Horizons.*   157
Figure 6.1   Tania León, Eun Lee, and Ivory Nunez-Medrano (lower
              right corner) at the Hostos Center for the Arts and
              Culture.   167

List of Music Examples

Example 5.1   Tania León, *Tones* (1970–1971), second movement, mm. 16–17, piano reduction.   133

Example 5.2   León, *Tones*, third movement, mm. 20–23, piano reduction.   134

Example 5.3   León, *Tones*, third movement, mm. 162–163, piano reduction.   135

Example 5.4   León, *Tones*, first movement, mm. 113–115, piano reduction.   136

Example 5.5   Tania León, *Haiku* (1973), "Haiku I" and "Haiku II," harmonic reduction.   139

Example 5.6   León, *Haiku*, "Haiku VIII," for solo flute.   140

Example 5.7   León, *Haiku*, "Haiku IV," harmonic reduction.   141

Example 5.8   Tania León, *Four Pieces for Violoncello* (1981), "Allegro," m. 5.   141

Example 5.9   León, *Four Pieces for Violoncello*, "Montuno," mm. 5–7.   142

Example 5.10   Cuban son clave rhythmic pattern.   142

Example 5.11   León, *Four Pieces for Violoncello*, "Lento doloroso, sempre cantabile," mm. 1–4.   143

Example 5.12   León, *Four Pieces for Violoncello*, "Vivo," mm. 7–8.   143

Example 5.13   Tania León, *Batá* (1985), mm. 1–2, piccolo.   146

Example 5.14   León, *Batá*, mm. 137–141, reduction: violin and cowbell parts.   147

Example 5.15   Tania León, *Carabalí* (1991), mm. 61–69, reduction: wind section.   149

Example 5.16   León, *Carabalí*, mm. 188–190, reduction: horns, trumpets, and trombone parts.   150

Example 5.17   Abelardo Valdés, "Almendra" (1938), riff from the montuno section.   150

Example 5.18   León, *Carabalí*, mm. 12–14, reduction: piccolo, flute, oboe, clarinet, contrabassoon, and horn parts.   151

Example 5.19   Tania León, *Indígena* (1991), mm. 91–93, trumpet part.   154

Example 5.20   León, *Indígena*, mm. 114–117, trumpet part.   155

Example 5.21   León, *Indígena*, mm. 165, piano part.   155

Example 5.22   Tania León, *Horizons* (1999), mm. 110–122.   158–159

Example 5.23   León, *Horizons*, m. 76, piano part.   160

Example 5.24   Tania León, *Axon* (2002), m. 7.   163

Example 5.25   León, *Axon*, m. 76.   163

Acknowledgments

This project reflects the interest and support of many individuals. Foremost, I wish to express my deep gratitude to Tania León for entrusting me with writing about her, her music, and her life. Without her commitment, patience, and generosity at every step of the road this project would simply not have been possible. I would also like to thank Brandon Fradd and The Newburgh Institute for the Arts and Ideas for commissioning the book and providing generous funding to conduct multisited archival and oral research, write the manuscript, and see it through publication. I am also eternally grateful to all the relatives, colleagues, friends, and students of León who shared their experiences and anecdotes with me. The list is too long to include here but their names are included at the end of the book's bibliography. I am especially thankful to Sergio Cote-Barco for accepting my invitation to be a "composer in residence" in Chapter 5. Sergio's refined ear and savvy listening strategies were fundamental in helping me develop a novel and rich contrapuntal way to analyze León's music.

I have been invited to share the ideas behind this book at several conferences and study groups. I want to thank their members and constituencies for patiently listening to my concepts as they were taking shape and for providing much-needed feedback. Certainly, these visits presented plenty of opportunities for debate and intellectual exchange. I first talked about this project at the 83rd Annual Meeting of the American Musicological Society in Rochester, New York. There, I benefitted enormously from the feedback provided by the session participants, Brigid Cohen, Laura Jordán, and Susan Thomas; the session respondent, Andrea Bohlman; the session moderator, Eduardo Herrera; and the many engaged audience members who provided feedback and suggestions, especially Ana Alonso-Minutti, Eric Johns, and Marysol Quevedo. I am particularly thankful to Daniela Fugellie for inviting me to share my work with her colleagues and graduate students at Universidad Alberto Hurtado's Instituto de Música in Santiago de Chile, where I also owe a debt of gratitude to Juan Pablo González for his enthusiastic welcoming. Likewise, my participation at the University of North Carolina's Symposia in Music and Culture was a unique moment to discuss my ideas with deeply respected colleagues, especially Annegret Fauser, David Garcia, and Mark Katz, and their graduate students. I am very grateful for this opportunity. I would also like to thank Emily Abrams Ansari and Catherine Nolan for welcoming me to the Graduate Colloquium Lecture Series at Western University to share my project. Finally, I am thankful to Matt Mendez and the musicology graduate students at Yale University's Department of Music, who invited me to speak about this research project at their Guest Lecture Series.

A number of archives and libraries and their staff facilitated my research and deserve special thanks here. They include Lenora Schneller and the staff at the Sidney Cox Library of Music and Dance and Bonna Boettcher and the staff at the John M. Olin Library, both at Cornell University; Anne Rhodes, Research Archivist for the Oral History of American Music at Yale University; Liza Vick, Head of the Otto E. Albrecht Music Library and Eugene Ormandy Music and Media Center of the University of Pennsylvania Libraries; April L. James, Reader Services Librarian and Eri Mizukane, Administrative and Reprographic Services Coordinator at the Kislak Center for Special Collections of the University of Pennsylvania Libraries; and the staff at the Music and Dance Divisions of the Dorothy and Lewis B. Cullman Center at the New York Public Library for the Performing Arts. In Cuba, I am indebted to María Elena Vinueza and the staff at Casa de las Américas' Departamento de Música, especially Carmen Souto Anido and Layda Ferrando, who always go out of their way to make my visits to their country productive and fond experiences.

My work could not have been carried out without the help of my research assistants in Cuba and the United States. In Havana, I could not have asked for better research assistants than Liliana González Moreno and Gabriela Rojas Sierra, who impeccably conducted research on my behalf when I was unable to be there, organized my research agenda before I traveled to the island to interview relatives and friends of León, and helped me secure permissions after my visit. In Ithaca, Martha Mateus, Frederick Cruz Nowell, and Carlos Ramírez were in charge of the often tedious job of transcribing countless hours of interview audio files. Thanks to Jordan Musser for his indexing and proofreading job.

Likewise, many individual friends and colleagues contributed to my research. I am forever grateful to all of them. They include Arved Ashby, Dan Blim, David Borden, Carole Fernández, Dana Gooley, Rob Haskins, Sara Haefeli, Ailer Pérez Gómez, Carmen Cecilia Piñero, Jesús Ramos-Kittrell, Lena Rodríguez Duchesne, Nairin Rodríguez Duverger, and Evis Sammoutis. For many reasons I had a hard time deciding on the title of this book, and I owe a big debt of gratitude to all the friends and colleagues who generously shared with me their ideas and feedback about the different versions of the title I entertained; they include Emily Abrams Ansari, Ana Alonso-Minutti, Catherine Appert, Marcos Balter, Seth Brodsky, Charity Anne Caldwell, Guadalupe Caro Cocotle, Sergio de Regules, Sam Dwinell, Kai Fikentscher, Brandon Fradd, Kyra Gaunt, Dana Gooley, Justin Grant, Alisha Jones, Kendra Leonard, Tamara Levitz, Ana María Ochoa-Gautier, Carmen Cecilia Piñero, Jesús Ramos-Kittrell, Nancy Rao, Will Robin, Diana Marcela Rodríguez, Brenda Romero, Suzanne Ryan Melamed, Dan Sharp, Susan Thomas, and Sean Williams. At Peermusic, I would like to thank especially Todd Vunderink, Karen Hayden, and Karen Heymann for facilitating all the scores of Tania León's music I requested and for granting permission to publish the music examples in Chapter 4. At the Dance Theatre of Harlem, I am also deeply thankful to Anna Glass and Theara Ward for sharing historical pictures from the company's archive. I am grateful to Ed Yim and Stephanie Polonio—former President and current Development Associate of the American Composers Orchestra, respectively—and to Jesse Rosen and Julia Gonzalez—current President/CEO and Executive Assistant to the President/CEO of the League of American Orchestras, respectively—for loaning me pictures of the Sonidos de las Américas festivals from their institutional as well as personal archives, and for generously giving me permission to use them in the book. I am also indebted especially to friends and colleagues who have provided kind and detailed comments and feedback on specific chapters of the book at various stages; they include Maria Cristina Garcia, Kyra Gaunt, Marc Gidal, William Robin, James Spinazzola, and María de los Angeles Torres. I also want to thank Richard Carlin for his editorial work with the manuscript in its final stage.

I would like to thank Laurie Matheson, Julianne Laut, and Jennifer S. Argo at the University of Illinois Press for their interest in my project, as well as Nancy Albright for her diligent and detailed work as copyeditor. I am also deeply thankful to Walter Aaron Clark and Robin D. Moore, the anonymous reviewers who initially evaluated the book proposal and who graciously revealed their identity to me after the book was put under contract; they read my proposal in great detail and provided invaluable suggestions to improve it. Finally, I am in debt to the anonymous reviewers who wrote the developmental reviews of the book at the end of the submission process. Their detailed reading and generous suggestions allowed me not only to polish the final manuscript but also to figure out how to speak about some of León's most recent works without disturbing the overall structure and flow of the book. They also warned me about certain rhetorical and argumentative shortcomings in the manuscript, which gave me the opportunity to go back to them and hopefully prevent undesirable future embarrassments. In the end, I remind the reader that I am solely responsible for any errors and oversights found in the book.

TANIA LEÓN'S STRIDE

INTRODUCTION
Notes on a Biographical Counterpoint

On Wednesday, June 5, 2019, Tania León presented the closing plenary lecture at the 74th National Conference of the League of American Orchestras in Nashville, Tennessee. Her talk focused on questions of equality, diversity, inclusion, and other professional challenges within the world of classical orchestral music today. She also warned her audience about the easy way in which inclusiveness can become unproductive tokenism. She illustrated her speech with anecdotes from her own life to highlight the benefits of inclusion and tolerance to produce a collective legacy that fosters solidarity and builds bridges: from her childhood in a poor neighborhood in Cuba to the fascination of discovering the skyscrapers of New York City when she moved to the United States; from composing ballets for Dance Theatre of Harlem to taking conducting lessons with Leonard Bernstein at Tanglewood; and from being music advisor to the American Composers Orchestra to founding Composers Now. The standing ovation she received at the end of her talk is an indication that—in an increasingly divided and polarized world—stories like hers and the values they underscore are vital and necessary sources of inspiration and encouragement.[1]

Tania Justina León Ferrán (b. 1943, Havana) is one of the leading American composers and musicians of her generation. Her music is frequently programmed in Europe, Latin America, Asia, and the United States, and she has received honors, awards, and commissions from some of today's most prestigious arts and culture institutions. León is also a sought-after conductor who is frequently invited to work with renowned orchestras and new music ensembles throughout the world. Nevertheless, although León has been able to find a place in the academic classical music canon,[2] the impressive scope of her artistic success has not yet translated into a serious academic study. Neither her music nor the personal experiences that have shaped her life and given meaning to her works have been the focus of serious scholarly examination.

León was only twenty-four years old when she moved to the United States in 1967. In Cuba, she was a promising young pianist known for having premiered works by some of the young up-and-coming modernist composers on the island and for participating in a number of experimental artistic projects. However, by the end of the 1960s, León felt that the Cuban music scene was limiting her artistic development and professional prospects. Since she was a young girl, studying piano at the conservatory, she had dreamed about continuing her piano studies in Paris. In order to pursue her dream, León left her native country precisely at the moment when the revolutionary Cuban regime began implementing a number of economic, social, and cultural policies that would lead to the Stalinization of the country's economy in the 1970s. León was never able to make it to Paris to study. However, in the United States, she morphed from pianist into composer and conductor. It was there that her artistic voice blossomed. This migratory rite of passage and the process of becoming a cultural citizen of her new country inspired her to find her individual artistic voice.

León's work with Arthur Mitchell and the Dance Theatre of Harlem in the 1970s was fundamental in this dual process of transitioning to a new culture and developing a personal musical style. It was upon Mitchell's request that she composed her first major work, when she was the company's music director. Her job at the Dance Theatre of Harlem led her to establish important links with African American artists and arts entrepreneurs. It also allowed her music to be heard at a number of important international venues. Nevertheless, throughout her career, León has been adamant about not being labeled and pigeonholed. She refuses to identify herself as a "black composer," a "female composer," or an Afro-Cuban individual. Her rejection of labels has irritated some musicians, artists, and intellectuals who believe in the strategic use of identity politics.

Respecting León's decision, I never refer to her in this text as a black or female composer nor as a black woman. However, I told her that I would be writing about her involvement in a number of very important African American cultural projects and networks in which she has been perceived as a black woman. For this reason, we agreed on the use of the term "woman of color" or "person of color" as descriptive phrases. The term "people of color" has been used in the United States since the late eighteenth century. However, it was only in the 1970s—in the politicized arena of post–civil rights racial justice activism—that the phrase became widely used to describe marginalized nonwhite people and to provide a space for antiracist, interethnic alliance.[3] Although the phrase is not unproblematic, León's choice of words is not surprising when one considers that they invoke precisely the racially volatile moment when she arrived in the United States.[4]

The fact that León has rejected identity labels for decades does not mean that she is unaware that there are groups of people who have been systematically and disproportionally marginalized and denied opportunities because of the color of their skin, ethnicity, gender, or sexual preference. She is not only outspoken about these issues—as her lecture at the Conference of the League of American Orchestras makes clear—she also has fought for equality, diversity, and representation through her work as a composer, community organizer, arts manager, and educator. Some people may think that León's actions contradict her rhetoric. I do not see it that way. Instead, I see her passionate rejection of labels and her fervent labor in favor of inclusion and community-building as expressions of her interest in understanding individuals' experiences on their own terms and in being a force for progressive change. In the end, I believe this apparent contradiction simply shows the complexity of life and identity, which often challenges the dogmas we often inadvertently embrace.

While writing and researching this biography, I had to negotiate ways to talk about León that respected her wishes to avoid labels but also allowed me to make certain critical interventions. This led me to conclude that the work these labels do, although strategically empowering, can also obscure the complex particularities of an individual's experience. Therefore, rather than dwelling on these identity markers, I focused on how fluidity and movement inform León's life in a wide variety of ways. León's life story reflects her fluid engagement with ethnic, racial, and gender-based influences, as well as musical genre, style, or highbrow/lowbrow practices. Paying attention to this fluidity enables the reader to better understand the multifaceted particularities of identity construction in León's life.

Writing Tania León's Biography: Rules of Counterpoint

Writing a biography is often a complicated and intellectually hazardous enterprise. The biographer risks reducing a complex life story to the simple, conventional, chronological plot that the lives of most outstanding individuals have in common: They were born; they succeeded in overcoming seemingly insurmountable obstacles; and they died and left a legacy that was eventually valued. Other than the fact that León is alive and her legacy is still in the making, this book could have followed a similar progression. Nevertheless, that would be a disservice to León and an oversimplification of her otherwise rich, complicated, and extraordinary life. Instead, I have chosen to break away from a strictly chronological narrative to focus on the issues that have helped me make sense of her life. This approach is not new; experimental takes on biographical writing have provided new models to conceive of the affective relationship between writer and subject as a productive, performative dialogue rather than an obstacle that may prevent a perceived "objective" storytelling.[5] Thus, my first disclaimer is that, although this work is based on thorough and systematic archival, oral, and ethnographic research, it does not pretend to be an objective narrative. The book is my subjective take on Tania León's life, her legacy, and some of the personal and artistic networks in which she has become the artist and human being that she is today.

I have used the idea of counterpoint as a metaphor for the kind of text I wanted to write. In doing so, I had to enter into dialogue with multiple voices that specifically address her life and its relation to unique historical moments, instead of simply writing about it in a chronologically linear fashion. To extend this metaphor, my interviews with León provided a cantus firmus in a continuous contrapuntal conversation with the composer's relatives, her professional acquaintances, her colleagues, her mentees, and those who have written about her and her music.[6] And just like when composing any successful contrapuntal musical work, the fundamental rules of counterpoint writing should be established beforehand. León and I established the rules of this biographical counterpoint during our conversations, as we tacitly negotiated the scope of the project.

This book is neither an uncritical hagiography of León nor an authorized biography. The fact that I was planning to write about a living composer who wanted her biography to be a celebration of her legacy made me hesitant to take on this project. Finding the right balance for this book in order to successfully navigate these concerns required a lot of direct negotiation with León, as well as unspoken give and take. Determining the extent of this project was the first item we needed to clarify. León wanted a traditional, all-encompassing biography, the type of "objective" narrative that outlined the facts about her professional life. On the other hand, I thought that for those facts to be meaningful to ordinary readers, they needed to resonate in significant cultural and personal ways. This meant that I needed to write about aspects of León's personal and private life that she was hesitant to share in a book. In the end, I was able to include most of those aspects of her life, but in a manner that was respectful of her desire not to speak in detail about certain things.

For the most part, this compromise worked well. However, it did create a problem after the first draft of the book had been written. In Chapter 2, initially,

Martha Mooke's voice—León's partner for almost thirty years—was featured prominently in dialogue with the voices of León's relatives in Cuba. However, while I was in the process of writing the book, their relationship ended in an unforeseen way. I eventually revised this chapter in order to avoid misrepresenting their relationship. I also removed any statements about it that may have caused León emotional pain.

The overall form of the book was designed in response to a specific request from León. Originally, I had developed a structure in which each chapter unfolded out of flashbacks that put in dialogue León's performance conducting Cuba's National Symphony Orchestra in Havana—which in the book's final version is described in the vignette that opens Chapter 1—with a variety of important moments in the composer's life. León thought that using that event as a focal point would give Cuba an overpowering presence in the book—and in her life as presented to the world by the book—which she did not think it deserved. I was very fond of that particular structure but, after a long conversation with León, I was convinced that she was right. Cuba and Cuban culture are indeed very important to an understanding of many moments in León's life. However, featuring that particular event so prominently in the book would have given too much voice to a regime that has also made her personal life *un yogur* (miserable).[7]

An important issue I faced while writing this book was how to present the candid statements that friends and relatives of León who still live in Cuba shared with me without putting them in jeopardy. This was especially important because many of them were either critical of certain policies of the Cuban regime, social dynamics among people on the island, or retold stories about their problematic or embarrassing encounters with Cuban authorities. Needless to say, León felt very strongly that we needed to avoid putting anyone into jeopardy by retelling these stories. Although a few of these anecdotes had occurred repeatedly in our conversations, we eventually decided to leave them out of the book to protect the individuals involved.

Another issue that we discussed was the selection of works to be included and analyzed in Chapter 5. León hoped I would give an in-depth analysis of what she considered her most important works. Instead, I wanted to use a representative number of works to map out the development of her unique stylistic features. I wanted to identify the presence of certain sonorities, technical procedures, and the persistence of certain ideas throughout her compositional output. Since my goal with the analytical discussion in that chapter was different from hers, we ended up not seeing eye to eye about the selection of works and their temporal scope. I intentionally focused on her works composed up to 2002, because I felt they provided enough material to trace the development of León's compositional voice. In this case, I went with my own preference over León's. I believe this disagreement was the result of different understandings of what this biography should do. I was never interested in writing the "final word" about León or her music. Instead, my intention was to write a cohesive story that would, at the same time, leave behind many kernels to be taken up by interested scholars in the future.

Tania León's Stride

Originally, this book was going to be titled *Becoming Tania León*. However, the recent publication of Michelle Obama's autobiographical bestseller, *Becoming* (2018),[8] made me reconsider this decision since I did not want the title of León's biography to be seen as somehow derivative. After a long process that helped me reconceptualize some of the premises upon which I had developed the narrative strategies behind the structure of the book, I settled for *Tania León's Stride. A Polyrhythmic Life*. The amendment to the title does not change the fact that rather than a book about a figure frozen in time that one somehow discovers as a complete entity, this story is about the processes and routes that led Tania León to become what she is today—in both her own words and in my eyes as her biographer.

The *Merriam-Webster Dictionary* defines the noun *stride* as "the most effective natural pace." The word implies confidence and assurance: a decisive, confident walk. Tania León titled her 2020 orchestral work *Stride* to reflect its subject, Susan B. Anthony, and her decisive, effective work toward the passing of the 19th Amendment in 1920. Following on that, "stride" highlights León's agency through the steady, forward steps that have established her career. This composition tells a story, as the reader will learn, that can be seen as an allegory of León's own story.

The second part of the book's title, "a polyrhythmic life," refers to the multiple cultures and sensibilities that, in a contrapuntal way, work together like a musical polyrhythm to give meaning to the composer's stride. In discussing polyrhythm, León has stated that

> [t]he inherent rhythmic complexities in the African music brought to Cuba imparted an incredible sophistication to the music that we refer to now as Cuban music. From the Abekuá to the Arara to the Yoruba, these rhythmical complexities subliminally embedded themselves in the consciousness of the people.[9]

Just as León understands polyrhythmic practices as central to the Cuban people's consciousness, polyrhythm underlies the composer's development of her own consciousness through the relational and polyphonic ways in which she has moved through space and time. The title of this book is an attempt to poetically insinuate movement, given that motion is one of the central leitmotifs in León's music and life.

In *Tania León's Stride*, I was interested in examining the affective ways in which individuals engage with the larger historical developments that historians often privilege. In that sense, reflecting on affect at specific moments in León's life—her family relations, the development of friendships, the personal motivations behind many of her professional projects—provides an effective point of entry into exploring how regular people move to the different beats that life throws at them: the Cuban revolution, the Cold War, the struggle for civil rights, or identity politics. These personal reactions to larger, apparently impersonal social and historical processes are central to understanding how individuals make sense of their world, not only intellectually but also affectively; yet, they are often neglected in academic scholarship.[10] Paying attention to an individual's affective motivations provides a unique lens for readers to make sense of how people navigate complex processes and social structures.

A Polyrhythmic Life

The book is divided into eight parts: an introduction, six chapters, and an epilogue. Each of the chapters explores León's life according to specific musical motives that I use as their titles to symbolize certain aspects of her experience: tonic; modulation and displacement; syncopation and color; direction; voice; and canon. The introduction explores the stories behind the book and, in doing so, sets the narrative tone for the six chapters that follow. Chapter 1, "Tonic: The House on Salud Street," focuses on the intimacy of home and family, including León's childhood. It tells the story of the composer's immediate relatives, a family of working-class migrants from the Cuban countryside living in Havana. It describes their cosmopolitan aspirations and their diverse political and religious beliefs, and it pays close attention to León's musical upbringing in relation to the political changes brought about by the Cuban revolution in the 1960s. This chapter provides previously unknown information about León's musical training, her participation in certain Cuban musical networks, and her musical activities in the Havana music scene of the 1960s. The chapter concludes by exploring the personal and professional circumstances that led León to leave Cuba and continue her musical training abroad.

The extraordinary dislocations that diaspora brings to the rhythms of everyday life inform Chapter 2, "Modulation and Displacement: *cubana de adentro . . . cubana de afuera*." I begin by examining the tensions between *cubanos de adentro*

(Cubans residing on the island) and *cubanos de afuera* (Cubans living abroad). These two politically, culturally, and racially diverse groups of heterogeneous, but opinionated, people have been at odds since the late 1960s. León's 1967 emigration trip to the United States serves as a chronological point of departure. I contextualize it within the particular political circumstances of the Cuban revolution at the time she left the island. This is followed by my discussion of the affective ways in which she has navigated antagonistic networks and discourses of identity in order to develop her own, more fluid, sense of belonging.

The contradictory takes on race that inform how we understand the world around us is central to Chapter 3, "Syncopation and Color: Adapting to New Life Rhythms." I explore León's experience of blackness in Cuba before and after the revolution, her participation in networks of African American expressive culture in the United States, and her reticence to be labeled an "Afro-Cuban" or "African American composer." This shows the complex ways in which conflicting experiences of race were essential for León to make sense of U.S. culture and finding an artistic voice. Through the stories of León's collaborations with the Dance Theatre of Harlem, Geoffrey Holder, and INTAR, I examine the instances of racism she has experienced while carrying out her professional duties as musician and educator.

Chapter 4, "Direction: Leading in Music, Leading in Life," takes the accidental concatenation of events that led León into an unforeseen conducting career to explore the idea of conductivity as a metaphor of leadership. Here, a conductor is not only someone who leads the way but also someone who creates the conditions conducive for things to happen. This chapter provides not only a narrative about León's conducting career—with an emphasis on her work with the Brooklyn Philharmonic, the New York Philharmonic, and the American Composers Orchestra—but also an examination of the professional, creative, and community networks through which León has become an influential mentor for younger musicians and a role model for several generations of artists. In doing this, I trace León's experience and influence as a professor, community leader, and cultural broker through personal and intimate dialogues with colleagues, students, and mentees in a wide variety of social settings.

Chapter 5, "Voice: Style and Idea in the Music of Tania León," explores the complex aesthetic, artistic, and cultural dynamics that have shaped how León developed a uniquely personal musical style and a compositional voice. I make a distinction between a composer's "voice" and their technique, following John Corigliano's opinion that a composer's personal style is the result of "the sonorities [they] come to just because [they] like them,"[11] while techniques are larger musical practices shared across compositional styles at specific moments in history. In this chapter, I examine both the sonorities León uses often "just because she likes them," and the techniques she uses that are part of larger, shared compositional rhetorical strategies. My intention is to provide a fuller account of an artistic voice that encompasses many voices.

I tell the story of the development of León's artistic voice through a counterpoint of multiple analytical voices, including: the composer's oral testimonies about her creative process; conversations she and I had while listening to her music; summaries of my conversations with composer Sergio Cote-Barco about León's music; as well as the voices of musicians who have collaborated with her and have firsthand experience playing her music. Each of these voices represents a different listening approach based on their trajectories as composers, musicologists, performers, and music critics. These approaches often privilege different musical features or aesthetic criteria when listening to a particular work of music. By extending Cote-Barco an invitation to be a "composer in residence" of sorts in this chapter, I do not intend to establish him as an authority of any sorts on the music of Tania León; I want to recognize the fact that by virtue of his being a Latin American composer studying at Cornell at the time I was working on this project he became a natural interlocutor as he was also interested in the music I was writing about. As a composer with expertise in Latin American modern music, he is trained in a set of listening strategies and priorities that were simply not on my radar as a musicologist because I am trained to listen for other things. Thus, by bestowing on him the honorary title of "composer in residence" in Chapter 4, I want to acknowledge the fact that my understanding of León's music was profoundly affected by my conversations with him. One always moves within intellectual networks and engages them when developing scholarly projects; he became part of my scholarly network almost naturally as we repeatedly bumped into each other in the hallways of Cornell's Lincoln Hall and as we learned about our mutual interest in León's music.

The type of communal listening strategy I attempt in this chapter is an exercise in what Dylan Robinson has described—following Ajay Feble, Donna Palmateer Pennee, and J. R. Struthers' formulation of the term "contrapuntal listening"—as more than merely "a model for the co-presence of difference" but "as a metaphor for democracy."[12] In contrapuntal writing "each voice must stand independently, but all voices are considered of equal importance and no single voice dominates";[13] contrapuntal listening aspires to this same type of utopian, democratic condition. It provides a multiplicity of listening strategies in which the copresence of difference is essential. Regardless of the fact that my authorial voice is behind the final narrative text, my intention is for that narrative to weave a pluralistic experience in which no single listening dominates (or at least, to produce a discourse that interweaves all of these listening experiences). I do this in order to override as much as possible the shortcomings embedded in individual and disciplinary listening regimes.

The analytical conversations in the chapter are organized around a selection of León's works: Preludes nos. 1 and 2; *Tones*; *Haiku*; *Four Pieces for Violoncello*; *Carabalí*; *Indígena*; *Batá*; *Horizons*; and *Axon*. These works provide a panoramic and diachronic overview of León's stylistic development as a composer. My goal is not to provide definitive textual readings of any of these works, but to trace León's technical and aesthetic choices that give meaning to her voice. I suggest that it is at the intersection of style and idea that the compositional voice emerges as a unique aesthetic feature. I invoke the notion of "performative composition," which I coined elsewhere in relation to Mexican composer Julián Carrillo's compositional practice, in order to highlight the active way in which composers fashion their musical persona in the act of assembling their music and as they "[work] out the details of [. . .] particular composition[s]."[14]

Chapter 6, "Canon: Representation, Identity, and Legacy," reflects on the ways in which León's life and works have been portrayed to create the idea of an artistic legacy. The chapter unfolds around three concepts: representation, identity, and legacy. The first part is an exploration of the ways in which Tania León has been represented in literature about music in the United States and Latin America. I pay special attention to examining the agendas behind the individual texts that mention her or her music since 1976 to the present. The second part is devoted to León's discourse of self-identification and provides a detailed exploration of the ways in which she rejects identity labels and the implications of this rejection. In the final section, I assess León's current legacy as a musician, artist, educator, and community organizer and put in further counterpoint with the narrative journeys explored in the previous chapters.

Finally, the epilogue, "Tania León's *Stride*: An Echo that Reaches Our Ears," takes a look at the premiere of *Stride*, the title of which I borrowed for this book, in order to move away from the polemics explored in Chapter 6 and return to León's actual work at the book's ending. By returning to *Stride* and the idea of León's personal stride, I summon certain personal and musical presences that illuminate the inspirations and motivations behind her life journeys. Thinking about her music in terms of presences that reverberate soundly beyond the moments and spaces of their inception reminds us that it is ultimately in her music and the echoes it brings back to our ears that we can find who Tania León really is.

1

TONIC

The House on Salud Street

Sunday, November 13, 2016. Havana, Cuba. 12:15 AM. Almost fifty musicians patiently wait on stage for the conductor to appear. They have finished tuning their instruments and seem eager to start the performance. The door to the off-right stage wing opens and Tania León appears, framed by the darkened house behind her. The audience breaks into a loud ovation as she walks slowly but confidently on the stage. The orchestra stands as she approaches the concertmaster to shake his hand. She climbs up the podium and, upon her command, the musicians sit down and prepare to start the concert. There is nothing new about this ritual; nevertheless, a somehow unusual sense of expectation and anticipation fills the Covarrubias Hall of the National Theatre of Cuba. León raises her hands, marks the beat, and the music starts with a sustained dissonant chord played by the strings, while a flute, piano, vibraphone, and clarinet take turns to present a rhythmically irregular and disjointed melody. First a short flute solo sounds over a static harmony played by the strings; then a clarinet takes over and energetically moves through a tricky rhythmic sequence in order to reach a soaring long note supported by a tremolando in the marimba. Then the whole orchestra bursts into a loud, dissonant texture that saturates the musical spectrum. The music continues to unfold with the mercurial alternation of loud orchestral tutti outbursts and short solo or chamber sections: sometimes colorful trumpet duels, sometimes sharp and groovy polyrhythmic percussion solos that loudly erupt from the back of the stage grab the listener's attention.

As the music unfolds, one hears an artful combination and juxtaposition of styles that produce a complex sonic palimpsest—one that abstractly evokes the *comparsas* of Havana and Santiago during Carnival[1] providing a space for the unlikely encounter of displaced sonorities reminiscent of Olivier Messiaen, Ernesto Lecuona, and Igor Stravinsky. Without a baton, with her bare hands, León avoids the flamboyant contortions one often witnesses on orchestral podiums. Instead, she holds together this intricate, flowing rhythmic and sonic structure with precise, well-defined, but economical gestures. Hers is a sober and pragmatic conducting style that is nevertheless breathtaking in its rhythmic precision and its ability to communicate through its elegant and minimal austerity. The music comes to an end with the slow fade out of a piano ostinato that once again conjures the timelines and rhythmic patterns that characterize Cuban popular music within a largely atonal setting. A standing ovation breaks the brief silence following the performance, the Cuban premiere of *Indígena* (1991), a work León composed more than twenty-five years earlier but that only now she has a chance to conduct in her native country (see figure 1.1).

Backstage, once the applause fades, a large number of people surround the composer. They are among her closest friends and relatives for whom this was the first chance to see their beloved Tania in action: her older nephew, Oscar Jr. (son of León's brother, Oscar José, and his first wife) and his wife Sullen, with their two daughters (Karla and Kalia); her younger nephew, Alain (the dedicatee of *Indígena*), with his son, Manuel Alejandro, and his mother, Caridad Rodríguez

FIGURE 1.1. Tania León and the National Symphony Orchestra of Cuba.

FIGURE 1.2. Marta Valdés, Juan Piñera, Tania León, and Alfredo Diez Nieto; Oscar Jr. observes the scene in the background. Reproduced by permission of Liliana González Moreno.

"Cachita" (Oscar José's second wife); and her sister-in-law, Yolanda (Oscar José's third wife), who took pictures throughout the performance. Also in attendance is her composition teacher, Alfredo Diez Nieto, 98 years old at the time; her dear friend and confidant, songwriter Marta Valdés, to whom she wrote dozens of letters in the 1970s, through the years she was unable to return to Cuba; and composer Juan Piñera (see figure 1.2). Many of León's most cherished friends and relatives on the island are there to hug her and share emotional tears.

There is one person missing, however: León's mother, Dora Ferrán—"Mima," as her children and close relatives affectionately called her. She passed away in 2014. Although Mima saw her daughter conduct her music when she was able to travel to the United States, for the composer this concert is a bittersweet moment. By having the opportunity to conduct the National Symphony Orchestra for the first time, León is finally recognized by the cultural scene of Cuba, the country her mother never wanted to leave. But this recognition, which would have brought so much pride to Mima, happens two years too late.

A Family of Nomads in Havana

Mima was born in 1925 in Sagua la Grande, a small city on the north coast of the province of Villa Clara, about 150 miles east of Havana. She was one of several children Estela Ferrán had with different men. There are no formal records of Mima's parents and most of what León knows about her maternal lineage comes to her through family legends. One of these stories relates that Estela was the daughter of a slave woman, born on a slave ship somewhere in the Atlantic Ocean during the Middle Passage.[2] Mima's biological father was a seaman from the south of France who had two children with Estela before leaving the family when Mima was seven years old.[3] As a child regarded as illegitimate by contemporary Cuban society, Mima used her mother's last name, Ferrán, although she was not registered and had no birth certificate until the mid-1940s.

According to León, Mima's life in Sagua was difficult. The Ferrán household was rather dysfunctional. Estela expected Mima and her siblings to work to help support the family as well as Estela's occasional partners. Finally, when she was sixteen in 1942, Mima grew tired of the situation and decided to leave the maternal house and move to Havana. She found work as a maid and cleaning lady there.[4] Life in the country's capital was much more cosmopolitan than in Sagua. For black people, social life revolved around the so-called *sociedades de color*, social clubs for people of African descent—although they were called "societies of Cubans of color" because open references to Africanness were discouraged in mainstream Cuban culture. Although these societies had some positive influence on their members' lives, they were not truly oriented toward celebrating their African heritage. On the one hand they provided a space for black people to enjoy various educational activities for the advancement of their communities, as well as entertainment, especially dances; on the other, articulating the racist rhetoric of the time, they attempted to "civilize" black people by eradicating cultural traces of Africanism conventionally considered too wild or savage. For example, the overtly sexualized rumba (a drumming genre of West African origins) was discouraged while dance styles with more prominent European features, like the popular *danzón de nuevo ritmo* (danzón of new rhythm), were privileged.[5] It was at one of these club dances that Mima met Oscar León a few weeks after arriving in Havana.

Tania León keeps a studio photograph of her parents from the early days of their relationship. They are both dressed in their best clothes. Mima sports a hairdo that emphasizes her straight hair and charmingly delineates the refined beauty of her face; her hands look meticulously manicured, and she wears a

FIGURE 1.3. Dora "Mima" Ferrán and Oscar León. Courtesy of Tania León.

stylish dress and earrings. If this picture is any indication, when Oscar first met Mima she was a sight to behold (see figure 1.3).

Oscar was working at the club as a ticket salesperson. When Mima approached him, he could only manage gallantly to say: "No, you can go in for free." Once she was in, Oscar gave the rest of the tickets that he was supposed to sell to another salesman, explaining that he had to go dance with that girl.[6] That was the beginning of a very complicated relationship that would bring Mima both immense happiness and deep sorrow.

Oscar León was born in 1921 in Cárdenas, a maritime port in the province of Matanzas, about 97 miles east of Havana. He was the son of José León, a first-generation Cuban of Chinese ancestry, and Rosa Julia de los Mederos, a mulatta, the daughter of a Spanish man from Galicia and a black Cuban woman (see figure 1.4). Both José and Rosa Julia were from Cárdenas, and moved to Havana after Oscar was born. Little is known about José's parents, although at some point the family's original Chinese last name was replaced by León. This suggests that José's father may have arrived in Cuba as part of the coolie system at the end of the nineteenth century. This system of indentured labor brought Chinese men to work under slave-like conditions in sugar plantations up until the 1870s. During this period, it was common for Chinese laborers to be given Spanish names or for them to take the last names of their master or godparent after conversion to Catholicism.[7] In the 1940s, Cuba had one of the largest Chinese communities in Latin America, and up until his death in 1957, José remained close to his Chinese roots. He worked as a dispatcher and accountant for a bus company called *Únicos de Cárdenas*, a co-op that provided transportation services between Cárdenas, his native city, and Havana. The company's main office was located at the corner of Teniente Rey Street and Paseo del Prado, across from the Capitol in the Centro Habana neighborhood, a short distance from the famous *Barrio Chino de La Habana* (Havana's Chinatown). León remembers her grandfather would spend most of his leisure with his Chinese friends and acquaintances at Restaurant Pacífico in Havana's Chinatown. She and her grandfather were very close, so she often joined them at these meals. While sitting at the round tables on the second floor of the restaurant, León learned to eat with chopsticks while enjoying the mysterious but melodic contours of her grandfather and his friends' conversations in Chinese.[8]

Rosa Julia, "Mamota," as her grandchildren called her, worked as a bureaucrat for the Ministry of Commerce, the governmental department in charge

FIGURE 1.4. Tania León's paternal grandparents, José León and Rosa Julia de los Mederos "Mamota." Courtesy of Tania León.

of regulating national and international trade, controlling prices, tracking the activities of corporations and public limited companies, and keeping records of patents and inventions. Government jobs like hers were not permanent; the personnel tended to change when a new administration was sworn in. Therefore, in order to make ends meet, Mamota also regularly worked at home, sewing clothes for people in the neighborhood. She also designed and made clothes. León has kept several photos of herself as a young kid wearing clothes made by her grandmother: a flamboyant mini dress inspired by Carmen Miranda (see figure 1.5); a more formal dress with hat included; and an elegant, white recital costume with a beautiful topknot. Mamota always made sure her granddaughter dressed appropriately for any social occasion.

León's grandmother was also a uniquely well-read individual who appreciated music despite not having received any musical training herself. She enjoyed literature and was particularly fond of the Russian classics. She was also a Marxist and a member of the Popular Socialist Party, one of Cuba's two leftist parties before the 1959 revolution. Her passion for education, the arts,

FIGURE 1.5. Two-year-old Tania León wearing a Carmen Miranda–inspired dress made by her grandmother, Mamota. Courtesy of Tania León.

and progressive social causes would greatly influence the lives of her grandchildren.

Soon after Oscar and Mima started dating, she got pregnant and the couple
moved in with his parents. Oscar wanted to have a son, so when Tania was born
on May 14, 1943, it exacerbated the problems that may have already existed in
the young couple's relationship. After Tania's birth, Oscar disappeared for several
days, which became a regular occurrence throughout his relationship with Mima.
When Estela Ferrán, Mima's mother, came to visit her daughter's first child, she
threw a coin on Tania's crib before leaving; this spiteful action foreshadowed
their future estrangement. On the other hand, Mamota brought a small gift for
the baby, a toy piano that was an omen of things to come.[9]

Mamota, was an enthusiastic *aleyo* (lay practitioner) of Santería, the syncretic
Afro-European religion that combines elements from Yoruba and Catholic faiths.
In Santería, it is customary for parents to bring their newborns to the *babalawo*,
the priest who possesses the ability to communicate with Ifá. Ifá is the only deity
in the Santería pantheon to whom Olorun, the Ruler of/in the Heavens, gave
the power to communicate with human beings. Through this ritual, the parents
would receive instructions on how to raise their child and information about
what the future will bring to the newborn.[10] Olorun, one of three manifestations
of the Supreme God, is usually associated with the sun. Because Mima was not a
follower of Santería, Mamota broke with tradition and took the role of the priest
herself; she raised baby Tania toward the sun to communicate with Olorun. Her
vision clear and powerful, she declared: "This girl will travel a lot and far during
her life."[11]

Many relatives describe León's father as a very intelligent man although no-
toriously lacking discipline. He first received a scholarship to study art and then
medicine, but eventually dropped out of school. Oscar eventually worked for
several U.S. and Cuban construction companies, first as a painter and later as a
technician overseeing the assemblage of industrial buildings. This professional
lack of discipline was reflected in his private life. For example, for a while after
Tania's birth, Oscar and Mima rented their own apartment; Mamota had paid
for its furniture. One day, Mima came back home to find her baby Tania sleep-
ing on a pillow on the floor and all the furniture in the apartment gone. León
assumes that her father sold their furniture probably to pay gambling debts.[12]

León's younger brother, Oscar José, was born in 1947 during one of the periods
when Mima and Oscar were back together. However, Oscar's continued absences
along with his constant womanizing made things very difficult for Mima. It was
clear that Oscar was not prepared to be a father to his children nor was he solely

committed to Mima. Nevertheless, although Oscar and Mima never married, he did recognize Tania and Oscar José as his legal children. León found out decades later in the 1980s, after Oscar's death, that during one of his absences, he had fathered another son, Juan Gabriel Amoros.[13] Aware that the volatility of their relationship did not provide the stability that Tania and Oscar José needed, Mima and Oscar decided their children should live with his mother, Mamota. Mamota's house on 617 Salud Street, between Oquendo and Soledad streets, in the Centro Habana neighborhood, would be home for Tania and Oscar José.

Childhood on Salud Street

A popular Latin American saying states that *"infancia es destino"* (childhood is destiny). And, indeed, Tania León's personal and professional lives were shaped by her childhood. Her tumultuous family life sculpted her later years, while her early musical experiences planted the seed for the development of her personal musical voice. If one could summarize León's childhood in three words they would be: family, absence, and music; these three words would also be essential to understanding her future paths in life.

León's childhood occurred during the politically contradictory last fifteen years of Cuba's Second Republic (1933–1958), which began with Fulgencio Batista, one of the leaders of the so-called *Revuelta de los sargentos* (Sergeant's Revolt). It put an end to the Machadato, the eight-year presidency of Gerardo Machado, in 1933.[14] Batista was Cuba's first mixed-race president and was a force for progressive change in the country early on. During his first administration, he established the more liberal 1940 Constitution, supported labor unions, and implemented social reforms, which led to the development of a strong sense of working-class identity in the country.[15]

Batista's successors, Ramón Grau San Martín (1944–1948) and Carlos Prío Socarrás (1948–1952), are generally recognized as having attracted investment to Cuba, leading to an economic boom that helped strengthen the middle class in the country's urban areas. Nevertheless, because these leaders consolidated power in the presidency, their governments undermined the division of powers on the island and eroded the legitimacy of the Cuban political system.

In 1952, Batista ran for president again. Facing a loss, he led a military coup d'état that reestablished his power. While he had been perceived as progressive during his first term in office, his second presidency was characterized by a myopic authoritarianism and a reversal of many of the forward-looking causes he had championed in the early 1940s. With military and strategic support from the United States, Batista suspended the 1940 Constitution, revoked many social and political liberties, jailed and tortured political dissidents, and presided over a deteriorating economy that created unemployment and a greater gap between rich and poor. Although Batista included blacks in his administration—and despite his own racial heritage—Cuban people of color remained underprivileged in the country's largely racist society. Batista's collusion with the Mafia led to further dissatisfaction with his government and placed the activities of U.S. organized crime at the center of Cuba's corrupt political system.[16]

The rise of corruption and the racial, social, and political abuses that occurred between 1952 and 1958 inspired several revolutionary urban- and rural-based groups to attempt to depose Batista. One of those groups, Fidel Castro's guerrillas, gathered enough momentum to eventually overthrow the regime in 1959. We will see how this social and political context is key to understanding León's largely black family's motivations and how their dreams changed with the advent of the Cuban revolution.

The house on Salud Street was in a working-class neighborhood, Centro Habana. It sheltered an interesting artistic community, including Joseíto, Odilio, and Orestes Urfé, who were León's neighbors. They were part of a renowned family of Cuban popular musicians from Madruga, a small city between Havana and Matanzas. The family's patriarch, José Urfé, was the composer of the classic *danzón* "*El bombín de Barreto*," which scholars claim first included the *son montuno* in the final section of the danzón, thus formalizing its traditional structure. His children include Odilio Urfé, a celebrated musicologist, pedagogue, and cofounder with his brother Orestes of the historical *Seminario de Música Popular* (Cuban Popular Music Seminar) and the *Charanga Típica Nacional*, an ensemble dedicated to playing sophisticated arrangements of traditional danzones; Orestes Urfé, a bass player who studied in Boston and became head of the bass section of the Havana Philharmonic Orchestra; and Joseíto Urfé, a sought-after pedagogue.[17]

Perhaps influenced by the neighborhood's musical community, Mamota pushed Tania and Oscar José to pursue serious musical studies. Mamota's family was poor but she made it a priority for her grandchildren to get a good education. Although elementary education was free and compulsory in Cuba, the shortage of good public schools meant she chose to send them to private institutions.[18] León and Oscar José attended private schools, including the Bravo Academy for elementary school, and eventually the Carlos Alfredo Peyrellade Conservatory, which put a considerable financial burden on Mamota and José. Although they split when their granddaughter was still very young, José continued to pay for their grandchildren's education. When he died, Juana Valles de Pérez-Goñi, the conservatory's director, granted scholarships to León and her brother. After José's passing, Marcelino Arango "*El Gallego*" ("The Galician"), Mamota's partner during the last years of her life, took on many of his responsibilities for the children.[19]

León says that Mima and Mamota claimed that, at around age four, she "used to go to the radio and look for radio stations that had classical music, something that in [her] home was not a common practice."[20] When Mamota noticed her granddaughter's interest in music, she talked to the family about enrolling her in music lessons. León started formal music training at the age of four at the Peyrellade Conservatory, where she took piano, music theory, and solfège lessons two days a week. Mamota was very strict and would not let León go out to play until she finished her homework and practiced piano. Oscar José affirmed how Mamota kept him from playing with his friends until he was done practicing: "Cry all you want today," Mamota would say, "tomorrow you will thank me."[21] This attitude and the conservatory's French curriculum, which emphasized fixed do solfège, allowed León to develop perfect pitch. León's talent was evident so early that José, her grandfather, bought her a vertical piano when she was only five years old (see figure 1.6). Fitting

FIGURE 1.6. Eight-year-old Tania León practicing piano at home. Courtesy of Tania León.

the instrument in the small living room of their house was a real challenge, but it proved to be an important asset for the family; not only León and her brother, but also her niece and nephew, Alain and Yordanka, decades later, learned to play music on its worn-out keyboard.

León was a dedicated student; she fully understood the sacrifices her grandparents made in order for Oscar José and her to have an education. She had excellent grades at the Bravo Academy and won many academic awards at the conservatory. When she graduated from secondary school she proudly wore the many medals she had received for her excellent grades and her many academic achievements (see figure 1.7). At the Peyrellade, León started taking piano lessons with Rosa Valle. By age nine, she was also studying privately with Edmundo López (1922–1992), who took her under his wing upon Orestes Urfé's recommendation.[22] León recognizes López as one of her most important childhood mentors. He introduced her to contemporary music through the study of Bartók's *Mikrokozmosz* (1926–1939).[23]

Josefina Ordieres, known as "Fifi," was one of León's best friends at the time and a piano student at the conservatory. She remembers that ten-year-old León already showed unique signs of compositional talent. According to Fifi, she used to talk on the phone every other afternoon to León; "many times, [Tania] would start composing and would call me on the phone. My mom would say: 'It is so late and you are still on the phone!' So, she would play the piano very softly for me to hear her latest [musical] witticism."[24] León clarifies that these were not her own compositions, but rather arrangements of the piano repertory that Fifi and she studied at the conservatory.[25] Nevertheless, León also recalls that "when I was about thirteen [years old, I] actually put together a song. I had a heartbreaking break-up with a boyfriend and this was how I dealt with it."[26]

In spite of not living with their parents and the long and continuous absences of their father, both Tania and Oscar José remember their childhood as a very happy time. The household's limited financial resources forced the family members to work as a team to achieve common goals, which often resulted in unexpected positive side effects. León remembers that during one of her father's sporadic reappearances she had to work with him "in order to actually keep the electricity running in the apartment. I learned through him how to put electrical wires together and how to make connections, and so I became his sideman. It was not, 'She's a girl; she's not supposed to do this.'"[27] Although Oscar was an absent father, León treasures the periods when she had a chance to spend time with him. Moments like this sweeten the memory of an otherwise bittersweet relationship that remained strained until Oscar's passing in 1980.

FIGURE 1.7. Tania León at the time of her secondary school graduation. Courtesy of Tania León.

On the other hand, León's relationship with her mother, Mima, was always one of love and respect. Like Mamota, Mima also washed and ironed other people's clothes. She often worked at the house on Salud Street because Mamota had a new wringer-washing machine, which gave her a chance to spend time with her children. León and Oscar José also developed very close relationships with their grandfather José and with El Gallego. Given that the Bravo Academy was on Neptuno Street, just a few blocks away from the Capitol and from the head-quarters of Únicos de Cárdenas, where El Gallego and José worked, respectively, the kids would often stop by to spend time with them after school.

Besides schoolwork and music lessons, León and Oscar José did what most kids do: they ran around the neighborhood playing with other kids; enjoyed games and sports; danced at community events; participated in extracurricular activities; and, as is the case with most restless kids, sometimes had minor problems with their neighbors. They also enjoyed listening to the radio. Oscar José recalls that they would spend hours listening to CMBF, Radio Universal, a station that broadcast only classical music, as well as Radio Cramer, a station devoted to the latest trends in U.S. popular music.[28] Their passion for popular music led the two siblings to put together a band of sorts along with the kids from the neighborhood. The group featured piano, violin, drums, and backing vocalists. "My brother always had a great initiative and he would get our friends together [to play]," remembers León, "I improvised songs for the small combo [. . .] and he and I would sing together. There was a lot of music at home."[29] Their band was not a commercial endeavor; it was simply a fun activity. However, it gave León a chance to experience her music played by other people for the first time.

León says that her family members were "bilingual" in their religious practices: "With the exception of my mother, who was more of a spiritualist [she had spiritual visions], they believed in Santería and Catholicism."[30] Although Mamota was never formally initiated in the religion, she attended Santería celebrations regularly. León recalls those evenings:

> I grew up watching all of those Santería things. They'd cut the chicken's head and they would put the blood in a small casserole. . . . And the drum, you know? If you do Santería you are surrounded by *Batá*; and not only Batá but also the dances and the chants, which are very interesting . . . I was always there but more like a spectator, looking at everything and absorbing it [but] I have never done any of that. I have nothing to do with Santería.[31]

FIGURE 1.8. Postcard of the Eiffel Tower sent to Tania Léon in 1952. The back reads: "Dear Tania: Affectionate greetings for you and your nice grandmother and mom. ¿Are you practicing a lot? Make good use of your time, I'll bring new things to teach you. See you soon, Edmundo López."

Although León was never trained as a Santería drummer, getting to know this music through these visits and becoming familiar with the complex rhythmic structures it is based on was a very important aspect of her musical upbringing.[32] Although she may have suppressed these memories for decades, they would be essential in finding her own compositional voice later in life.

The sea is omnipresent in Cuba's emotional life. It promises so much beyond its horizon but also separates Cubans from those dreams. As a kid, León enjoyed walking along Havana's beautiful *malecón* (seawall), always wondering about life beyond that sea. One of her earliest experiences of the world beyond that sea occurred when Edmundo López, her piano teacher at the conservatory, traveled to Paris and sent her a postcard of the Eiffel Tower (see figure 1.8). León was nine years old and became fascinated with the idea of Paris. Maybe her dream of visiting this exotic city was inspired by this moment, when Mamota's early prophecy ("this girl will travel a lot and far during her life") was echoed by Edmundo's gift. Oscar José remembers that "the postcard sent [Tania] into a dream. After that she kept saying that one day she was going to go to the country of the Eiffel Tower, that she was going to go to France. It became my sister's obsession."[33]

"*Ya llegaron de la sierra*": A Time for Revolution

On Wednesday, December 31, 1958, people in the United States may have been listening to Domenico Modugno's "Volare" or Dámaso Pérez Prado's "Patricia" on the radio. But they were largely unaware that, in Cuba, Ernesto "Ché" Guevara and Rolando Cubela were delivering the final blow to Fulgencio Batista's regime at the Battle of Santa Clara. Fidel Castro's insurrection against the Cuban government had started five years earlier. In 1953, Castro led an attack on Santiago de Cuba's Moncada Barracks; it was a military failure but a symbolic success for the rebels. However, it wasn't until the unsuccessful attempt to assassinate Batista on March 13, 1957, that the government's reaction to the rebellion started to have a negative impact on Cuba's people. To its increasingly brutal repression of dissidents, the government added a number of harsh economic measures that led to a stagnant economy and a withdrawal of U.S. support. By the end of 1958, it was clear that the Batista regime was in trouble and there was an oppressive sense of uneasiness and uncertainty among *cubanos de a pie* (regular Cuban people). On the night of December 31st, Tania and her friends went to the rooftop of Mamota's house to light some fireworks in celebration of New Year's Eve. Oscar José recalls the occasion: "My grandmother was very upset with all of us because she said the cops could think we were signaling someone

. . . it was a dismal end of the year for everyone . . . and then, the following day the revolution triumphed."[34]

Fidel Castro and his *barbudos* (bearded ones) enjoyed a massive popular reception when they entered Havana on January 8, 1959. Cubans from all levels of society were thrilled with their march on the capital and came out to welcome them loudly. This early sense of anticipation, hope, and faith in the revolution can be heard in "Los barbudos," a cha-cha-chá by Fajardo y sus Estrellas, one of the many songs inspired by this momentous occasion:

> *Ya llegaron de la sierra*
> *porque los mandó Fidel*
> *libertaron nuestra tierra*
> *y nos dieron la paz al volver . . .*
> *Todos gritan:*
> *"¡Han triunfado!"*
> *"¡Que viva Fidel!"*
> *"¡Vivan los barbudos!"*

> They already came down from the sierra
> because Fidel sent them
> They liberated our land
> and gave us peace back . . .
> Everyone screams:
> "They have triumphed!"
> "Long live Fidel!"
> "Long live the bearded ones!"[35]

Mima had foreseen this moment years earlier when, after one of her spiritual visions, she told her daughter that "some men with a lot of hair will come and they will change everything."[36]

The reaction within León's family was mixed. While Mamota supported the revolution, Mima was more ambivalent about it. Many of her acquaintances disagreed with the revolution's goals and, after Castro's victory, were planning to emigrate to the United States. The younger members of the family also had mixed views of Castro. León was not interested in politics, but recalls that she did not like Castro for purely personal reasons; she did not like his "bullying tactics and how he resorted to disparaging and insulting"[37] those who did not agree with him. She remembers that she would go up to the *barbacoa* (makeshift mezzanine) in Mamota's house during the radio broadcasts of his long speeches in order to play records by Chopin to avoid hearing Castro's voice. Her brother was more receptive to the barbudos's nationalist rhetoric. León remembers that years later, Oscar José announced his decision to quit music studies and accept a scholarship from the Cuban government "because the revolution needs men."[38] Regardless of the change in government, the economic situation of the family changed very little after 1959: Mamota and El Gallego kept their jobs at the Ministry of Commerce and the Capitol, while Mamota continued washing and sewing other people's clothes.

León graduated from the Peyrellade Conservatory with bachelor degrees in piano pedagogy and music theory and solfège in 1960. Soon after, she wrote a letter to composer Harold Gramatges (1918–2008), who was the Cuban ambassador to France from 1960 to 1964. León asked him about scholarship possibilities to study in Paris. Gramatges wrote a handwritten response, encouraging her to think about going to Warsaw instead. Gramatges' recommendation was not surprising given the presence of Leo Brouwer (b. 1939), Cuba's musical enfant terrible, at the Warsaw Autumn Festival in 1961, which helped in establishing links between the Cuban and Polish avant-garde music scenes.[39] His letter was disheartening for a young pianist whose lifelong dream had been to study in Paris. His response, along with the family's precarious financial situation, may have been important factors in León's decision to put on hold her cherished childhood dreams. Instead, she matriculated at the *Escuela Profesional de Comercio de Marianao*, in the outskirts of Havana, and a year later graduated with a bachelor's degree in accounting. On graduation, she started working as a bookkeeper at the same government office that had employed Mamota for many years.

In the meantime, Oscar José continued his music studies at the Peyrellade Conservatory and started sitting in on classes at Havana's *Conservatorio Municipal de Música*. It seemed like he was making real progress and thus it came as a big surprise when he announced his decision to quit music. In 1963, after finishing secondary school, and taking into account the family's economic situation, Oscar José accepted a scholarship from the revolutionary government to study at the *Instituto Hermanos Gómez* to prepare for a technical career. In 1964, the government enacted mandatory military service for young men, which could be fulfilled by attending some technical institutes, including the Hermanos Gómez.[40] This may be one reason that Oscar José decided to enroll at this institute. After graduation, Oscar José got a job at the *Instituto de la Pesca*, where he remained until his resignation in 1996.[41] Interestingly, after more than thirty years, he returned to music and became a prominent restaurant pianist, which eventually led him to be hired to play at a hotel in Andorra.

León spent the best part of the early to mid-1960s checking receipts and managing transactions behind a bureaucratic desk, certainly a dispiriting experience for a young, talented woman. However, she was able to continue working on her musical craft. Her piano training at the Peyrellade Conservatory had been rather ecumenical; she mastered the music of canonical European composers from the Classical and Romantic periods, along with the study of some modern repertory on Edmundo López's instigation. She also studied the music of classic Cuban composers like Ignacio Cervantes (1847–1905) and Ernesto Lecuona (1895–1963). León states that

> in the smaller countries, those that become their classics are really nourished [. . .] [T]herefore, for us to study Chopin and to study Lecuona, it was on equal terms [. . .] You couldn't learn the 24 Études by Chopin without learning the Lecuona Dances or the Cervantes Contredanses [*sic*].[42]

This emphasis on Cuban music during her early years inspired her interest in deepening her knowledge of Cuban popular music after graduating. Undoubtedly, the best place to do this in early 1960s Cuba was Odilio Urfé's Seminario de Música Popular Cubana. Created by Urfé in 1949 as *Instituto de Investigaciones Folklóricas* (Institute for Folkloric Research), the revolution brought this initiative a new name and mission, and state sponsorship, in 1963. Under its new name, it was transformed into a conservatory to provide musical training to popular musicians who had received none in its location at the *Iglesia de San Francisco de Paula* in the *Habana Vieja* (Old Havana) neighborhood.[43] Since León's childhood, Orestes Urfé, Odilio's brother, had been very supportive of her musical studies. Invoking this, she asked Odilio to allow her to continue her training at the Seminario. At this school, she studied advanced harmony, counterpoint, and composition with Alfredo Diez Nieto (b. 1918) and Gramatges, who encouraged her to compose her first serious classical works. She also studied danzón performance practice with Jesús López (1905–1972), a former pianist with the legendary charanga *Arcaño y sus Maravillas*.

In 1964, León started taking piano lessons with Zenaida Manfugás (1932–2012) at the newly founded Alejandro García Caturla Conservatory in the Marianao neighborhood. Manfugás was a black pianist who had recently returned to Cuba after several years of studies in Madrid and Paris. She was quickly gaining a reputation as one of the most talented and accomplished Cuban pianists of her generation. León's lessons with Manfugás were thorough; she was an excellent pedagogue with an eccentric personality who kept her students constantly on their toes. But outside of Manfugás' classroom, student life at the conservatory could also be a lot of fun. León recalls, "[A]t the end of the day, when classes were over, we [students] would hang around and the jam sessions would begin. We would create pieces out of our spontaneous improvisations and marvel at our inventions."[44]

At one of these sessions, León met a young virtuoso, Paquito D'Rivera (b. 1948). D'Rivera was a clarinetist who was already making a name for himself in the Cuban classical and jazz music scenes. Manfugás was a friend of Enrique Pardo (1905–1996), D'Rivera's clarinet teacher, and wanted to couple her best student, León, with Pardo's best student for a chamber music concert. León and D'Rivera played a program consisting of clarinet and piano works by Louis Spohr, Johannes Brahms, and Mikhail Krein, as well as a solo clarinet piece by Esteban Eitler, at Havana's *Palacio de Bellas Artes* (Palace of Fine Arts) on December 2, 1964. Besides this recital, the duet also played a concert sponsored by the *Brigada Hermanos Saíz* (Hermanos Saíz Brigade) on April 11, 1965.[45] The program was similar, but it also included two works for solo piano composed by Tania León, Two Preludes and *Rondó a la criolla* (Creole Rondo).[46] As an encore, the duo played an instrumental arrangement of "Ciego reto" ("Blind Challenge"). León had composed this song earlier for her brother's combo, but it gained wider recognition when Elena Burke (1928–2002), the legendary bolero singer, added it to her repertory. The second recital is the earliest record of León's music being performed in concert. When Edmundo López, her old piano teacher, heard these pieces he said, in an almost prophetic tone, "we may lose a pianist but we will gain a composer."[47]

León's reputation as a pianist was on the rise. One of the concerts in the series organized by the Hermanos Saíz Brigade was devoted to the music of some of Cuba's most promising young composers: José Loyola (b. 1941), Roberto Valera (b. 1938), and Carlos Malcolm (b. 1945). Loyola recalls that "it was the premiere of my first published work, a piano piece. . . . It was the 'Son' from my *Tres piezas cubanas*, the first piece of a cycle of three pieces; and it was the more complex to play. Tania did it. So, Tania was the first performer of my music. . . . The concert finished with a work for chamber orchestra; for strings, wind quintet, and piano. Tania played the piano in that piece too."[48] The invitation to play the more difficult music of Cuba's star composition students—pupils of José Ardévol (1911–1981), Federico Smith (1929–1977), and Leo Brouwer—shows that by 1965 León was already regarded as one of the most respected young classical pianists in Havana.

If attending the García Caturla Conservatory gave León a lot of exposure among young Cuban musicians, taking classes at the Seminario provided her many opportunities to expand her musical networks. Marta Valdés (b. 1934) was already a well-known singer and songwriter in the Cuban *filin*[49] scene when she decided to attend the Seminario to take music theory and composition lessons. Valdés met León there:

> One day I was going back home when I heard this piano; and I thought "Oh my God! What is that?" I opened the door and saw a very young woman playing. So, I asked the director [Odilio Urfé] and he said "that girl is a neighbor of my relatives. She is a very talented student." [Most of us, students at the Seminario] were popular musicians but she was not. This young woman had a classical music background; nevertheless, she became friends with everyone and we learned to love her.[50]

By 1966, León had already requested permission to leave Cuba, which led concert producers to stop offering her paid contracts. Notwithstanding, Valdés invited her to participate in a production of Bertolt Brecht's *El alma buena de Sechuán* (*Der gute mensch von Sezuan*) by *Grupo Teatro Estudio*.[51] Despite León's youth and lack of experience, the songwriter thought she was the ideal pianist to play the complex changing meters and irregular rhythmic patterns of the incidental music that she had composed for the occasion. Valdés' description of their working process sheds light on León's sense of humor which, beyond the serious professionalism that characterizes her work, to this day colors her professional and personal relations:

> There was a very funny moment in one of the songs that [actor] Sergio Corrieri was supposed to sing and in which I had to play a cymbal. It was a song about elephants and I had to hit the cymbal very loudly. So, that stuck with me. After that I became *platillo* [cymbal] and [Tania] became *tecla* [piano key]; she always calls me platillo and I always call her tecla.[52]

This collaboration with Teatro Estudio was León's only paid job as a musician in Cuba before she emigrated to the United States in 1967.

In 1966, León was already married to Eduardo Viera, a textile engineer who had recently come back from studying abroad and whom she met at the house of a neighbor who was also an engineer. This was a sort of furtive relationship that, in order to progress, León had to defend from Mima and Mamota. Although she had a few boyfriends before Eduardo, she always had problems with Mima and Mamota accepting them. When León was fifteen years old, she told her grandmother about her boyfriend, a Chinese Cuban kid; Mamota replied: "No, that cannot be because you are going to be famous. You are studying to have a career. Your name will be on theater billboards. So, you will go and tell that boy that you are very sorry but that you cannot be in a relationship with him."[53] León was such an innocent and obedient girl that she actually told the boy they could not be together because she was going to be famous. Her subsequent boyfriends did not fare much better with Mima and Mamota; if Mima liked one, Mamota did not, and vice versa. In order to avoid this trouble with Eduardo, León simply showed up at home and told her relatives "this is Eduardo, he is my boyfriend, and please do not get in the way."[54] Mamota was so upset that she refused to attend their wedding ceremony.

After Tania and Eduardo got married she moved out of her grandmother's house and moved in with Eduardo and his parents, who had a bigger house in the Cerro neighborhood. Eduardo was an educated and sensitive man whose interests included classical music and ballet. He was very supportive of León's professional goals as a pianist and encouraged her to compose even before she was really interested in that. León remembers him often uncannily saying "You should compose an opera."[55] Furthermore, and most importantly, Eduardo was also supportive of her dreams to study music in Paris.

The mid-1960s were very important in the development of Cuban culture under the aegis of the revolutionary regime. The nationalization of the music industry had taken place in 1961, but it was only in 1964 that the Cuban government created EGREM as a national recording label in an attempt to overcome the problems that the 1962 U.S. embargo against Cuba created for its music industry. However, the shortage of quality plastic for the production of vinyl prevented EGREM from properly supplying the local market—jukeboxes almost disappeared because new records were not available—and weakened its ability to promote Cuban talent beyond the island. Some scholars have argued that this situation affected not only the visibility of Cuban musicians but also their creativity, as the development of new genres or styles of Cuban popular dance music was severely crippled.[56]

In 1965, Fidel Castro constituted the Cuban Communist Party and its Central Committee, a political and bureaucratic reorganization that put the country on a path toward Stalinization. This became increasingly apparent with the widespread repression and censorship that came during a period known today as *Quinquenio gris* (gray quinquennium or five years), from 1971 to 1975.[57] This radical turn of events in Cuban cultural life coincided with León finally making up her mind to leave Cuba to continue her music studies abroad. By now it had become clear for her that her country was in no position to help her by providing a scholarship to pursue what she thought was her destiny, studying piano in Paris. Thus, having grown tired of recording financial transactions and balancing books, León decided to leave Cuba without a scholarship and without help from the government. She just needed to figure out how to do it.

Family, Community, and Destiny

Although Tania León had a troubled relationship with her family through her childhood and years of music study, the idea of family has always been very important to her. Her unique experience growing up in Cuba in a matriarchal family—where two very strong, hardworking women were central in defining family dynamics and the collective sharing of responsibilities in the household— as well as in a neighborhood in which neighbors were almost considered family members, may have made León's understanding of family more fluid and in a way more communitarian. One can only imagine how hard it must have been for someone like her to leave her family behind and start from scratch, by herself, in a new country. Nevertheless, this desire for community is something that León has carried with her throughout her life. Learning to deal with distance, to love unconditionally from afar, to mediate between contrasting ideologies, and to put differences aside for the sake of common goals has enabled her to develop a strong family network even when living thousands of miles away from her relatives. This ability to build bridges, to maintain and strengthen family ties against all odds, and to empathize with other people's pain has been essential in helping her deal with the hard times in her life. It has also been fundamental in shaping her personal as well as professional and mentoring relationships. Growing up in the house on Salud Street indeed provided León with a moral and affective outlook that would shape her life beyond the dusty streets of her Havana neighborhood.

2

MODULATION AND DISPLACEMENT

cubana de adentro . . . cubana de afuera

On April 18, 2015, I had the opportunity to watch Tania León conduct live for the first time when she led the Fromm Players performance of *Indígena*, one of León's signature compositions. This work can be performed in its original large chamber-ensemble setting as well as by a symphony orchestra. Matthew Guerrieri, music reviewer for the *Boston Globe*, recognized León's composition as the concert's highpoint, highlighting how the composer "conducted her own stylish, convivially fractious 13-player [ensemble, and how the music presented] Latin rhythms and notions ebulliently piled around Peter Evans' extroverted trumpet solo."[1] For me, the most memorable experience of the evening was discovering León's restrained but precise and effective conducting style, which was just what these expert musicians needed to provide a memorable performance.

Just a little over a year and a half later, León was invited to conduct *Indígena* for its Cuban premiere performed by the National Symphony Orchestra in Havana. This is a work that several professional conductors I have informally talked to consider to be difficult to lead. However, the work seemed to have been selected because León thought it may be the easiest to put together given the small amount of rehearsal time. Nevertheless, the Cuban musicians' performance lacked the precision one usually hears when listening to this popular composition. León felt a bit frustrated about it. After analyzing a video of the concert, it became clear to me that the issues that upset her were the result of mistakes, rhythmic errors, and ensemble coordination problems one would not expect to hear from any professional orchestra used to playing contemporary music.

Contrasting these two performances leads one to wonder why it may have been particularly difficult for these professional Cuban musicians to play under León's baton. Researching into the current status of contemporary music in Cuba reveals how much the local classical music scene has changed almost fifty years after she left the island. Once a haven for contemporary avant-garde music, Cuba has slowly become very conservative in the last couple of decades.[2] Neither audiences nor musicians are really used to the musical experiments that defined the Cuban avant-garde in the late 1960s and early 1970s. In a musical world that privileges the programming of Mozart, Beethoven, Grieg, and orchestral versions of Cuban popular music, Cuban audiences may have found listening to León's modernist music a novel and stimulating occasion. But for Cuban musicians, it may have been an extra challenge to come to terms with an unfamiliar musical style, as well as the music's complex rhythmic patterns.

The dynamics that arose between León and these musicians during rehearsals and the subsequent concert underscore the cultural differences between *cubanos de afuera* (Cubans from abroad, especially those who left the country after the revolution) and *cubanos de adentro* (Cubans from inside Cuba, those who still live on the island). They are also a metaphor for the complex dynamics the composer had to continuously negotiate as a Cuban living in the United States who still had relatives on the island.

A few days before the Havana concert, the *New York Times* hailed the significance of the occasion by stating that "although her works have been performed in Cuba before, León [has] never performed there."[3] For most Cubans, this was the first opportunity to see León as a professional musician and to have a peek into the life of a displaced artist. León has been a central figure in the contemporary music scene of the United States for over forty years; but up to that moment, she had been largely rendered invisible in her native country.

On November 25, 2016, only nine days after this concert, Raúl Castro appeared on national Cuban television to announce that his brother, Fidel, the founder, leader, and pragmatist ideologue of the Cuban Revolution, had passed away. The news, loudly celebrated and painfully mourned by many on both sides of the Florida strait, symbolized the end of an era: a period that emotionally marked the life of León as well as that of more than one million Cubans who were forced to leave their country for political, economic, religious, or familial reasons since the triumph of Castro's revolution in 1959.

1967, *Año del Viet-Nam Heróico*: Leaving Cuba

In 1967, the Cuban Revolution celebrated its *Año del Vietnam Heróico* (Year of Heroic Vietnam). Ché Guevara's call to "create two, three . . . many Vietnams"[4] was becoming a familiar slogan posted on public walls around the island. On May 29th of that year, León traveled to Varadero to board a plane that would fly her to Miami. She had been living in a kind of limbo for almost two months since the Cuban government had unilaterally canceled her original departure date on April 4th at the very last minute. Right before boarding the plane, León handed her passport to a migration officer who, without thinking much about it, canceled it, thus annulling her Cuban citizenship.[5] This was a complete shock to León, because she was unaware that this was a possible outcome of her leaving the country. She walked the last couple of meters toward the airplane as a citizen of nowhere. Adding to her distress, right before boarding, a black militiaman blocked the flight of stairs and rebuked her by asking: "What are you going to do there?" León was the only person of color on the plane, and, for many, the soldier posed a sincere question: Why would she abandon her country and a revolution that sought to bring equality to people of color in Cuba? As the plane took off, she looked through the window to catch a last glimpse of her island. All she could see was a giant sign written with stones on Varadero beach: "*Patria o Muerte. Venceremos!*" (Country or Death. We Will Be Victorious!). Reading that slogan was the painful moment that made her suddenly aware that she was leaving her country for good.

León left Cuba on one of the *Vuelos de la Libertad* (Freedom Flights), the air bridge administered by the U.S. and Cuban governments in response to U.S. President Lyndon B. Johnson's speech at New York's Statue of Liberty on October 3, 1965. He had declared: "Those who seek refuge here will find it. The dedication of America to our traditions as an asylum for the oppressed will be upheld."[6] Regardless of how we judge Castro's regime today, as Silvia Pedraza states, the 1960s

> were some of the leanest and most idealistic (years) of the Cuban revolution. To spread access to a basic education and health care, young, educated Cubans went to live in the countryside, working in the Literacy Campaign to educate the illiterate peasants and in public health campaigns to provide basic health care.[7]

A person of color emigrating from Cuba was not the most common sight during those early years. The first and second waves of emigrants after the Cuban revolution were largely members of the overwhelmingly white, economic elite of the country. They sought to escape the political turmoil as well as "to access greater economic opportunities than were provided in a socialist society that instituted a new ethic of sacrificing individual consumption to achieve collective goals."[8] These emigrants were portrayed in Cuba as selfish people who did not care for the well-being of their fellow countrymen and were often called *gusanos* (worms).[9]

As much as it caused León a great deal of anxiety, the militiaman's question was based on a real lack of understanding as to why a person of color would leave Cuba precisely at the moment when exceptionally far-reaching anti-discriminatory laws had been passed in the country. This had also been the reaction of some of her colleagues when they found out she was leaving for the United States. "There is nothing for you there,"[10] was the recurring mantra she heard from them, including some of the most prominent Cuban musicians of the day. However, León's decision to leave Cuba had nothing to do with the polarized politics that were engulfing her country in the late 1960s. To this day, León maintains that she was a naïve, twenty-four-year-old woman, unaware of the practical implications of her trip abroad. She believes she was inadvertently trapped in a political turmoil that had nothing to do with her musical aspirations. Nonetheless, and much against her own wishes, the turmoil consequences would impact her life in many unforeseen ways.

León had requested the support of the Cuban cultural elites in her search for financial aid to sponsor her trip abroad to study, but these efforts had been unsuccessful. In order to support her family, she had put her artistic dreams on hold for several years, but by 1965 she was determined to find a way to fund her long-awaited study trip to Paris. An option opened when the Vuelos de la Libertad started operating on December 1st of that year. A few years earlier, one of León's conservatory classmates had moved to Miami with her family. With their support, León got an application form from Cuba's *Acción Católica* (Catholic Action)—a Vatican-sponsored organization critical of the authoritarian path that the Castro government already seemed to be taking—to leave the country via the Freedom Flights air bridge. For León, it was an exclusively financial decision. Neither she nor her family had the money to pay for a flight abroad. She remembers that

> this was the free trip out I was able to get. My family had no money to pay for anything. . . . And this was my own thing; since I was nine years old I had been saying that I was going to study in Paris at the conservatory. To tell you the truth, this was a moral matter for me because I saw my family struggle so much to give

me an education; and one of my dreams was to have the resources, you know, to get my grandmother, my mom, and everyone [in my family] away from all that poverty.[11]

Registering through Acción Católica ensured that the program would pay for her trip. León's plan was to fly to the United States only as a temporary move; the final step was still to go to Paris and continue her music studies there. She was not completely unaware of the polarized situation she would encounter by leaving Cuba for the United States. It was sure to create difficulties for her with the Cuban government and its followers, the Cuban exiles she was about to meet in her new country, and the U.S. government. In fact, the Cuban government was increasingly tightening its emigration policies, especially in relation to the United States, as it became more and more politically and economically dependent on the Soviet Union. Stuck in an unknown country, without money, without a passport, and in a legal limbo, León would be unable to return to her country and visit her family and relatives for twelve years.

Probably the most painful moment in all those years of absence was being unable to return to Cuba when Mamota died. The night before León boarded the plane in Varadero, Mamota took her cane and with great difficulty walked to Mima's house, where her granddaughter was staying overnight. She hugged Tania tightly and begged her not to leave, assuring her that everything was going to change for the better.[12] With tears in her eyes, León could only manage to say, "You made me believe in this. You gave me wings to fly and now you do not want me to fly."[13] That was the last time León saw Mamota; she passed away in 1971, just four years after her granddaughter left Cuba. Needless to say, León was not permitted to travel to Cuba to attend Mamota's funeral.

Cuba from Afar

León had planned to stay in the United States for only a short time, save some money, and continue her trip to France. Because she didn't have a passport, it was impossible for her to leave. After a few days staying in Miami, she asked to be resettled in New York City. Finding herself with a canceled Cuban passport was an unexpected burden that, added to the stress of having no money and speaking no English, made her situation more uncertain.

An extra source of anxiety was having to inform Mima and Mamota that she had lost her Cuban citizenship and had no legal way of returning to them. In the late 1960s, calling her grandmother from the United States created many problems; "she had to call [the] long distance operator and the long distance operator had to call the operator in Cuba."[14] They had to limit their conversations to topics that possible government eavesdroppers would not find suspicious, and there was the real possibility that mean-spirited Cuban operators would sabotage the call for no reason. The process was even more difficult when León wanted to talk to her mother. The "operator in Cuba had to call the neighbor of Tania's mother" says Martha Mooke, Tania's former partner, "because [she] didn't have a phone in her house. So, for Tania to call her mother it could have been a two- or three-hour-long process just to get the line and then, once the neighbor answered the phone, the neighbor had to run around the corner and get her mother to come and answer [it]."[15]

Political differences with her relatives were yet another source of apprehension for León. She felt that under the pressure of distance and separation such disagreements could lead to undesirable family misunderstandings and break-ups. "My father and my mother were two persons who were very involved in the process that Cuba was going through," explains Yordanka León, Oscar José's daughter, "they were people who truly believed in the revolution. And at that time, it did not look well to have a relative living abroad. I was very young but I remember neighbors throwing eggs at other neighbors [who had relatives abroad]. I never saw my parents do that but I did see neighbors doing it. People had to keep up appearances."[16] Fortunately for León, these differences never led to an unforgiveable misunderstanding, because she and her brother agreed that family ties were more important than ideological differences. "We have different ways of thinking but that never affected our personal relation," says Oscar José, "Tania was always my sister, I was always her brother. Yet, there were moments of tension, I won't deny it. There were difficult, sour moments; but we always found a common ground and understood each other."[17]

On the other hand, the uncertainty of León's status in the United States was a hard blow on her marriage to Eduardo Viera. Originally the couple did not think that León's trip would mean them splitting. However, the fact that she was unable to return to Cuba meant that the marriage was, in practical terms, over. Eduardo had a son from a previous marriage and, even in the unlikely case that he could legally establish a way to travel abroad, he was unwilling to leave his son behind. Their dissolution of marriage was granted in 1973, the year León became a U.S. citizen.

Although her closest friends and relatives in Cuba knew, many of León's friends and classmates were unaware of her departure. Paquito D'Rivera says

I found out [about her departure] through her father. . . . I do not remember which year but I know he was the first one who told me about Tania. Back in those days, when someone left the country they would completely disappear them. Nobody will speak about them. They did no longer exist. Even the relatives would stop talking about them; and some would not even talk or write to them. But not her father. I used to bump into him very often and he always told me about Tania's success. He was very enthusiastic about her [life in the United States].[18]

José Loyola left Cuba in 1967 to study in Poland and only found out that Tania had left when he came back home in 1973.[19] On the other hand, Guido López Gavilán remembers that everyone noticed her sudden disappearance because "she was one of the most prominent students of our generation . . . and she only reappeared in our circle when she organized the *Sonidos de las Américas* Festival in the late 1990s."[20]

Living in the United States, León also quickly realized that—because she was a Cuban who had left her native country in the midst of the tumultuous political polarization of the time, with the help of an organization that openly criticized the Cuban government—she was expected to sympathize with the Cuban exiles in their opposition to the Castro regime. Even if she did not do so, there was always the potential of her being used as a pawn in a larger geopolitical game she was not interested in playing. Her refusal to engage with the Cuban exiles' rhetoric put her in a difficult position. Many viewed her with suspicion, which would eventually lead to bitter and unfortunate fallings-out with friends and acquaintances.

1979: Seven Days that Shook Tania León

In 1979, a softening of the U. S. relations with Cuba led to a chance for León to return to her country for the first time. This trip allowed her to reconnect with her family whom she had not seen in 12 years. But it also led to her discovery of how much her presence in Cuba and her accomplishments abroad were rendered invisible by the Castro government. From beginning to end, this trip was an emotionally draining experience for León.

Lourdes Casal Valdés (1938–1981) was a Cuban poet and activist who, accused of counterrevolutionary activities, had been forced into exile in the United States in 1962. Until the publication of her book *El caso Padilla: literatura y revolución en Cuba*, in 1971, Casal had been a critic of the Cuban government. Nevertheless, she was also one of the first Cuban exiles allowed to legally travel back to Cuba when the Castro regime invited her to visit the island and "witness the accomplishments of the revolution."[21] In 1973, she lived in Cuba for five months. After this experience Casal became an activist supporting Cuban exiles who wanted to reestablish links with their native country and negotiated with the Cuban government for the possibility of family reunification trips.[22] This possibility became more real after President Jimmy Carter allowed the travel restrictions to Cuba to lapse and opened an Interests Section in Havana in 1977. U.S. citizens, who were not allowed to travel to the island since the U.S. embargo was imposed in 1962, were now permitted to do so.

In New York City, León knew Casal through their involvement with INTAR, a Hispanic theater company founded in 1966 by Max Ferrá (1937–2017). Ferrá had left Cuba in 1958, shortly before the revolution. León began working with INTAR in 1974, when she composed incidental music for Mario Peña's play *La ramera de la cueva*. Thanks to their friendship, once Casal finally arranged for a group of Cuban exiles to travel to Havana from New York City in February 1979, she included León's name on the list of selected travelers.

Oscar José reflects on the discussions that were triggered when the alignment and changing policies in the United States and Cuba finally allowed for the return of the invisible and nameless Cubans who had left the country:

> My sister came in the first flight from New York to Havana. That was an event that brought a lot of discussion to the country . . . it brought an earthquake because the Revolution had talked so much against that policy that allowing it took "God and His Holy Help." It was terrible! A lot of people were saying that we should not receive back [those who left].[23]

The day León returned to Cuba, the canceled passport from 1967 stayed behind. She entered the country as a U.S. citizen with a permit from the Cuban government to stay on the island for seven days only and with the requirement that she had to stay at a hotel, not with relatives. In many ways, these were seven eye-opening days for the composer. Although she had become a visible figure in the 1970s New York music and theater scenes, in Cuba she was completely unknown as a composer or conductor. The Cuban government was particularly adamant about rendering invisible the prominent artists and musicians who had left the country after the Cuban revolution.[24] In a style that resembles the erasure of Stalin's enemies from the history of the Soviet Union, the names, works, and images of many of these artists were expunged from Cuban books and media and tacitly forbidden from being mentioned in public discussions, regardless of the degree of success they had abroad. This was particularly crude and pronounced during the so-called *Quinquenio gris*, a five-year period of unprecedented censorship and repression that started in 1971, soon after León's departure from the island.[25] However, her case was a bit different from that of more established Cuban artists and musicians—such as Guillermo Cabrera Infante (1929–2005), Aurelio de la Vega (b. 1925), or Celia Cruz (1925–2003)—because she was not well-known before leaving Cuba, remained largely apolitical abroad, and refrained from publicly criticizing the Cuban government. As she recalls:

> I have gone through a lot with these Cuba issues but I have never been a spokesperson for any of that because I always tried to protect my family. If you said anything against Cuba, [people in] Cuba would know it immediately. And if you said anything here, [the Cubans in the United States] would want to take you as a spokesperson against Cuba. I could never lend myself to that type of prostitution; neither for one side nor for the other.[26]

Despite León's determination to avoid taking sides in Cuban politics, her name and artistic activities were still rendered invisible. She was not mentioned in the first edition of Helio Orovio's *Diccionario de la música cubana* (1981). According to Guillermo Rodríguez Rivera, Cuba's *Instituto del Libro* (Book Institute) "ordered [Orovio] to eliminate exiled and emigrated [musicians]."[27] At any rate, other than her close friends and relatives, nobody in Cuba knew of her or her work in New York City or elsewhere. Thus, her first journey back to the island, as well as subsequent trips through the 1980s and 1990s, remained strictly family affairs. She had no formal relation with the Cuban music establishment until Sonidos de las Américas, the American Composers Orchestra's festival she co-founded in the 1990s, was dedicated to Cuba in 1999.

León's return to Cuba in 1979 was a very happy and emotional occasion for the family. They got together regularly at Mima's house and at Mamota's house on Salud street; even Oscar, Tania's father, attended those gatherings. But this homecoming was as emotional as it was shocking for León. Not only had her family changed during the twelve years that she could not return to the island—old family members had died and new ones were born, which had been a draining source of sorrow for her in the United States—it was that, without her realizing, she had also changed. "Why does she speak so funny?" asked Alain, León's three-year-old nephew. His blunt statement appalled her. She arrived in the United States without knowing a word of English and had a hard struggle to learn the language and assimilate into a society that was completely foreign to her. But apparently, this also disguised her Cubanness, her accent. Her voice—the most intimate and bodily connection between her inner self and her social self as a Cuban woman—had changed. Her Cuban family, her closest relatives, did not find it familiar anymore. It was as if Alain's question tacitly implied "you do not belong here anymore."

Despite these feelings of alienation, the short February trip allowed León to reconnect with relatives and old friends; meet new family members; and marvel as well as be shocked by the city, the people, the scents, and the flavors she had left behind (see figure 2.1). She invited Mima and her father to spend her last night in Havana at the famous nightclub, the Tropicana. Without her knowing, Oscar arranged for Paquito D'Rivera to come to the club that night. "I was ashamed to show up empty handed," remembers D'Rivera, "so I bought a seashell outside of the club and gave it to Tania as a present."[28] It was a happy reunion and León has kept this seashell in her house to commemorate the occasion. That night, León was able to spend time with her mother, reestablish ties with her father, and re-acquaint herself with D'Rivera, who would defect to the United States two years later, in 1981. The following morning, Oscar José went to the Habana Libre hotel to say goodbye to his sister. He brought with him Odilio Urfé, León's old neighbor and former mentor, for an emotional farewell that had the composer in tears hugging her brother for several minutes.

A second trip back to Havana in June of that year further signaled the distance between León the New Yorker, the public figure, and León the lost daughter, sister, aunt, and pupil. This trip was also the result of Lourdes Casal's negotiation with Cuban authorities to set up a well-orchestrated meeting between Cuban artists abroad and Cuban officials. This time, León had the opportunity to truly spend quality time with her father. León remembers, "That week [my father and I] went together everywhere and it was he who told me, after listening to my music, [. . .] that it was very interesting but that [he wondered] where was I in all of that."[29] Having her nephew question her accent and having her father question her artistic voice during those trips made a powerful impression on León and sent her into a deep reflection upon her personal and ethnic identities as a diasporic Cuban individual.

Before León's second visit to Cuba, Oscar had sent her a program of the *Danza Nacional de Cuba* that featured Yoruba traditions.[30] Founded by choreographer Ramiro Guerra Suárez (b. 1922) in 1959, the company's mission was to combine American contemporary dance techniques, classical European ballet, and Afro-Cuban folk styles. Guerra's *Suite yoruba* (1960) remains one of the standard works in the company's repertory and is widely viewed today as the foundation of a uniquely Cuban dance style.[31] During her second visit to Cuba,

FIGURE 2.1. Tania León, Mima, and Oscar José León during one of the composer's first trips back to Cuba. Courtesy of Tania León.

Oscar took his daughter to an impromptu *bembé* celebration at a private house.[32] León remembers:

> [T]here was a moment when I wanted to leave the house—it was doing something to me. I felt the drums. [...] It was overwhelming ... my return to Cuba ... the reunion with my family after all those years. My father repeated once again, "*Why don't you use something in your work that is ours?*" He did not suggest that I specifically use the *tambores* or anything like that—he was referring in general to elements of our music.[33]

The night before her departure, Oscar skipped the farewell dinner Mima had prepared to bring all the family together. León felt her father's absence was yet another blow in the history of emotional agony that characterized their relationship. She was not ready to forgive him easily this time. When Oscar showed up at the lobby of the Habana Libre when León had to take a bus to the airport, she ignored him. It was the last time she would see her father. On January 1, 1980, Oscar wrote a letter to León asking for her forgiveness and pledging to start their relationship anew; three months later, on March 6th, he passed away. The days they spent together in Havana in 1979 were some of the few moments in their entire relationship that León felt really close to her father. She remembers those days with a mixture of melancholy and remorse: "I was working on forgiving him [when he died]. That letter is the only thing I have from him."[34] The experiences they went through together would stay with León forever and would significantly shape her future creative output.

On her return to New York, León began work on a new composition, *Four Pieces for Violoncello* (1981), which reflected the distress of losing her father. The second movement is "a eulogy, but it [was] filled with great pain. I called the third movement, *Tumbao* (groove) [. . .] As the cello begins to express *el tumbao*, that's where I first introduced the elements of Cuban music that would appear in my later work."[35] *Four Pieces for Violoncello* marked the beginning of a new aesthetic path that responded to León's father questioning her artistic voice. Ten years later, she began a project that directly addressed the other emotional shock she experienced during these trips: her young nephew's questioning of her accent. León indicates that *Indígena* was dedicated to Alain as a response "after that little kid said that I spoke strangely."[36]

A Family's Special Period

In the Fall of 1989, Tania León met Martha Mooke, who worked for her publisher, Peer Music. León was in the process of revising *Batá* (1985, rev. 1988) for its final publication, and had to visit the company's office in New York City regularly. A Jewish woman of Russian and Polish descent who grew up on Staten Island, Martha was also a viola player interested in contemporary music, so they often bumped into each other at concerts or other music-related events around the city. Slowly, their relationship became closer. This was the beginning of a long relationship that would last for almost thirty years.

In 1990, Martha visited Cuba for the first time so she could meet Tania's relatives. The trip took place just a year before Cuba entered the so-called *Periodo Especial* (Special Period; 1991–1999), one of the most economically depressed phases in the country's modern history. Since the financial fiasco caused by the failure of the *Zafra de los Diez Millones* (10-Million Ton Sugar Harvest) in 1971, the Cuban economy had been subsidized by the Soviet Union. Its dissolution in 1991 meant that Cuba was left to fend for itself. Drastic fuel, electricity, and food and medicine shortages became the norm through the 1990s. As the Cuban government attempted to deal with the economic crisis, regular Cuban people resorted to all type of imaginative and dramatic solutions, from "raising pigs in bathtubs" to eating "mashed banana peel and fried grapefruit peel."[37] A thriving black market developed because of these scarcities. In 1994, the dire situation of many Cubans tired of the economic hardships of the Special Period and the bureaucratic obstacles that made it difficult to leave the country generated the *crisis de los balseros* (Cuban rafter crisis).[38]

In the middle of the Special Period, Yordanka León informed her aunt that she wanted to leave the island. It was not the first time they had discussed this; Yordanka was only thirteen years old when she first told León about her desire to "leave Cuba, visit other cities and places, and study abroad"[39] back in 1987. However, by 1994, Yordanka had graduated from basic and middle music levels at the *Escuela Elemental de Música Manuel Saumell* and the *Escuela Nacional de Instructores de Arte*, with a specialization in choral conducting. She started experiencing problems at her job after expressing her desire to study abroad; one of her supervisors actually asked government officials to formally veto her exit visa petition.[40]

León's story from almost thirty years earlier was happening again. However, there were no Freedom Flights for those who wished to leave the country now. The government's bureaucracy continued to be an unsurmountable obstacle. León's intervention was essential for Yordanka to be able to leave Cuba legally. She asked her friend Barbara Held, a flutist from the United States who was living in Barcelona and married to the well-known Catalonian arts collector Rafael Tous, to help. Tous' foundation awarded Yordanka a scholarship to study at the conservatory in Barcelona. León still needed to pull some strings among the contacts she had at various Cuban music institutions. In the end, Yordanka was allowed to travel abroad. She lived with Barbara and Rafael for a couple of years. After finishing her studies, Yordanka auditioned for the choir of the *Palau de la Música Catalana* and was hired as a singer. She currently lives in Barcelona, where she is married and makes a living as a vocal instructor and as an opera singer at the *Gran Teatre del Liceu*.

Eventually, the country's socialist constitution had to be reformed during the Special Period in order for the government to hold onto its power. Some of the government's initiatives included tolerating incipient forms of private entrepreneurship, the decriminalization of circulating the U.S. dollar, and attracting foreign investment, particularly in the area of tourism, which was seen as the country's economic panacea.[41] The government's emphasis on tourism led to a new openness in the cultural arenas. Eventually, this preceded not only a reassessment of the contributions of *cubanos de afuera* to Cuban culture—a rehabilitation of sorts—but an expansion of the notion of national identity as also being shaped by the Cuban diaspora.

Sonidos de las Américas-Cuba:
Spring in New York City at the End of the Special Period

On Tuesday, March 2, 1999, the *Sonidos de las Américas-Cuba* Festival launched with a sold-out concert at Carnegie Hall's Weill Recital Hall. The event, entitled "Dance Date" with Cuba, featured music by Cuban classicists Ernesto Lecuona, Gonzalo Roig (1890–1970), and Alejandro García Caturla (1906–1940), as well as more recent works by living composers Harold Gramatges, Odaline de la Martínez (b. 1949), Aurelio de la Vega, and Tania León. This was the first of sixteen concerts in a festival featuring programs that combined music by Cuban composers in the diaspora and Cuban composers from the island. This was the sixth and final edition of *Sonidos de las Américas*, a festival created by the American Composers Orchestra and its Music Director, Dennis Russell Davies (b. 1944), and Tania León. The goal of the festival was to make U.S. audiences aware of "an abundant and rich body of music, which like the music of U.S. composers, is infrequently performed on concert programs in the United States."[42] The previous editions had been dedicated to the music of Mexico, Venezuela, Brazil, Puerto Rico, and Argentina. However, this sixth and last edition was probably the most emotionally meaningful for León. It provided a unique space for the encounter of composers and musicians who, in some cases, had not seen each other in nearly forty years.

León had to work especially hard to organize this edition of the festival, particularly to clear the path for a delegation of Cuban musicians to visit the United States. She had originally planned to present the Cuban edition of the festival earlier. However, the anti-Cuban political climate that followed the Cuban Air Force's shoot-down of two aircraft operated by *Hermanos al Rescate* (Brother to the Rescue)—a Miami-based activist organization—in 1996, and the U.S. Congress' subsequent passing of the Helms-Burton bill, made the project politically impossible. It was only three years later, in 1991, when President Bill Clinton eased the Cuba travel restrictions that had been reinstated by the Reagan administration in 1981, that Sonidos de las Américas-Cuba became feasible.

Assembling a list of invitees and making their travel arrangements required coordination between León, officials in Cuba, and the U.S. State Department. She and Michael Geller—the newly appointed Executive Director of the American Composers Orchestra—had to get State Department permission to meet with Cuban composers and UNEAC (*Unión Nacional de Escritores y Artistas de Cuba*) officials at the U.S. Interests Section in Havana. Once Sonidos de las Américas-Cuba was approved, León went to visit Alicia Perea (1934–2015) in Havana. The composer had met Perea in the early 1960s, when the former was a student and the latter a piano accompanist at the Peyrellade Conservatory. In 1999, when the festival was being planned, Perea was president of the *Instituto Cubano de la Música* (Cuban Music Institute), the bureaucratic office that oversees and regulates musical life on the island. She was in a perfect position to help León coordinate the organization of the event.

Although León wanted a delegation of composers and musicians that represented a broad aesthetic spectrum of Cuban musical practice, she was also interested in making sure that some important musicians as well as some of her former mentors were included in the list. It was agreed that the selection of music by Cuban composers to include in the festival would be a joint effort. On the island, a local committee would place a call for scores, while, externally, a selection committee in the United States would evaluate the works submitted. José Loyola remembers some of the details of the process in Cuba:

> I was told "We need you to send some of your works." So, I did. The [scores] were sent to the United States . . . and my work [*Homenaje a Brindis de Salas*] was selected there. I never knew for sure that I was going [to New York] until the Instituto de la Música announced here that I had been selected.[43]

In the end, Loyola was able to attend the festival.

For others in Cuba, the selection process was far from being stress-free. Juan Piñera (b. 1949) explains how the conversations among Cuban musicians unfolded:

> I can tell you that out of the Cubans who were here [in Cuba] there were indispensable names; people who could not be left out that in the end were left out, sometimes because they wanted specific works [to be performed] and sometimes because they did not want to be with one another. But out of everyone there were two persons who had to be in the list, one was [Tania's former] teacher, Alfredo Diez Nieto . . . the other one was me, because we had similar ways of approaching things. Tania did something few persons do. She treated all aesthetic, political, ideological positions, and questions of fame, very ecumenically . . . She tried to have them all and [here] it was truly an agonizing experience. I tried to be helpful, I even gave up my place so Carlos Fariñas, who is an indispensable name in Cuban classical music, could participate. But it was fruitless because in the end, my friend Fariñas was very intransigent.[44]

According to León, Carlos Fariñas (1934–2002) said that unless his Cello Concerto was played, he would not travel to the United States.[45] That was not the only problematic situation. Aware of their great importance in Cuban musical life, the Festival issued a couple of direct invitations, among them to composer and guitarist Leo Brouwer and pianist Frank Fernández (b. 1944). León reveals that, a few weeks later:

> We received a phone call telling us that Frank Fernández did not want to come. In a case like that, like Leo [Brouwer]'s, there is nothing I could do . . . Years later, Fernández bumped into my brother and asked him how he could contact me because he had been unable to come to the Cuba Festival. . . . My brother told him "Listen, it was you who did not want to go!" And [Fernández] said "Who said I did not want to go?" So, he found out right there that someone had backstabbed him. He is still trying to figure out who did that to him.[46]

In the end, the Cuban delegation included composers Juan Blanco (1919–2008), Alfredo Diez Nieto, Harold Gramatges, Guido López Gavilán, Jorge López Marín (b. 1949), José Loyola, Edgardo Martín (1915–2004), Juan Piñera, and pianist Huberal Herrera (b. 1929). The participation of Cubans from abroad included composers Aurelio de la Vega, Orlando Jacinto García (b. 1954), Keyla Orozco (b. 1969), and Ileana Pérez-Velázquez (b. 1964) as well as pianists Nohema Fernández (b. 1944) and Santiago Rodríguez (b. 1952), among others. Figure 2.2 shows some of these musicians during a pre-concert talk.

As could be expected in the polarized atmosphere of U.S.-Cuban relations, not everyone was happy about the festival. Some members of the Cuban exile community were very antagonistic, including musicians who were actually included in the program. Music critic Greg Sandow reports that Aurelio de la Vega

FIGURE 2.2. Pre-concert talk during Sonidos de las Américas-Cuba. From left to right, Ileana Pérez-Velázquez, José Loyola, Keyla Orozco, Tania León, Juan Piñera, and Orlando Jacinto García. Reproduced by permission of American Composers Orchestra.

told him "he'd had phone calls [from members of the Cuban exile community] urging him not to participate [in the festival]," and that Paquito D'Rivera, whose music was programmed in the festival, accused the event of being communist propaganda.[47]

In Cuba, the presence of Cuban musicians at the festival was used as propaganda that had nothing to do with León's original intentions. *Granma*, the official newspaper of the Central Committee of the Cuban Communist Party, published a review that described the event as a triumph for the Cuban delegation without even bothering to mention the Cuban exiles in attendance.[48] Mima sent León a copy of the review and reminded her, "that's for you to see how they treat people here."[49] *Boletín Música*, the journal published by Casa de las Américas, Cuba's institution in charge of promoting cultural relations with Latin American and Caribbean countries, covered the event in a similar vein. Although it included the names of León, Aurelio de la Vega, García, Orozco, and Pérez-Velázquez, the article did not mention that they were all Cubans living abroad.[50]

Regardless of these setbacks, the event was the successful point of artistic and personal encounter it was meant to be. José Loyola mentions that, while he was waiting for a concert to start, a black woman approached him. Showing him a picture in the program, she asked him:

"Are you this one here?" And I said, "Yes." And then she asked me "Are you [living] in Havana or are you here in the United States?" So, I told her, "No, I am in Havana." So, we started a conversation and it turns out she was Zenaida Manfugás! I had not seen her since the 1960s. I met her later at the closing event at Carnegie Hall and we had a chance to talk a lot . . . This happened thanks to Tania's idea to get people from here and from there together.[51]

The festival fostered many encounters like this one. Especially noteworthy was the meeting of Aurelio de la Vega and Harold Gramatges, two of the most prominent Cuban composers of their generation—one a fierce critic of the Cuban regime and the other an unapologetic supporter of the government. They had not seen each other in over forty years (see figure 2.3).

Cristina Eguizábal from the Ford Foundation, one of the cosponsors of the event, described it as "the most public meeting yet of Cubans on both sides, a step toward ultimate reconciliation."[52] Several years later, Juan Piñera summarized the occasion:

It is painful that some people forget moments as important as that one. Because very few of us [Cuban musicians] can have our music played at a theater as important as Carnegie Hall . . . [Tania] fought to have as many of us as possible [from here and from there] participating [in the festival]. She struggled against

FIGURE 2.3. Conversation between Harold Gramatges, Alfredo Diez Nieto, and Aurelio de la Vega. Reproduced by permission of American Composers Orchestra.

intentional and unintentional acts of forgetting here and there. So, generosity . . . that is my image of Tania, a very generous woman.[53]

Ultimate reconciliation between *cubanos de afuera* and *cubanos de adentro* may take a very long time through a conscious effort from both sides to truly understand and respect each other's positions. As much as the festival did a lot of good, it also showed the ugly side of U.S.-Cuban politics. Tania was particularly hurt by the criticism of some Cuban exiles, who disregarded their lifelong friendships in order to further political agendas. When Paquito D'Rivera characterized the festival as communist propaganda, it was particularly painful for her, because she had always been very supportive, personally and professionally, of D'Rivera, especially when he first defected to the United States.[54] Although D'Rivera and León remain friendly to this day, his allegations reveal her continuing difficulties dealing with the more militant members of the Cuban exile community.

Excitement and Frustration at the
II *Festival de Música de Cámara Leo Brouwer*

Regardless of the bridges that León had tried to build with the organization of Sonidos de las Américas-Cuba, her music remained unheard in Cuba. It was not until 2003, when pianist Ursula Oppens (b. 1944)—León's friend and frequent collaborator—received an invitation to perform in Havana that one of the composer's works was heard live in Cuba for the first time since she moved to the United States. On May 11, 2003, Oppens played the Cuban premiere of León's *Mística* (2003) for solo piano at the *Basílica Menor San Francisco de Asís* in Old Havana. The piece was written for Oppens, who had recently given its world premiere in Chicago, so it was an obvious choice for her to play in Cuba. *Mística* is dedicated to León's mother. As it happened, the concert was given on Mother's Day, and although the composer was unable to attend, Mima was there. León says that "when [Ursula] finished playing the piece, she stood up and said 'Tania's mother is here' and gave her the score. I wanted it to be [my mom's] Mother's Day present."[55]

Seven years later, in 2010, León received an official invitation to have her music performed in Cuba. It came from Isabelle Hernández, Leo Brouwer's manager, who was the director of the *Festival de Música de Cámara Leo Brouwer*. Brouwer states that the festival was created in order to break the inertia of conservative music programming that dominates orchestras and other musical ensembles in Cuba. "We present chamber music concerts with an unusual repertory," explains the composer, "we are never going to play Mozart or Beethoven in those concerts."[56] Hernández adds that for this particular event:

> I decided to program a concert of Cuban women composers living abroad. Of course, the first person to come to mind was Maestra Tania León. So, I put together a program with her, Magaly Ruiz, and Keyla Orozco. I believe the concert was called "Cuban Women in Other Lands." I got [León's] e-mail and contacted her. She was very efficient. She accepted the invitation right away. I told her what were the instrumental formats we had and she sent three or four pieces. We selected two. And she was always very generous. She accepted to fly to Cuba and pay for her trip. I believe she was very happy because her music may have been played in Cuba only once before. So, the concert at the Basílica de San Francisco de Asís was a very beautiful moment.[57]

The pieces selected for the festival were *Arenas d'un tiempo* (1996), for clarinet, cello, and piano, and *Alma* (2007), for flute and piano. The event was announced in *Juventud Rebelde*, the newspaper of the *Unión de Jóvenes Comunistas* (Union of Young Communists):

> The feminine mark, from the 19th century until today, will also be present [at the festival . . . including female Cuban [composers] in the diaspora who have produced their work in other countries without losing the beat and the deepest essence of their identity. It is the case of Magali [*sic*] Ruiz, Keyla Orozco, and Tania

León, the last one a resident of New York for several decades now, with works that breath Africanness from its more authentic source, stripped of superficiality, folkloric effects, and vacuous ornaments.[58]

What is most striking about this announcement is not only that a government-sanctioned newspaper like *Juventud Rebelde* was reporting about a group of Cubans living abroad that it would have completely ignored in previous decades, but that it refers to their music, especially León's, as deeply and authentically Cuban.

This new attitude was further reinforced by flutist Niurka González, a member of *Duo Ondina*, the ensemble in charge of playing the Cuban premiere of *Alma*. When asked about the technical and stylistic challenges in León's music, González stated:

It is a very difficult piece. Technically it is very complex for the flute [. . .] and rhythmically it is a very complex world. [. . .] It has a very impressive Cuban and African influence, but it is not something you see by simply looking at the score. But when you start working on it and start listening to the rhythmic layers, it is amazing the influence of Cuban and African rhythms. It is like it is all there, underneath, and suddenly it blossoms. [. . .] I believe it is a deeply Cuban piece. It has beautiful rhythmic elements that could get easily lost, if the performer does not have the cultural knowledge about the richness of Cuban music.[59]

Evidently, the antagonism expressed toward people who chose to leave Castro's Cuba—who were denied their Cubanness (rhetorically and formally, as in the period when their passports were canceled), were referred to as *gusanos*, and had their names removed from history books and even family conversations— was not necessarily the norm anymore.[60] It is tempting to read the openness that the festival showed toward *cubanos de afuera* as being influenced by the Obama Administration's 2009 lifting of all restrictions on family traveling and remittances to Cuba. The repercussions of this act certainly showed the importance of the Cuban diaspora on the economic and emotional lives of those living on the island.

Despite having had the chance to listen to her music live in the company of her eighty-five-year-old mother in her native country, León's sense of excitement was diminished by some negative experiences she had during the festival. First, the biographical note that she had sent from New York had been edited, removing information about her post as Distinguished Professor at Brooklyn College and the Graduate Center at the City University of New York. Whether this was done intentionally or not is unclear, but the incident left León with the impression that there were aspects of her life Cuban authorities were not willing to publicly celebrate or even acknowledge. The second problem may have been more upsetting; it took place at the second concert's reception. "My relatives went back home and Juan Piñera stayed with me," León explains, "so, I asked if Juanito could come to the reception with me."[61] Because Piñera was Cuban, the authorities did not allow him to attend the reception, hitting Tania like a bucket of cold water.[62] She was further frustrated by the fact that her name and her musical activities abroad were suspiciously absent from media coverage of the festival.[63] If the invitation and concerts provided moments to rejoice, they were also a reminder of the less-than-fair treatment that many *cubanos de afuera* as well as *cubanos de adentro* receive in Cuba.

All in all, León was very happy to be able to attend the two concerts at the Festival Leo Brouwer with her mother and enjoyed the experiences greatly. The renowned black Cuban painter Manuel Mendive (b. 1944) came to one of the concerts and Mima was ecstatic to be able to take pictures with him. Her mother was also honored to hear Brouwer publicly praise Tania and see many black people come close to her daughter and whisper in her ear how proud they felt of her.

However, after 2010, Mima's health started to deteriorate. She passed away on May 3, 2014. Unlike when Mamota and Oscar died, León was able to be in Cuba for her passing. Mima died peacefully with Tania and Oscar José holding both her hands. The decision was made to cremate her body. León kept the urn with the ashes but gave a small portion to her brother, her nephews Oscar Jr. and Alain, and her niece Yordanka. The loss of her mother was a very hard blow for León. Like the loss of her father thirty-four years earlier, it made her deeply question her identity and place in the world.

Cubana de adentro . . . cubana de afuera

In the summer of 2016, León received a letter from Guido López Gavilán, director of the XXIX Havana Festival of Contemporary Music. It was an invitation to conduct a work of hers with the National Symphony Orchestra of Cuba as part of the festival in November 2016. In a way this invitation was a seventeen-year-late act of reciprocity, because León had invited López Gavilán for Sonidos de las Américas in 1999. The invitation was made possible by a new political climate of openness generated by Barack Obama and Raúl Castro's announcement about the normalization of diplomatic relations between the two old Cold War rivals on December 17, 2014. The fact that two other composers of the Cuban diaspora,

Ailem Carvajal (b. 1972) and Orlando Jacinto García, were also invited made it seem like reconciliation was indeed a tacit theme of this particular edition of the festival.

Returning to Cuba as a professional musician inspired a new clash of emotions for León. On the one hand, her return as a conductor and composer was a way to share her most intimate artistic being and her public persona with her family and friends. She could honor the memory of those departed who had believed in her from the beginning, encouraged her education in Cuba, and emotionally supported her life abroad from afar. On the other hand, it presented her with the unpleasant opportunity to compare the professional life she made for herself abroad as a woman of color with the often negative, everyday professional and musical experiences of her peers on the island. On November 9th, she conducted the first rehearsal of *Indígena* with Cuba's National Symphony Orchestra (see figure 2.4).

The problems began right away. "There were a lot of supportive musicians in the orchestra but a few were somewhat upset. Especially men," recalls León, "I was conducting and [a musician] was laughing with a small group of people in the back. You know they make their little groups . . . I looked at him and he

FIGURE 2.4. Tania León conducting a rehearsal of *Indígena* with Cuba's National Symphony Orchestra. Reproduced by permission of Liliana González Moreno.

continued with his party there." At some point, León asked the group of men why weren't they playing and the violinist sarcastically responded "if you want us to play then write [the music] down," referring to the passages of open notation that León uses in *Indígena*. Alain, León's nephew, who was watching the rehearsal felt outraged by the guy's lack of respect and yelled: "¡Respeto, coño!" (Respect, damn it!) The violinist jumped down from the stage and began arguing with Alain. The situation escalated as other members of the orchestra tried to separate the two men. Some of the orchestra's musicians sided with their colleague, claiming this type of *pejepalera* (phony) music was too complex and León's working methods too unfamiliar. León was in a state of complete shock as the violinist left the rehearsal.

After some time, once he calmed down, the violinist rejoined the orchestra, which had continued the rehearsal without him. At that point, León stopped the music and addressed the orchestra:

> It is unbelievable we could behave like this. I just want you all to know that this young man [Alain] is my nephew. He is sitting there because he wanted to hear this music, which I dedicated to him. It was inspired by our first encounter when he was just a kid. So, he reacted emotionally when he saw that someone was not paying attention to what I was saying.[64]

Although the violinist later apologized to her, the situation was very unpleasant for León and those who attended the rehearsal.

This was not the only incident with the musicians. The concertmaster skipped most of the rehearsals. When León asked Enrique Pérez Mesa (b. 1960) why he wasn't attending, he told her not to worry, stating that the violinist was a very good musician and would be able to sight-read during the concert. This situation combined with the musicians' lack of familiarity with contemporary music notation and performance practice made León's work with the orchestra very hard. She was pushed to enforce an iron discipline on the orchestra members if the performance of *Indígena* was to happen. She requested more rehearsal time and eventually had a recording of the piece played through the hall's loudspeakers for the musicians to get a sense of what the music should sound like. Regardless of the shortcomings on the day of the concert—for instance, musicians who were unable to technically play their parts—Pérez Mesa and composer Roberto Valera recognized León's superb conducting technique. Pérez Mesa actually sat with the orchestra during rehearsals in order to closely follow León's working strategies and technique. When it was over, the orchestral musicians themselves thanked León for the discipline and commitment that she had demanded from them.

León believes that the difficulties she faced reveal not only problems of discipline and training within the orchestra, but also larger issues about machismo and chauvinism in Cuban society at large. These were exacerbated by having her, a woman of color and a Cuban from abroad, in a position of authority.

For Liliana González Moreno, the musicologist in charge of covering the event for the local media, these situations exemplify the complex relationship *cubanos de adentro* have with *cubanos de afuera*. In a conversation about changing ways of understanding Cuban identity, González Moreno suggested to León that, in fact, the musicians treated her just like they would treat any other Cuban woman. González Moreno shared this exchange from an interview she conducted in Havana with the composer:

> **González Moreno:** Being Cuban in Cuba or living somewhere else. That sensation of coming back home and people knowing you are Cuban but not living in Cuba. . . . How did you feel about that?
>
> **León:** Well, I have never stopped being Cuban.
>
> **GM:** I mean, as a musician.
>
> **L:** I understand. But for example, I was born here; and one is always like the elephants, who know where they were born. When they come back they recognize the aroma, the visual impact. . . . There are forms of expression that are the same while others are completely different . . . even the dancing styles, there may be something from those moments when I used to dance [here as a young woman] but there are also very different features due to the mixture of influences that Cuban people have had [through] their contact with other cultures; different from what I have had . . . but I do not need to go to the beach or drink a mojito in Cuba to know that part of me feels alive [here] . . .
>
> **GM:** I think what has happened is that we are moving beyond the *cubano de afuera* and the *cubano de adentro*. It was a time that marked us a lot.
>
> **L:** Yes.
>
> **GM:** Because now we can be in both places [on the island and abroad] we are beginning to treat each other in the same way. The way they treated you is the same way I am treated; they did not establish any differences. And I think there is something sad about that. Because [they do not recognize who] you are, and that you are coming here, making a great [personal] effort; paying for everything yourself . . .
>
> **L:** That is very interesting because I never saw a difference between the *cubano de adentro* and the *cubano de afuera*. Even when we did not have the kind of exchange we have now, I always treated the *cubano de adentro* equally. . . . And it always bothered me a lot when Cubans treated me as if I was *de afuera*. I perceived that not only in the United States, also when I came to visit my mom and I had sad and uncomfortable experiences with [her] neighbors. One may

56

perceive things differently but I believe human beings are all the same regardless of the languages we speak. Also, one communicates with the eyes, with the body, with our attitudes. I mean, the language of [body] movement. . . . So, that time [of separation] has affected us all, creating a false [dichotomy].[65]

Notwithstanding their different interpretation of the problems she encountered with the orchestra—whether they came about due to having León as a disruptive element of the musicians' everyday local power dynamics or as an example of how men routinely deal with women in Cuba—León felt gender dynamics at odds with those she experiences in her everyday professional life in the United States. She was also aware of the lack of presence of contemporary music in Cuban cultural life and felt she had to address it. When talking to the audience at the end of the concert, she stated her support for "contemporary music, the music of our times, the music written by living composers."[66] Regardless of her desire to bridge the gap between *cubanos de afuera* and *cubanos de adentro* by invoking a shared sense of memory or humanity, the different cultural routes followed by León and these Cuban musicians throughout their lives created different professional expectations. For the *cubanos de adentro*, acknowledging the composer as a *cubana de afuera*—with the perceived privileges this may have afforded her—could only produce further tensions.

Several days after León returned to New York from her trip to Cuba, she learned that Fidel Castro had died. Her first reaction was to think: "It's about time!" However, instead of celebrating the passing of the man who had created the conditions for the emotional displacement of many Cubans, she cried bitterly. It was the recognition of her own emotional displacement and her becoming a *cubana de afuera*. It was the culmination of years of grieving from afar the passing of relatives and friends instead of being able to share her pain at home with her family, or enjoying the birth of nieces and nephews that, instead, she knew only through pictures. While her music had given joy to strangers around the world, her loved ones were unable to experience it in their country—which filled her eyes with tears. However, one thought comforted her: "Look, Fidel Castro always did as he pleased, and that is what I am doing [with my own life], you know? Exactly the same."[67]

Of Returns, Reinventions, and Emotional Displacements

For León, traveling to Cuba has been a source of both distress and happiness. On the one hand, her trips have allowed her to become aware of her displaced life. After her first trip to Cuba in 1979, she began problematizing the compositional voice that she first developed in the United States. The sounds she produced in her new country, the result of her life in the cutthroat music scene of 1970s New York City, seemed foreign to those living in her native country. This was made even more striking when she was questioned by, of all people, her father, that largely absent figure in León's life, as to why she didn't embrace the sounds and rhythms of a musical world that had always been present in her life. While she was a public figure in New York, a powerful new voice in a vibrant music scene, she was completely unknown in Cuba, which was another source of her cognitive displacement. León's diasporic experience reflects the emotional displacement of all migrants whose loved ones stay behind but who cannot leave behind the fragrances, the sounds, the colors, and the everyday itineraries of the land they left. It is the identity displacements of those who discover themselves through the emotional connection to a country they deeply love but that may not love them back. It is the political displacement of individuals who are constantly pushed by others into defining themselves because defining themselves helps those others to also define their own identity.

The idea of a return to a shared homeland that was left behind is central to any diaspora. However, the specific political and economic circumstances of the Cuban experience have given rise to contradictory discourses, representations, and expectations about that homeland among Cubans in Cuba and those in the diaspora. It is often nostalgically assumed that going back home is about getting in touch with our "roots" and reestablishing friend and family ties. As much as returning home could be about that, León's case shows that it is also, if not primarily, about discoveries and self-discoveries. It is about finding out not what we are, but how we came to be what we are, and what we are *not* in the different spaces where we exist. It is also about what we could have become: it is a painfully emotional journey to learn not only about the routes that led us where we are, but also about a future that could have been but never was.

3

SYNCOPATION AND COLOR
Adapting to New Life Rhythms

In 2011, Rolling Potter, then Dean of the College of Fine Arts and Communication at the University of Central Arkansas, became fascinated with two John Adams operas, *Nixon in China* (1987) and *Doctor Atomic* (2005). He was especially interested in the fact that they dealt with somewhat recent political events. Potter started thinking about commissioning an opera based on a historical event that would have both local and national relevance. The story of the Little Rock Nine, a moment at the center of the civil rights movement of the 1950s–1960s, seemed to be dramatically, politically, and geographically perfect for such an opera, especially given that 2017 would be sixty years since the event occurred.[1] Once the funding and commission details were arranged, Potter placed a phone call to Tania León. He thought she would be the ideal person to tackle this opera because of her strong ties to many African American expressive-culture projects and institutions.

León admits that when she was invited to compose this opera she did not know the details about the story of the Little Rock Nine. So, she did her research. She learned about *Brown v. Board of Education*, the 1954 Supreme Court decision that made segregation in public schools unconstitutional. This ruling eventually opened the door for nine African American students to attend Little Rock Central High School as an integrated school. However, Arkansas governor Orval Faubus opposed school integration and sent the National Guard to prevent the nine students from entering the school. León saw the infamous picture of a dignified Elizabeth Eckford being harassed by a mob of hateful white students.

She learned about President Eisenhower's decision to federalize the Arkansas National Guard and send troops from the 101st Airborne Division to escort and protect the students between classes. She discovered the insults and indignities, the verbal and physical abuse that Minnijean Brown had to endure before she was expelled from the school when she fought back. She discovered that only one of the nine students, Ernest Green, was able to graduate from Central.

León watched newsreel footage of these events, talked to the surviving participants, and was horrified by the whole affair. She accepted the commission and became part of a team that also included two celebrated African American intellectuals, Thulani Davis as a librettist—who had experiences writing similar politically and racially charged librettos for two operas by Anthony Davis, *X (The Life and Times of Malcolm X)* (1986) and *Amistad* (1997)—and Henry Luis Gates Jr.—whom León met during a residency at the Bellagio Center in 1992—as historical consultant.[2]

Although the particular story of the Little Rock Nine may have been new to León, she knew of the violence against African American activists during the civil rights movement. Since her arrival in the United States, she was aware of the idealism and nobility of this crusade and experienced the aftermath of the movement and its earliest political and social repercussions. León's experiences as a woman of color during this period shaped her becoming a cultural citizen of the United States, as well as an artist and composer. They are fundamental to understanding the nuances of the musical palimpsest she composed to honor one of the more contradictory moments—disgraceful and dignified at once—in U.S. history.

1967: A Woman in New York

Tania León arrived in Miami on May 29, 1967. She recalls the occasion in a series of surrealistic sounds and images: a crowd of people yelling anti-Castro slogans, alongside cries like "we'll finally have a chance to drink Coca Cola!" and a priest blessing people while they lined up to kiss his ring.[3] The head of the family who had sponsored León's trip was a manager at a Publix, a chain of supermarkets in Florida. Given that she was an accountant, he had lined up a job for her as a cashier at the store. León spent a couple of sleepless nights thinking about her future. She did not have a valid passport; she did not speak English; and she was stuck thousands of miles away from her dream of continuing piano studies in Paris. Regardless, she did not quit her job as an accountant in Havana and risk the safety of her relatives on the island to land a job as a cashier in Miami.

León also quickly discovered the growing resentment among native M[ ]ians toward the newly arrived Cubans, whom they believed were taking jobs. The newcomers were greeted with chauvinistic signs like "No Pets, No Children, and No Cubans!"[4] That was not for her. It took her only a couple of days to gather the courage to go to the Catholic church that handled her immigration case and ask the staff to relocate her to New York City. Luckily, they understood that, given her training and aspirations, New York City, not Miami, was the right place for her.

Sara "Sarita" Checa, and her husband, Fernando, lived in Fordham, in the Bronx. Although their apartment was small, they welcomed León and let her stay on their living room couch for several weeks. Driving from the airport to Sarita and Fernando's place, she noticed the typical Manhattan buildings with outside fire-escape stairs and could only say, "María! María!" to the astonishment of her hosts.[5] The only image she had of her new city came from Maria and Tony's love duet in *Amor sin barreras* (1961), as Robert Wise and Jerome Robbins' film *West Side Story* was known in Cuba in the 1960s.[6] In 1967, the Bronx, traditionally an Irish and Jewish settlement, was going through a radical social and economic transformation. Many of the older white residents were moving away while thousands of African Americans and Puerto Ricans were moving to the area due to slum clearance in Manhattan.[7] This was León's first encounter with the complex dynamics between race and class informing U.S. everyday life; it was also her first encounter with the type of racial and social turmoil that had triggered the civil rights movement.

León met Sarita back in Havana, where she worked as a copyist for composer José Ardevol. In 1965, she and her husband left Cuba via Mexico and settled in the Bronx shortly thereafter.[8] They were the only persons León knew in New York City when she landed there. Soon after León's arrival, Sarita helped her search the yellow pages trying to find opportunities appropriate for her training as a musician. Sarita was especially interested in finding professional organizations that could help León transition into the music scene of her new country. They found the address of the American Council for Emigres in the Professions, an organization founded by Else Staudinger in 1940 "to facilitate the rescue and resettlement [of] designated refugees [intellectuals] in obtaining passage to the United States"[9] during World War II. Originally created to coordinate this rescue program, the Council was still actively helping with the relocation of newly arrived artists and intellectuals in New York City in the early 1970s. A few days after finding out about the Council, León went to their headquarters on 46th Street. She was fortunate to encounter a couple of fluent Spanish speakers, who were able to introduce her to Margaret Bush, the director of the Council's Music Department.

After an initial moment of awkwardness trying to communicate with each other, Bush pointed to a piano in the room and asked León to play something. Having just landed from Cuba, where weeks earlier she was still practicing piano several hours a day, León felt confident enough to try one of the most technically demanding works in her repertoire. She does not remember if she played one of Chopin's Ballades or one of Schumann's Symphonic Etudes Op. 13, but she recalls the mixture of incredulity and astonishment on Bush's face when she finished her performance.[10] Bush was so impressed that she arranged for the Council's support in securing practice space for León at the organization's music studios near Lincoln Center, and arranged for an audition for her to attend the New York College of Music (NYCM). After the audition, the jurors awarded León a scholarship, which allowed her to join the NYCM as an advanced undergraduate student. On September 14, 1967, less than four months after she entered the United States, León enrolled as a piano performance major at the NYCM. Her Cuban music training allowed her to easily test out of the solfège and music theory classes. However, because she did not speak English and the schools' curriculum required a few classes she had not taken in Cuba, she could not enter as a graduate student.[11]

Life as a student at the NYCM was both rewarding and challenging. Early in her first semester, León was sitting in a class unable to understand the instructor who, frustrated, asked her in front of her classmates to leave his classroom, admonishing her not to come back until she was able to speak English fluently. She felt terribly humiliated but, instead of discouraging her, this public embarrassment motivated her to enroll in an intensive English class at New York University.[12] Regardless of these setbacks, León's musical talent made her quickly a visible force among both undergraduate and graduate students. By the end of her first year at the NYCM, she was selected to participate in a broadcast for the National Educational Radio Network, the forerunner of National Public Radio, to play with the college's orchestra; by the end of her second year, she made her solo debut with a recital at the Museum of the City of New York, where she played works by Schumann, Beethoven, and Chopin.[13] León graduated with a Bachelor of Science degree on February 22, 1971, two and a half years after the NYCM merged with the School of Education of New York University.[14]

That year, the American Council for Emigres in the Professions recognized León's early achievements in this country with the Alvin Johnson Award, which she received from the hands of Puerto Rican congressman Herman Badillo.[15] At the time, León was still going by her married name, Tania Viera; it was not until 1973, when she received U.S. citizenship, that the dissolution of her marriage to Eduardo Viera came through. Media outlets continued to refer to her as Tania Viera, Tania Viera León, or Tania León Viera as late as the early 1980s. However, by the time she received her degree and the first of many awards to come, León's musical life had been turned upside down by a chance encounter in the summer of 1968.

Dance Theatre of Harlem: A New Musical Path

During her early life in the United States, like most immigrants, León had to take on many different jobs to make ends meet. She played piano at a restaurant, delivered packages, worked as a messenger, and even took advantage of the accounting skills she had acquired back in Cuba. A couple of weeks after arriving from Miami, she took a job as an accountant at Gilbert Systems, a maker of women's clothes on 34th Street and 9th Avenue, which enabled her to move out of Sarita and Fernando's apartment.[16]

On a summer evening in 1968, one of León's classmates at NYU, Laura Wilson, asked her if she could take her place as a piano accompanist for a ballet class at the St. James Presbyterian Church in Harlem. León recalls the moment:

> One day, Laura got sick . . . so she said, "Tania, do me a favor. Could you go and play for me at this dance school? I cannot do it, and I do not want to lose the spot." I said, "Okay, what do I have to do?" She gave me the books—marches, waltzes, mazurkas, everything. "You listen to the beat that the teacher gives you or she might say, 'I need a waltz,' whatever."[17]

The dance school where Laura worked as an accompanist was the Harlem School of the Arts. It had been founded a few years earlier, in 1964, by the influential soprano Dorothy Maynor (1910–1996), the first African American woman to sing at a Presidential Inaugural Gala, in 1949.[18] The school's mission was to provide a sense of community to children and families in Harlem through exposure to the arts, while offering "a means by which black Americans [could] establish agencies to help them benefit from their talents."[19]

Accompanying the ballet lessons was not a difficult job for someone with León's skills and experience. However, her broken English and the Czech instructor's equally poor language skills made their initial conversations a bit tricky: "You can imagine what that was like. We communicated using hand gestures," she remembers.[20] There was a fifteen-minute break between lessons. Trying to make the most of her time with a piano, León went over the repertory she was working on. Although she was absorbed by the beautiful sound of the grand piano, she could not help but notice a man walking by the classroom door: "This man just came out of nowhere. He was very handsome. So, I was like, 'Who is this guy? Where did he come from?' Because it was everything [not just that he was very attractive], but the way he carried himself, his demeanor. It was everything."[21] The man left without saying a word to her and the dance lessons resumed. At the end of the day, when León was by herself improvising on the piano, he returned, entered the room, and walked directly to her. His big smile somehow paralyzed her and, trying to smile back at him, she was only able to utter: "No English."[22] In a mixture of Spanish and Italian, the man was able to convey to her that he liked her playing and the way she accompanied the dance lessons, and wanted to discuss with her the possibility of a more permanent job.

The man was Arthur Mitchell (1934–2018), whom Dorothy Maynor had just invited to start a dance program at the school.[23] Although he was only thirty-four years old at the time, Mitchell was already a legend in the ballet world. In 1955, he was the first African American to join the New York City Ballet permanently, and eventually became the first African American to rise to the position of principal dancer in a major ballet company. As one of the stars of the dance troupe, he found himself at the center of a nasty situation when George Balanchine created a duet for him and white ballerina Diana Adams as part of his 1957 choreography for Stravinsky's *Agon*. At a time when Jim Crow laws were still enforced in the southern United States, the pairing of a black man and a white woman dancing on stage was received with far less than unanimous approval. To his credit, the Russian-born choreographer resisted the pressure of racist audiences and commercial sponsors and refused to change the pairing. Although Mitchell would go on to dance this number with white partners all over the world, it was not until 1968—three years after Jim Crow laws were legally overruled by the Civil Rights Act of 1964 and the Voting Rights Act of 1965—that he was allowed to dance *Agon*'s pas de deux with a white ballerina on national television in the United States.

In 1966, Mitchell had participated in a cultural exchange program to help establish Brazil's *Companhia Brasileira de Ballet*.[24] On April 4, 1968, Mitchell was on his way to Brazil to continue work on this project when he learned about the assassination of Martin Luther King Jr. Enraged and saddened by this tragedy and the riots that followed in over one hundred cities in the country—including numerous businesses robbed and set afire in his native Harlem—Mitchell decided to leave the program in Brazil and return to his country. Mitchell explains:

> I sat there [on the plane] the whole time, thinking to myself, "Here I am running around the world doing all these things, why not do them at home?" I believe in

helping people the best way you can; my way is through my art. But sometimes you need a splash of cold water in your face to make you see the right way to do it.[25]

Dorothy Maynor had encountered racism throughout her singing career, having been prevented from appearing on the opera stage due to her skin color—regardless of the excellent reviews her vocal recitals generated through the 1930s and 1940s.[26] She knew exactly what Mitchell had to fight against in his artistic life, as well as the kind of pain that prompted him to try to give something back to the African American community. It seemed almost natural to have him start the dance program at the Harlem School of the Arts.

However, Mitchell was not just thinking about teaching African American kids how to dance ballet. His goal was to establish the first permanent African American ballet company in the United States, and for that he needed a music director. Meeting León, a formidable pianist who knew how to improvise and accompany dance lessons, presented him with an opportunity. "This was divine intervention," said Mitchell, "that [she was] in New York and looking for a job. So, I said, 'Why don't you take the job' [. . .] She said 'yes.'"[27] Two weeks after their chance meeting, León was the company's official pianist. When León showed up for the first lesson, Mitchell asked her not to play from any of the music scores she had brought. León remembers:

[He] said, "Do not play anything from the scores. Do whatever you want." So, I would improvise. And at some point, people started talking about what we were doing in the lessons. I mean, I would improvise at the piano and that would inspire him to also invent things.[28]

In Mitchell's words, "She started playing for class and we got along very well and the dancers liked her [. . .] So, she would count, musicians would count, and I would count; but we always ended up together."[29] The chemistry between León, Mitchell, and the dancers was almost palpable. León was not only able to adapt quickly to the way dancers count—which is quite different from the way musicians count—she was also able to contribute creatively to the rehearsals through improvisation in a way that fueled the choreographer's imagination.

The Harlem School of the Arts' dance program opened on July 8, 1968. A few weeks later, Karel Shook (1920–1985), Mitchell's former ballet master, joined the project as its codirector. Lincoln Kirstein and Georges Balanchine, for whom Mitchell had danced at the New York City Ballet, were supportive of the school and acted as mentors. When the relationship between Mitchell and Maynor became strained and their partnership ended a few months later, they helped him obtain funding that allowed for the expansion of the program into an independent dance school and company.[30] On February 2, 1969, with support from the Ford Foundation, Dance Theatre of Harlem was born, using space at the Church of the Master, at the corner of 122nd Street and Morningside Avenue in Harlem, to hold classes (see figure 3.1). By that time, being the program's music director demanded more from León than just providing music for daily rehearsals. León also had to hire staff for the new company's music-education program and teach music lessons.

FIGURE 3.1. The first Dance Theatre of Harlem company at Church of the Master. Photograph by Marbeth, courtesy of Tania León.

FIGURE 3.2. The Dance Theatre of Harlem Orchestra. Photograph by Marbeth, courtesy of Tania León.

Eventually, she organized the company's orchestra, which she made a point of making completely integrated (see figure 3.2).[31] Slowly, León's musical life started to revolve more and more around Dance Theatre of Harlem.

One of the features that characterized the new company early on was its lecture-demonstration or open-rehearsal series. These were open workshops that allowed members of the community to get a glimpse at the inner workings of the company. Virginia Johnson, one of the first dancers to join the company, remembers that

> one of the ways that Arthur Mitchell created the Dance Theatre of Harlem Company was [through] this thing called a lecture-demonstration that we did in public schools and community centers all over the country [. . .] So, he [needed to unify a group that] had dancers who [studied] in all kinds of different schools and [had] all kinds of different backgrounds and all kinds of different levels [. . .] So, the lecture-demonstration was the way that he did it. It was a public, about an hour-long, program that started at the barre. It explained what the roots of classical ballet were and how you prepare yourself to be a dancer. And so, you know, three times a day the curtain would open and we would do a classical ballet barre, and he would explain. And Tania was involved in that.[32]

Watching Tania play for these workshops and Mitchell's desire to have original work as part of the company's repertoire gave him the idea to commission a ballet from her. He recalls: "We always did lecture-demonstrations because we were building an audience; and so [Tania] would play all the lecture-demonstrations, and she got to know what I wanted [. . .] And so I said, 'Well, Tania, I'm going to do a new ballet why don't you write the music?' And she said 'Okay.'"[33]

This ballet was *Tones* (1970–1971), León's first formal composition. She had composed a few piano pieces and songs in Cuba. Some of these pieces had been premiered and at least one of them had achieved a certain level of success (the song "Ciego reto"). However, none of them featured the kind of technical range Mitchell's ballet required; León often refers to the pieces she composed in Cuba as the music she wrote "before she was a composer."[34] Asked about how this commission took place, León states that:

> [Mitchell] asked me to write a ballet and since I never say no to anything—especially after I learned who he really was, which was something that blew my mind. So, I said "of course, *caballero* [gentleman]." Everything started that way. We started to work together. He created *Tones* in front of me. I mean, every portion of it [we did together]. I had to learn how dancers count so I could make [their dancing] fit with the music I was inventing . . . because I truly invented that music. I invented it in the sense that I had never [formally] studied composition. So, I invented it [. . .] I went down to the library and checked out some music theory and composition books, and I learned by myself from them how things worked. That's how I wrote that ballet.[35]

The difference between how dancers and musicians count was at the center of *Tones* as a musical work. Although the specifics of counting vary depending on particular choreographies and styles, the main difference between how musicians and dancers count is that, while musicians count beats within measures, the dancers' count "sometimes corresponds to the number of measures, but sometimes corresponds to a multiple of the number of measures."[36] These different counting systems are not necessarily mutually exclusive but may result in dance syncopations across the music.[37]

León kept in mind these counting peculiarities as well as their possibilities for syncopation when improvising at the piano for Mitchell's lecture-demonstrations. They also informed the rhythmic unfolding and melodic inventiveness of *Tones*. When the company performed *Tones* in London in 1974, ballet critic John Percival commented on the choreography's "ingenious variants on standard classroom technique and conventional double-work."[38] Given that these lecture-demonstrations were to be the natural outlet for the ballet, it made sense that the music and dance dynamics at the center of the workshop informed its aesthetic outlook.

Virginia Johnson recalls dancing to *Tones* at these workshops: "*Tones* was a crucial part of the lecture-demonstrations; so, that was early [. . .] [It] eventually had three movements, but in the first year [we did these lecture-demonstrations] it was *Tones* as a one-movement work that we did three times a day."[39] León's ballet was a signature piece of the company's early public presentations and was performed repeatedly at open rehearsals and other concerts even before its final version was finished in the spring of 1971. In fact, when Dance Theatre of Harlem was invited to the First Bermuda Arts Council Summer Festival in 1970, the concerts on July 19–20 opened with *Tones*. León's ballet continued to be presented throughout that summer's Caribbean tour in Nassau and Curaçao, as well as the company's concerts at the Naparima Bowl in Trinidad on October 27, 1970. At these events, *Tones* was performed along with other works choreographed by Balanchine and Mitchell, including Brazilian composer Marlos Nobre's *Rhythmetron* (1968), a modernist piece for percussion that Mitchell had choreographed a few years earlier for the Companhia Brasileira de Ballet. Furthermore, when the Dance Theatre of Harlem made its official debut at the Guggenheim Museum in New York City on January 8–10, 1971, Mitchell included in the program three works, *Tones*, *Fête Noire*, and *Rhythmetron*. León's work was also featured at the company's Chicago debut later that year and through its first European tour, which took them to Italy, the Netherlands, and Belgium in the summer of 1971. The work was presented so often that the company eventually made a recording of the music score (see figure 3.3). Virginia Johnson recalls that

FIGURE 3.3. Arthur Mitchell and Tania León during the recording of *Tones*. Photograph by Marbeth, courtesy of Tania León.

the complete, three-movement version of *Tones* was finished for their concert at *Teatro Nuovo* in Spoleto during that tour. For most of these concerts, León was billed as musical director, composer, and sound technician.

When Mitchell asked León to write *Tones*, he was very particular about the kind of approach he wanted her to take to the music. Having worked under Balanchine at the New York City Ballet, he was interested in the kind of neoclassical, austere, modernist, non-Romantic aesthetic that company was known for. Although he was founding the first African American ballet company, he also wanted to avoid standard prejudices against African Americans. He explains, "*Tones* was one of the first ballets I ever choreographed. And . . . let me put it this way: You must understand we were always fighting the prejudices that people had about black people, [that] they should always sing spirituals."[40] Mitchell wanted to break away from the stereotype that African Americans performers were only good at African American expressive culture.

Accepting Mitchell's commission inspired a 180-degree turn in León's music career. She became fascinated with the idea of being a composer, which led her to enroll in a master's program in composition at NYU and to eventually abandon her dream of becoming a concert pianist. The move had a lasting impact on her life, just as the modernist character of her music was also important to shaping the company's artistic trajectory.

Dance Theatre of Harlem's quick success inspired an intense touring schedule locally, nationally, and internationally. This meant that León had to spend a lot of time on buses, planes, and in hotel rooms with other members of the company. This time allowed her not only to forge friendships that have lasted a lifetime, but also to develop the sense of community and even family she intensely craved and needed since leaving her native country. Virginia Johnson remembers that those tours inspired moments of true emotional and intellectual intimacy:

> I call Tania one of my best friends [. . .] We were often roommates in those first years when we were on tour. [. . .] So we would have these long conversations where we would solve the world['s problems]. And we would talk about art, we would talk about who we were [. . .] and what we could do as artists. [. . .] What could we do to lift people up and make them feel human, and generous . . . and open.[41]

The company's 1971 Caribbean and European tours created serious practical problems for León and Mitchell. Because she was music director as well as *répétiteur*—in charge not only of supervising the musical life of the company but also of accompanying dance rehearsals at the piano and coaching dancers on music-related matters—León was an essential member of Dance Theatre of Harlem. However, she still did not have a U.S. passport and her Cuban passport remained void since she immigrated to the United States. She had to travel with an advance parole permit, which theoretically allowed her to reenter the United States while waiting for her immigration status to be resolved. Nevertheless, an unforeseen difficulty when the company was leaving the country forced the plane to return to the United States. León remembers:

> The plane had to come back and they [the immigration officers] would not let me leave the country again. So, Arturo had to put on a fight and create a hassle. He said that I was the music director of the company and that nobody was going to get on that plane if I did not get on with them.[42]

In the end, the immigration officers agreed to add an extra clause on León's paperwork in order for her to be able to reenter the country again.

This was the first of several incidents created by the advance parole document that set León apart from the rest of the Dance Theatre of Harlem crew. During their first European tour, the company had to take a train from Italy to Holland. At the border, Swiss officers checked the travel documents of all the company members, but were particularly distressed with León's advanced parole permit, a kind of document they had not previously seen. León and Mitchell remembered the occasion when I interviewed them in Mitchell's New York City apartment a few weeks before his passing:

Tania Leon: It's something that happened in Germany too.

Arthur Mitchell: They said "Oh she's a communist!" And I said, "She's not a communist. She's from Cuba." I said, "No, no!" And we were on the train, you know, and I would say "Oh God! We have to do this again." I mean it was always . . .

T.L.: A problem with me . . .

A.M.: Always something. And I said. "Tania, I'm behind you." It was one of the saddest moments I ever had in my life. Then we went to Yugoslavia. And they would say, you have to get your luggage and put it in the middle of the airport.

T.L.: But in Germany the company left . . .

A.M.: Yeah! They took you off the train!

T.L.: They took me off the train and I had to stay in Germany and then continue to another country. And [the company members] didn't know what was going to happen to me . . . and me neither!

A.M.: And . . . her passport was both American and Cuban. And they didn't understand it, the German [officers]. So, right there.

T.L.: I had a piece of paper from immigration [the advanced parole permit] . . . and they didn't understand that.

A.M.: It was so sad!

T.L.: It's what happened to me.

A.M.: And I said, "You betta'!" I mean, I would fight the directors. And they [in Yugoslavia] said, "Oh! This is Yugoslavia, and we're sort of pro-communist." I don't care. What is that? You know? I said, "*Taniecita* [Little Tania]; I love you, *mi corazón* [my heart]!! We'll get you! We'll get you!!" Oh God![43]

Eventually, León was able to rejoin the company in Amsterdam for the rest of the tour. These experiences gave Mitchell and the members of the company a glimpse into the unique hardships and challenges Cuban émigrés like León had to face at the time. As sad as these moments were, they presented León's coworkers with an opportunity not only to better understand her but also to strengthen their bonds of friendship through acts of solidarity.

Mitchell always referred to Dance Theatre of Harlem as a family. In those years, he and León grew very close. He learned about the problems she had sending money to her mother in Cuba or even just calling her on the phone. He described their bond as

more of a friendship than a working relationship. I understood what she was fighting [for] all the time because we were fighting [for] the same thing [. . .] So we knew each other as human beings. And she was very concerned with her mother [. . .] She would try to send money to the family. She would send food to the family. So, I grew up knowing about her family. [. . .] She was like my little sister, you know. And then she was going to get married[.] I met her husband . . . and I'd write and send letters to her mother and her brother [in Cuba].[44]

León's first years in the United States were very hard. She was alone in a new country, with no prospects of seeing her family and the husband she had left on the island in the foreseeable future. Mamota, her beloved grandmother, the person whom she grew up with, died soon after she left Cuba. After her divorce from her first husband was finalized, León remarried, but the marriage was short-lived and emotionally painful. These setbacks were incredibly tough for a family person like León, who until a couple of years earlier was still living in close physical and emotional proximity with her family.

"A picture is worth a thousand words," is a popular English-language adage. In the case of Tania León, two pictures of her taken in those early years by Marbeth Schnare (ca. 1947–2006)—the photographer who documented the activities of Dance Theatre of Harlem for decades—illustrate perfectly how these adversities took a toll on her body and spirit. The sorrow in León's eyes in the first photo is distinct; she seems very fragile and her body language, with her head tilted

FIGURE 3.4. Karel Shook, Tania León, and Arthur Mitchell. Two pictures that tell a story. Photographs by Marbeth, courtesy of Tania León.

down and slightly to the right, makes her look withdrawn (see figure 3.4, picture on the left). Behind her, Arthur Mitchell places his hands on her shoulders in an unmistakably protective gesture, while a very serious Karel Shook looks directly into the camera. Unhappy with the results, the photographer suggested that they try again. León recalls, "They asked me to smile, but I was very sad. I was even wearing a wig because I was losing my hair out of so much stress."[45] The second picture, taken immediately afterward, shows León trying to smile and Mitchell smirking behind her (see figure 3.4, picture on the right).

Having no relatives around her in the United States, she was able to endure these hardships thanks to the emotional support and friendship of Mitchell and her friends and colleagues from Dance Theatre of Harlem.

Those early years with the company were fundamental in León's process of adaptation to U.S. culture; not only in terms of understanding the dynamics of the job market and the type of work ethic expected from her in a U.S. music scene like New York City's, but also in relation to the most basic aspects of surviving everyday life. When she and Mitchell first met, she did not know who he was. It was only after she saw him on stage at the Lincoln Center that she realized he was one of the biggest stars in the ballet world. This realization made her even more excited about the prospect of working for him. As she told me:

Arturo had no money but I did not care. Let's make this [ballet] company! And people from all over the place started coming . . . someone from Jamaica, someone from somewhere else. It was quite impressive.

Alejandro L. Madrid: And did they make you feel part of the team right away?

T.L.: Well . . . you have to understand that I did not speak English. One of them, Walter Raines [1940–1994], became almost like my brother. You cannot imag-

ine how much he helped me with [the language]. Marbeth, the photographer
. . . they all helped with my English. So, I never felt like I was with one side
or the other.

A.M.: What about issues of race?

T.L.: It was a very strange thing. It was like [they were] embracing and rejecting
[me] at the same time. It is just that it was a different idiosyncrasy, a different
way of thinking, a different way of behaving.[46]

Clearly, León's encounter with Mitchell and her taking the job at Dance Theatre of Harlem were central to her beginning to make sense of her new life in the
United States. Joining an African American dance company helped her understand that, as a foreign woman of color, she was perceived by black and white
people alike as a black woman, regardless of how she saw herself. In the long
run, working with Mitchell and learning about racial dynamics in the United
States also helped her manage the expectations that her presence generated
among the particular artistic groups that she joined.

From Dance Theatre of Harlem to *The Wiz*

On July 18, 1973, *Westport News* announced a dance demonstration by the Dance
Theatre of Harlem at Connecticut College as part of the American Dance Festival. The featured attraction of the evening was the premiere of *Haiku: A Dream
for Brown Eyes* (1973), with choreography by Walter Raines and music by Tania
León. It was described as a ballet that "uses the Japanese form of poetry, haiku, as
starting point, unfolding 17 connecting scenes to create a 'visual' haiku. Japanese
flutes, strings, percussion and a Moog Synthesizer merge in a score composed
by Tania Viera Leon [*sic*], which adheres to ancient Japanese traditions."[47] *Haiku*
was the third work by León commissioned by the company; she had also arranged *The Beloved* (1972) in collaboration with Judith Hamilton, which was
choreographed by Lester Horton.

Haiku is particularly relevant within Dance Theatre of Harlem's repertory and
León's oeuvre. Its non-African aesthetic reinforces one of the early goals of the
company, to avoid going "into the overtly political" that would blatantly reflect
the unprecedented social moment that African Americans were experiencing
in U.S. history. Virginia Johnson explains it succinctly:

It was very exciting. It was the time that we were living in. It was the civil rights
movement. It was the Black Power movement. It was people gaining a self-gen-
erated sense of identity . . . because we [African Americans] did not have that
before. [However, instead of focusing on that] Arthur Mitchell's choice was to

establish this high bar. [As if] saying "This is what classical ballet can be." The works we did in that time period were really about reflecting on what was the norm in this art form and our doing it. [. . .] Our protest was by doing those ballets that everybody thought belonged somewhere else.[48]

A ballet like *Haiku*, with its overt musical and literary references to Japanese culture reflected the cosmopolitan humanism that underlay Mitchell's understanding of the significance of Dance Theatre of Harlem as a cultural project. This work also points toward León's understanding her music in a new way; *Haiku's* twofold character (as a ballet as well as a concert piece)[49] shows a composer moving beyond the ballet idiom into the concert hall.

Nevertheless, regardless of Mitchell's universalist approach to aesthetics, the company's audiences, especially when they performed abroad, expected them to engage with issues related to black aesthetics. The opportunity to address this concern came soon after with two projects celebrating Afro-Caribbean and African American heritage: *Dougla* (1974) and *Spiritual Suite* (1976). Premiered on April 16, 1974, at the ANTA Theater in New York City, *Dougla* was the result of a collaboration between León and the legendary Trinidadian-American dancer, choreographer, actor, and visual artist Geoffrey Holder (1930–2014). The ballet is a celebration of *creolisation* and *métissage* (miscegenation or racial mixing), especially in the context of Trinidad, where the word "dougla" is used to name the mixed offspring of Indian and African parents from the British Caribbean islands. The choreography is a stylized representation of an Afro-Indo wedding ceremony punctuated by lavish and colorful costumes and stage design. Its sensuality is highlighted by an energetically percussive music score created by León and Holder. Here, repetitive African drumming and timelines (cyclic rhythmic clave patterns) dominate a musical texture that sporadically intersperses melodic flute episodes played over the repeated rhythmic loops of the percussion. The overall musical and aesthetic result is radically different from anything León had done for the company before. If *Tones* and *Haiku* were abstract modernist hymns of universalist appeal, *Dougla's* hypnotically primitivist Afro-diasporic specificity made it into a cultural manifesto of sorts for the company.

Clive Barnes, writing for the *New York Times* about the premiere of this work, noticed the ambivalence toward an African American dance company that many still saw as stepping onto an artistic turf where many believed they did not belong:

Mr. Mitchell's dream of classic dance as a black expression is not easily assimilated, if that's the word. European court dances and their ultimate refinement are a long way from the African heritage of black America. But Americans must absorb cultures—all except the Indians are strangers in what sometimes seems to be a never-never land. The American black speaks the language of Shakespeare. He did not choose it—but he has it. And the language of classic dance is his, too. [. . .] Everyone has known—most of all, I suspect, Mr. Mitchell—that Mr. Mitchell's peers and his press have been not easy but tolerant to the company. [. . .] Classic ballet is the main concern of the Dance Theatre—it was formed for that purpose. However, no classic ballet company restricts itself to classic ballet, and it is natural for the Harlem dancers, when moving outside the academic vocabulary, to move toward their own background. This is the root of "Dougla," the Geoffrey Holder ballet that ended the program.[50]

Dougla seemingly spoke to both those who believed Dance Theatre of Harlem should stick to African American cultural manifestations—either people who wished African Americans sang "only spirituals," as Mitchell said, or white supremacists who felt that African Americans dancing ballet was a corruption of "white" culture—as well as those who expected the company to engage with the pressing concerns with identity politics that U.S. mainstream culture was undergoing at the time.

Holder's idea to have an Afro-Caribbean percussion ensemble used as *Dougla's* musical accompaniment inspired León's first attempt at engaging Afro-diasporic drumming traditions in her music. She had, of course, grown up with similar rhythms that she heard at Mamota's Santería gatherings in Havana. However, if Holder was clear about the central position that the Afro-Caribbean drums were to have in the ballet, he was uncertain how this would be handled in the music itself. León recalls that while working together on the musical score:

He told me what he wanted with the drums and I took it from there. [. . .] He whistled to me this [flute] part because he did not know how to write music and everything else was my invention. He said that everything had to be over a continuo of drums and I had to invent everything else; especially the rhythm[ic patterns] they [the drummers] should play.[51]

While the general idea and the melodic cell that originates the melodic material throughout the work came from Holder, the actual composing and the details of the musical arrangement were done by León. This makes sense given that Holder was not formally trained as a musician or composer. The *New York Times* praised *Dougla* for "its constant interplay between intense sophistication and atavistic brutality [which] is consistently surprising and impressive."[52] The ballet became a central work in the Dance Theatre of Harlem's repertory, but it was also a classic adopted by other companies, such as the Alvin Ailey American Dance Theater, a modern dance company with whom Holder also collaborated.

In August 1976, the Catholic Church organized its 41st International Eucharistic Congress in Philadelphia. The conference, which convened in the United States for only the second time, was an interfaith ecumenical gathering of church leaders that coincided with the two-hundredth anniversary of the Declaration of Independence. In recognition of recent events in U.S. history, it devoted a number of sessions to social justice and the black tradition in worship.[53] As part of this focus, the congress commissioned a new ballet from Dance Theatre of Harlem as part of two evening concerts entitled "Dance in Praise of Him" on August 5 and 6. The new ballet, *Spiritual Suite*, composed by Tania León and choreographed by Arthur Mitchell, was dedicated to Dr. Martin Luther King Jr. It featured the legendary African American soprano Marian Anderson (1897–1993) reading a text written by Karel Shook in celebration of Dr. King's life (see figure 3.5).[54]

Scored for narrator, two sopranos, chorus, and amplified ensemble, *Spiritual Suite* is divided into three contrasting movements. The texture in the first and third movements feature very busy and prominent drum and percussion sections performed over sustained harmonies sung by the chorus that often move through

FIGURE 3.5. Tania León and Marian Anderson discussing *Spiritual Suite*. Photograph by Marbeth, courtesy of Tania León.

dramatic glissandi gestures. The second movement is a beautiful and lyrical melody played by the piano over slow-moving harmonies sung by the chorus. Mitchell's choreography features groups of female and male dancers often taking turns dancing on stage. The dancers' collective motion in the first two movements emphasizes circles and communal interaction, while the last movement shows a more geometrical distribution of dancers on the stage with individual movements reminiscent of urban popular dance. It is as if Mitchell wanted to develop a hybrid style somehow between the more mechanical, symmetrical, and geometric style of his early modernist, neoclassical choreographies—such as *Tones*—and the more exuberant popular style that had made more recent ballets—like *Dougla*—extremely successful.

Spiritual Suite's philosophical, spiritual, or religious overtones are more ambiguous, especially given the particular Christian/Catholic context of its commission and premiere. Marian Anderson cries at the beginning of the third movement, "He has been taken away and the pain will remain forever." Here the "he" is very clearly Martin Luther King Jr. However, the concerts were advertised as "Dance in Praise of Him," where the "Him" could be easily read as "Jesus Christ." Shook's text takes advantage of the striking parallels between the two leaders who were sacrificed in their struggle for justice for their people. By keeping its subject unnamed, Shook provides an opportunity to metaphorically collapse them into each other, particularly in the religious context surrounding the performance. One could read this work's ambiguity as being in the tradition of the religious resistance of syncretic religions like Santería, Candomblé, or Mexican Catholicism, where non-Western, subaltern deities are celebrated and prayed to through the images and names of Catholic saints.

The Philadelphia performances took place in the midst of the Dance Theatre of Harlem's 1976 tour of England. The company's tour was already scheduled and it did not include performances of *Spiritual Suite*. That may be the reason why the ballet was never staged again. Although there are no commercial recordings or videos of *Spiritual Suite*, there are existing videos of the work's rehearsal and premiere.[55]

By the end of the 1970s, León's work with Dance Theatre of Harlem had made her a visible figure in the New York music scene and beyond. In 1976, Lukas Foss (1922–2009) invited her to cofound the Brooklyn Philharmonic's Community Concert Series, a post she would hold until the end of Foss' tenure with the orchestra in 1990. In 1978, following their successful collaboration on the production of *Dougla*, Geoffrey Holder invited León as music director and conductor for *The Wiz* (1974), the African American retelling of the classic novel

The Wonderful Wizard of Oz. León joined the successful production for the last year of its four-year Broadway run. At the same time, León was becoming a sought-after composer, with more projects and commissions for new music landing on her desk.

León's busy schedule prevented her from focusing on Dance Theatre of Harlem as completely as she had for the past ten years, and it became clear it was time to part ways. In an attempt to avoid hurting Arthur Mitchell's feelings, she wrote a very long letter to him detailing the reasons she had to leave the company. She expressed her deep sense of gratitude for an opportunity that had completely transformed her life, welcoming her into a new family, and opening doors for her she could not have even dreamed of when she arrived in New York City thirteen years earlier. She felt she had done what she had to do for the company, and that, given the wide variety of her artistic interests, she did not see herself remaining the music director of a dance company for the rest of her life.[56] Although Mitchell was upset about her leaving, he ultimately understood León's reasons and came to support her efforts: "I was always behind her to keep developing in every way [she] could think of."[57] In 1980, she formally left her position as music director of the company; it was time for her to fly alone and follow her own path.

Musical Life beyond Dance Theatre of Harlem

León collaborated with a number of alternative and independent theater projects while she was still working for Dance Theatre of Harlem. One of the most important was INTAR, a Hispanic theater company founded in New York in 1966 by a group of Cuban and Puerto Rican artists led by Max Ferrá. León had developed a friendship with Manuel Martín Jr. (1934–2000), who had several plays produced by this company. Martín was a Cuban theater director and playwright who, like León, had left Cuba to pursue educational opportunities, rather than for political reasons. León composed music for several plays that he wrote or directed, including *La ramera de la cueva* (1974) and *Carmencita* (1978). She also acted as music director for *Swallows* (1980), a musical theater piece inspired by Martín's visit to his native country when Cuban refugees first were allowed to return in 1979, and *Rita and Bessie* (1988). She also worked as sound designer for Max Ferrá's 1979 Spanish production of Héctor Quintero's play *Rice and Beans* and as music director for Ferrá's 1989 production of Dolores Prida's *Crisp*.

León's and Martín's collaborations on *Carmencita* and *Rita and Bessie* are especially noteworthy. *Carmencita* is Martín's adaptation of Georges Bizet's classic opera *Carmen* (1875). The plot remains basically the same as in the original version. However, the action is transferred from Spain to New York City's Latino neighborhood, El Barrio, and the main male character is transformed from a bullfighter into a baseball player for the New York Yankees. Throughout the play, the dialogue is performed in English and the music sung in Spanish. Carmen's dance moves and the music that triggers them were also changed from flamenco to Afro-Caribbean rhythms and salsa. This production ran for twenty-four performances at INTAR's new theater on Broadway's Theatre Row, as well as several street performances throughout the summer of 1978.[58]

Rita and Bessie is a musical theater piece based on the provocative idea of a fictional encounter between two giants of Afro-diasporic popular music: Cuban *vedette* (singer and actress) Rita Montaner (1900–1958) and U.S. blues singer Bessie Smith (1894–1937). Famous as a Cuban *zarzuela* and popular-music singer,[59] Montaner was the first singer to record one of the earliest global megahits of Cuban music, "El manisero" ("The Peanut Vendor") in the late 1920s, while Smith was crowned "The Empress of the Blues" during the 1920s and 1930s.[60] Plotting the fictional encounter of these two legendary, gifted, and strong women allowed Martín and León to use the musical contrast between blues and Afro-Cuban music to comment on issues of racial and gender inequality that they had come to know very well.[61] For *Rita and Bessie*, León made arrangements of popular songs for an ensemble of alto saxophone, piano, and percussion, and acted as pianist and music director. The play was produced in the summer of 1988 by Teatro Duo/Duo Theatre, Martín's company, on which advisory board León served at the time.

Through those years, León also collaborated in musical theater projects with mainstream companies. From 1983 to 1984, she was music director of Joseph Papp's off-Broadway and Broadway productions of *The Human Comedy* (1983), with music by Galt MacDermot. In 1980, the John F. Kennedy Center for the Performing Arts commissioned her to write the music for Wallace Chappel's production of Wendy Kesselman's *Maggie Magalita*. This drama won the 1980 Sharfman Competition of the National Children's Art Festival. It tells the story of an adolescent Hispanic-American girl struggling between her desire for assimilation and her family's attempt to keep their native traditions, especially language, alive. *Maggie Magalita* premiered at the Kennedy Center's Terrace Theater in 1980 and was subsequently restaged in 1986 at New York's Lamb's Theatre, receiving mixed reviews. However, León's original music, colorful and vibrant, shows how she could navigate the world of classical music while successfully mastering the unique intricacies of popular music. The instrumental exuberance and rhythmic drive of "La conga de Maggie Magalita"—a short number from the musical scored for flute, piano, double bass, drums, and percussion—is a good example of how León thrived composing music based on the *guajeos* (vamps) and timelines that characterize rumba and salsa music.[62]

A collaboration for which León has not received due credit—because she declined to join the production team when the project went public—is Julie Taymor's stage adaptation of *The Lion King* (1997). Taymor stated that if she was going to "bring Africa to the stage in a positive, powerful, and beautiful way [. . .] she was not going to cast white people in most of the roles."[63] Taymor set out to develop a project that would create a significant aesthetic and political impact from its outset. Tania León was the obvious choice for its musical director. León worked with Taymor as conductor in the preparation of the musical's first workshop and its presentation to Disney's artistic producer, Michael Eisner. When Disney decided to produce the show on Broadway, they offered León a contract to write some of the arrangements. However, as she recalls, "they only pay you by arrangement and the arrangement belongs to them. They do not pay you any royalties. So, I said no."[64] The studio also offered León a contract to serve as the show's music director for a year. Nevertheless, remembering the busy schedule that she had when working in *The Wiz*, and the restrictions these working conditions imposed on her other artistic endeavors, she declined: "I said I could only do it for six months. [. . .] It was not what I . . . well, in the end you cannot get into a fight with Disney."[65]

In addition to her musical theater work for traditional companies, León also collaborated with a number of experimental groups. One of the most important for its impact on her musical output was her work with avant-garde theater director Robert Wilson (b. 1941)—to whom she was introduced to by composer Julius Eastman (1940–1990)—in the premieres of several of his minimalist, oneiric collage-like dramas. León served as musical director for Wilson's *Death, Destruction & Detroit* (1979) and *Edison* (1979), and as composer of some of the original incidental music for *The Golden Windows* (1982). This was the beginning of an important working relationship that would culminate in their collaboration on the revised productions of León's first opera, *Scourge of Hyacinths*, in 1999 and 2001.

Throughout her career, León has connected with a variety of African American and Latino artistic projects. In 1985, she accepted an invitation to work as a conductor and music advisor for the Alvin Ailey Dance Theater Company.[66] León remembers Ailey (1931–1989) as "a very charming man, with an incredible sense of respect. [Someone] I loved to work with."[67] One of the toughest projects that León and Ailey worked on together was *The Magic of Katherine Dunham* (1987). It was a celebration of the work of the famous African American choreographer consisting entirely of restored versions of her dances. León recalls, "It was an all-evening ballet and I made the arrangements for all of that."[68] It was difficult to recover the dancer's works, because she had to gather "people from that village and that other village" and ask them, "'[Do] you remember how this was done?' 'I do not know. It was twenty years ago.'"[69] Although putting together the celebration of Katherine Dunham was an incredibly daunting task, León has particularly fond memories of conducting *Revelations* (1960). Ailey's signature work, *Revelations* is a moving exploration of the history, faith, and traditions of the African American people and their journey from slavery to freedom, through spirituals, gospel, and blues music. León could easily relate to these musical styles.[70]

Two of her other significant artistic Afro-diasporic projects are her collaboration with Dominican jazz pianist Michel Camilo (b. 1954) on *Batéy* (1989) and *Drummin'* (1997), a hybrid percussion project celebrating multiculturalism. Both have an experimental, yet communitarian, character, and push and question traditional boundaries. *Batéy* is a work for vocal ensemble and percussion composed as a duo between León and Camilo. Inspired on the idea of the *batey*—the settlements in Cuba and the Dominican Republic where black slaves working on sugar plantations lived—as a space for liberation and self-expression, the work finds a common musical language between the worlds of jazz and classical music by incorporating a number of Afro-Caribbean and Afro-diasporic musical practices. When listening carefully, one hears hints of rumba *guaguancó*, bebop, batá drumming, and gospel singing combined into an invented musical language, or, in Leon's words, "a created language [with] traces of Spanish."[71] This musical hybrid metaphorically resembles the pidgin languages that displaced people have had to create in order to communicate with each other when living in strange lands without sharing a common language. This experience is shared historically by many peoples in the Caribbean, especially as a result of the slave trade and colonization.[72] León and Camilo chose this topic as an homage to their common ancestry, as she relates: "Michel [Camilo] and I have been touched by those people because his family, from his mother's side, is of Africano [*sic*] extraction—mine as well. We decided to do this piece and dedicate [it] to our grandmothers, who are the link we have to that continent."[73]

Drummin' is a piece that brought together different indigenous music drumming communities from around the world—Japanese *taiko*, Peruvian and Haitian drummers, African Yoruba, Native American, and Cuban Santería drummers—with Miami's New World Symphony Orchestra. The idea was to bring together musicians from a wide variety of cultural backgrounds under the banner of rhythm, a shared experience for them all. León composed a piece of music that incorporated elements from all of their different drumming traditions; but, because most of the musicians were not used to reading Western music notation, she also had to come up with strategies to enable them to play together at the same time.[74] The piece allowed plenty of freedom for the different drumming circles to incorporate their own musical mastery, but it also presented several problems. Besides trying to coordinate musicians who were not able to read Western music notation and who had never played together before, León had to coach conservatory-trained, orchestral musicians on how to flow within the freedom of the drummers. In the end, the project was a true exercise in diversity and open-mindedness; it required all of the musicians to truly listen to each other and to be willing to step out of their comfort zones to make the music happen. *Drummin'* premiered in 1997 in Miami and was presented again, two years later, at the 1999 *Hammoniale Festival der Frauen* in Hamburg, Germany.

Although she formally stepped down as music director of Dance Theatre of Harlem in 1980, León kept strong ties with Arthur Mitchell and the company and continued collaborating with them. Besides composing *Belé* (1981) for them—a second collaboration with Geoffrey Holder—she continued to participate occasionally in their shows as conductor, especially for their international tours. One of the most significant occasions for her was the company's tour of segregated South Africa in 1992. The invitation came from the Market Theatre, an internationally influential antiracist theater in Johannesburg, in partnership with the City of Johannesburg's Department of Arts and Culture, a major South African bank, and the U.S. Embassy. It was just a little over two years after Nelson Mandela (1918–2013) was released from his 27-year imprisonment, as negotiations to end the apartheid system were taking place. Aware that the international boycott against South Africa's apartheid was still in place, but that it was an important and delicate political moment, Arthur Mitchell sent a letter to Mandela before accepting the invitation. He hoped that the visit of his company could "contribute to the broadening of cultural links between our people."[75] Mitchell recalls that:

> Mr. Mandela said, "Mitchell, I want you to come to South Africa. You've proven that any child given the education can do anything they want." And I said, "That's how we feel!" And so, we broke it into groups; and Tania went with the first group and she was doing master classes and working.[76]

FIGURE 3.6. Arthur Mitchell, Tania León, Nelson Rockefeller, and Nelson Mandela during the Dance Theatre of Harlem South African Tour. Photograph by Marbeth, courtesy of Tania León.

After a long negotiation, and with the public endorsement of many local anti-apartheid political factions, Dance Theatre of Harlem performed at the Civic Theatre, a theater "long regarded as an elitist white venue"[77] that was trying to remake its brand, on September 16, 1992. The program included, besides classic choreographies by Balanchine and Fokine, Tania León's and Geoffrey Holder's *Dougla*. As part of their visit, Dance Theatre of Harlem offered their signature lecture-demonstrations, master classes for aspiring South African dancers, lectures and workshops on many aspects of theater production—and, of course, they had a chance to meet Nelson Mandela (see figure 3.6).

Nelson Mandela publicly welcomed and endorsed the company's tour as "an inspiration to our artists, who have struggled to maintain their vision and creativity despite brutal apartheid oppression."[78] The visit also allowed for the return to South Africa of dancers Augustus van Haeerden and Felicity de Jager, "who emigrated [from there] because apartheid limited the artistic prospectus of nonwhites"[79] and had never performed professionally in their native country. The company's two-week visit, featuring the work of a successful black troupe that shattered many common racist misconceptions and prejudices against blacks, positively encouraged further anti-racist debate in the country and beyond.[80]

Scourge of Hyacinths:
An Opera for the Münchener Biennale

In 1990, the avant-garde composer and violinist Leroy Jenkins (1932–2007) was in Munich attending the premiere of his dance-opera *Mother of Three Sons* at the Münchener Biennale. Its director, German composer Hans Werner Henze (1926–2012), asked him if he could recommend exciting New York composers who might be good candidates to compose new operas for the biennale. Among the names proposed by Jenkins was León, who had premiered some of his works at the Brooklyn Philharmonic's Community Concert Series. Henze invited León to be a jury member for the 1992 biennale; after he got to know her and her music better, he asked her to accept a commission to write an opera for its 1994 edition. Because she had helped to commission and produce several operas for the Brooklyn Philharmonic Community Concert Series, León was aware of the possibilities of the genre but also the difficulties and impracticalities of staging it. Maybe for this reason, León hesitated:

> First of all, it never crossed my mind because nowadays . . . contemporary opera? Who's going to write contemporary opera and have it produced? So here [Henze] goes, telling me he believes I can write an opera. And of course, when someone like that tells you that, you write an opera.[81]

Henze and León first considered writing a libretto based on *La mascherata* (1941), a novel by Alberto Moravia (1907–1990) set in Mexico, but the Italian novelist had recently died and there were problems with his estate.[82] León also considered the works of Octavio Paz (1914–1998) but was unable to get in touch with the Mexican writer. Because she wanted to use a Spanish work for the opera, she also considered Carlos Fuentes (1928–2012), but again, it did not work out.[83] Later that summer, during a residency at the Rockefeller Foundation's Bellagio Center, León met Henry Louis Gates Jr. (b. 1950). Gates suggested that she use as the basis for her opera *A Scourge of Hyacinths* (1991), a radio-play by his friend, Nigerian Nobel Prize winner Wole Soyinka (b. 1934) (see figure 3.7). Soyinka sent León a copy of the play, which, through flashbacks, tells the story of Miguel Domingo, a Lagosian sentenced to death for his alleged participation in a political crime.[84] León was completely captivated by it:

> The book starts with [Miguel's] mother praying to Yemoja and I connected that with my grandmother and mother praying to Yemayá, which is the same Goddess but in Cuba. I said, "My God! What a coincidence! What a strange thing!" So,

I told Henry, "Yes. I am going to do this." Then I told Henze and he went crazy [with the idea] and said "Yes, that's it!"[85]

Once they agreed that Soyinka's play was the right story for the opera, Henze and the Nigerian writer met in London to discuss the details of the commission and decided that it would be best for León to write the libretto herself. According to León, Henze thought this was a good idea because it would allow her to get more familiar with the text and make the process of composition easier.[86]

León's final libretto, which divided the play into two acts and twelve scenes, stresses the political aspect of Soyinka's play, its denunciation of state authoritarianism, critique of corruption, and defense of human rights. But, it also puts an emphasis on the emotional and dramatic character of human relations that occur in convoluted political moments. If León's music for the opera "evokes the power of percussive African rhythms [and] masterfully portrays the depth of black Africans' beliefs and prayers,"[87] as Eulalia and Cecilia Piñero Gil have argued, it is precisely because the composer was able to immerse herself not only intellectually but also emotionally in its dramatic plot. León remembers that "when I was composing *Scourge of Hyacinths*, especially when I was working on the mother's aria . . . I kept crying because I got so deep into the characters, almost as if I were an actor."[88]

In the summer of 1993, while León was composing the opera, Mima, her mother, traveled to the United States to stay with her for a brief period of time. León wrote about how this had an emotional impact on her as she struggled to compose an aria for this opera:

FIGURE 3.7. Wole Soyinka, Tania León, and Henry Louis Gates Jr. Courtesy of Tania León.

When I was composing the Yemayá scenes and their prayers, I tried to remember the songs of the ceremonies from my childhood. They were not clear in my memory until my mother surprisingly came to visit me in the summer of 1993. She sang for me what she still remembered from the Cuban chants to call Yemayá. I composed Tiatin's prayer out of those fragments of her memory. My mother's simple singing touched an emotional well in me, which enabled me to compose Tiatin's music almost off the cuff.[89]

The fragments Mima was able to remember were the inspiration León needed to quickly finish the aria.

With a stage design by Mark Lamos and a cast of singers from Opera Ebony, the New York–based African American opera company, *Scourge of Hyacinths* was premiered at the Münchener Biennale on May 1, 1994. After its run at the festival, the opera received the BMW *Musiktheaterpreis* for the best opera performed at the biennale.[90] A slightly revised version for full orchestra, with staging and design by Robert Wilson, was presented in 1999 at the *Grand Théâtre de Genève* in Switzerland, the *Opéra de Nancy et de Lorraine* in France, and the *Neues Festspielhause* in Austria, as part of a program of celebrations commemorating the fiftieth anniversary of the Universal Declaration of Human Rights.[91] This version was staged again at Mexico City's *Palacio de Bellas Artes* during the 2001 *Festival del Centro Histórico*. Among the numbers written for *Scourge of Hyacinths*, Tiatin's moving aria, "Oh Yemanja (Mother's Prayer)," has been particularly successful, having been periodically programmed and recorded independently from the opera.[92]

Tania León and the African American Experience

When Helen Walker-Hill was researching her book *From Spirituals to Symphonies: African-American Women Composers and Their Music* (2001), she invited Tania León to participate. León ultimately declined to be included because she thought the project's focus on black women composers was too narrow. Although there is no section in the book devoted to León, Walker-Hill quoted the composer at the beginning of the book to explain her absence:

I am tired of all our labels . . . I am not a black conductor . . . [I] am not a woman conductor. . . . The fact that I am in this physical costume does not describe my energy, does not describe my entity. My chosen purpose in life is to be a musician, a composer, a conductor. This is the way I am making my contribution to mankind.[93]

This statement may seem like a contradiction to those who know the centrality of a number of African American artistic and cultural projects to León's development as a composer and musician. Walker-Hill was sympathetic to León's objections to being represented by just one particular aspect of her life and artistic experience. However, she had her own theory as to why this was not troubling to some of the other composers who accepted her invitation to be included in her book. One of those composers, Mary Watkins, believed that León's concerns were due to the fact that "her experience is not that of one growing up African American."[94] Walker-Hill shared and expanded on this idea in the book's introduction, where she states that the great majority of composers in her study

> are proud to be identified as African American women, and they are aware of the unique and highly political history of black women in the United States, a history that is not likely to have been absorbed or experienced by those who, like Tania León, have grown up outside this country. Almost all of them have their roots in a black American world that is unknown to most whites and common knowledge to most blacks.[95]

However, while it is well-known that León objects to being identified as a black or a female composer, I would contend that her reasons have nothing to do with not understanding the experiences of black women.

Watkins and Walker-Hill are correct when they point out that Tania León did not grow up African American. Nevertheless, regardless of León's upbringing in Cuba, the fact is that in the United States she is often seen as an African American, and consequently treated by most white people as being African American. If anything, the racism experienced by African Americans is often further exacerbated when people notice León's foreign accent. As for León's relationship to that "black American world that is unknown to whites," it would be unfair to say that her upbringing in Cuba prevents her from understanding it. It is true that León's racial experience in Cuba was different from that of African Americans, but it is also true that she became a composer, conductor, pedagogue, and community activist in the black American world invoked by Walker-Hill. León's artistic collaborations and everyday life experiences concerning race as well as her trajectory as an "artivist" *avant la lettre*, documented in Chapter 4, help us understand these apparent contradictions as central to the complex identity constructions and experiences that inform the development of her personal political agenda.[96]

It is telling that, when asked about how she felt as a member of an all-black dance troupe, León asserted:

> It is just that it was a different idiosyncrasy, a different way of thinking, a different way of behaving. I have never avoided looking in the eye. I never look down. And that was something I noticed a lot among people of color at the time. They did

not look in the eye, especially if the other person was white . . . And I understand them perfectly well.[97]

This statement embodies the source of, as well as a response to, the misunderstandings León's position about race often generates.

In Cuba, León grew up in a working-class, multiracial neighborhood where being black was not a problem. This is not to say that there is no racism in Cuba—clues, hints, and oblique references to it are peppered throughout her childhood—but rather that León's experience was different. "My brother and I," León explains,

> did not live during that period when Cuba had the clubs for people of color where my parents met. I went to a school with many students [who looked] like me. At the conservatory nobody ever made me feel like I was different [. . .] and the same thing happened at the commerce school.[98]

Leon concludes, "In my school there were people of all colors; we were all together in the same classroom. We played together. I did not live all the tragedy [of racism]"[99] (see figure 3.8).

As a child, León was protected by her family, especially by Mamota and Mima, who were adamant about keeping her from experiencing the racism they had lived through in their lives. Nevertheless, Mamota was also interested in her knowing

FIGURE 3.8. A picture of Tania León's integrated class in elementary school. León is fourth from the right, second row. Courtesy of Tania León.

about important figures of African-diasporic origin, not only in Cuba but also in the United States. She told León about Josephine Baker (1906–1975), Marian Anderson, and Paul Robeson (1898–1976), musicians who León would eventually meet or collaborate with in one way or another.[100] "What I realize today," León concludes, "is that she was creating a consciousness in me. She wanted me to realize that they were musicians of color [and] they had gone to Europe and had conquered the world. It is like she was trying to tell me, 'If they did it you can also do it.'"[101]

These experiences would seemingly confirm what Walker-Hill and Watkins say about León: She grew up unaware of the history of abuse of blacks in the United States, which prevented her from empathizing with their sense of belittlement. Nevertheless, León has made clear that she understood very well why African Americans avoided looking white people in the eye. This came through her personal experiences living and working in the United States.

When León left Cuba, the Castro regime was engaged in a propaganda war against the United States. As part of that battle, images of the repression of the civil rights movement in the U.S. were common in Cuban television. Mamota, who did not want her granddaughter to leave Cuba, emphasized the racial abuse blacks had to face in the United States that was awaiting her. So, when León arrived in New York and saw what was going on, she panicked. "It was true what my grandmother told me," she recalls,

> what they were talking about [on] Cuban television [. . .] because the year I arrived was when they allowed [people of] two different races to get married . . . I started watching Martin Luther King's marches on TV, all of those things with the dogs and [repression with] police clubs. So, I thought, "Oh my God! It was true. Everything I heard back in Cuba was true" [. . .] I thought it was all propaganda, but no, it was true.[102]

León was horrified by what she learned, but her experience did not end there. Racism was something she experienced in her own life and witnessed on a daily basis where she lived and worked. But the fact that she was offered a job with Dance Theatre of Harlem almost as soon she arrived in the United States, and subsequently was involved with so many African American projects during those early years, was an immense educational experience concerning the politics of African American identity at the time. These were spaces where she could enter into these conversations about racism, giving her direct contact with many of the activists who were fighting these fights.

Martha Mooke, who was León's partner for almost three decades, puts the composer's experience of institutional racism in the United States in a more personal perspective:

[With her I got into] situations where [I got to see] something I would never have known about [otherwise, because of the color of my skin and the color of my eyes]. Going into a store and being followed, or having the perception of being followed by a store worker, or being stopped in the car [. . .] I have seen it enough and I have to respect that. I did see a police officer give her a hard time for no reason [. . .] I know she's worked extremely hard and had a lot of doors slammed in her face, and a lot of people tell her "You will never make it because of the color of your skin or the accent, or your music or whatever." And she has overcome all of that to be where she is today.[103]

Colleagues and students also witnessed León deal with racism in the workplace. Jason Stanyek, who was León's undergraduate composition student in the late 1980s, witnessed instances of racism against her at Brooklyn College:

I have distinct memories of particular professors speaking disparagingly about her and just be blunt racist. [I had a professor who] never stopped talking crap about her, and it was quite obvious that—even to an 18-year-old, a 19-year-old—that was racist. You know, the kind of language he used. I remember distinctly him not being happy about her being a composition professor at the university that he had been at for a long time.[104]

León has also discussed how those instances of racism affected her work at Brooklyn College and the student's curricular offerings:

One day I was in a classroom by myself, grading exams, when [a professor] came in and told me that he believed they had given me the position for my color and not my talent. So, I exploded in a faculty meeting and told them I was not going to put up with those things. [. . .] [Then], when Dorothy Klotzman stopped conducting the [conservatory] orchestra, she left it to me. And I invited Tan Dun, David Lang, Chen Yi, Pauline Oliveros, Philip Glass. We played their music. But then I had to go to Germany to conduct my opera [in 1994] and they gave the orchestra to this man, the same man who made my life miserable there. They did not want to give the orchestra back to me—even though I had just received this big award for my opera—because this guy said there was too much contemporary music. And when the students complained that there was not enough contemporary music, the answer was that this guy was going to have the orchestra until he retired.

Carol Oja, León's colleague at Brooklyn College from 1988 to 1997, considers that this particular faculty member may have felt threatened by:

Tania's musicianship [and] talent—talent in the body of an Afro-Cuban woman— it was just hard for him to handle, and he did his best over the years to make sure that she conducted the orchestra as little as possible [. . .] She was just kind of kept from fully functioning in those worlds, especially with the orchestra.[105]

In a more general impression of her former colleague's dealing with racism, Oja adds that she has seen many times how white people try to "keep her in her place. She is permitted to sit at the banquet, but she has a seat way down at the end of the table and not really probably even given a full meal. And yet, she speaks up. And of course, this causes irritation."[106] Years later, upon reflecting on the university's systematic lack of recognition of León's work and the unnecessary obstacles she had to face there, retired faculty member Wiley Hitchcock (1923–2007) confided to newly hired professor Ellie Hisama his sadness that Brooklyn College never "realized what they had with Tania."[107]

León has a deep knowledge and understanding of the "black American world" that Walker-Hill invokes in her book's introduction. She has been an important part of many cultural projects that have been central to the confirmation of that world and has also individually experienced the structural prejudices that have belittled African Americans for many generations. Nevertheless, she has chosen to deal with these issues in a different way, refusing to be defined solely by a single identitarian experience. But it is this experience of racism and its systematic reproduction in the reaction to her work with a variety of African American artistic projects that informed her transition into the culture of the United States, her adoptive country. Arthur Mitchell explained it succinctly when he said he "understood what she was fighting [for] all the time because we were fighting [for] the same thing."[108]

4

DIRECTION

Leading in Music, Leading in Life

On April 16, 2015, I conducted a public conversation with Tania León at Harvard University. After the event, León and I had dinner with Carol Oja, then chair of Harvard University's Department of Music, and a number of the program's graduate students. Many of the students came from ethnic backgrounds that are underrepresented in academic music programs, which made me think how lucky they were to have someone like Tania León as a role model. I mentioned how wonderful it was to have such a diverse representation around the table. This prompted Oja to reminisce about the years she and León overlapped as faculty members of Brooklyn College's Conservatory of Music in the late 1980s and early 1990s. Oja mentioned how students of color would flock unto León's office, often staying in line for several hours in order to talk to the composer about academic as well as personal issues.

León belongs to a generation of musicians and artists who had very few or no role models from their ethnic or cultural background when completing their academic study or beginning their professional careers in the United States. One can count on the fingers of one hand the number of female conductors truly active in the music scene of the 1970s when León began her career. The same can be said about people of color holding permanent teaching positions in composition programs at universities or conservatories in the United States or Europe. Individuals who could be seen as role models by aspiring music students and artists of color were few and far between. For Tania León, being one of the first—or one of the few—as a teacher, composer, and conductor meant that she had to break through innumerable explicit as well as intangible barriers and, in the process, upset many self-appointed gatekeepers. Yet, when León made it, she did not forget about how hard she had to struggle to get there. Helping others—intellectually, artistically, financially, and very often also emotionally—became a mission as important to her as her quest to develop into the best possible conductor and composer that she could be.

In this chapter, I take the idea of the conductor not only as a leader—in the sense of someone who leads the way—but also as someone who creates the conditions conducive for things to happen. This concept of leadership ties together Tania León's work as a conductor, cultural broker, and mentor. I explore the concatenation of events that steered her into unforeseen career paths and into becoming a central figure in the establishment of a number of influential cultural projects, professional and creative networks, and arts organizations.

The Baton and the Fulfillment of Artistic and Social Responsibilities

During the summer of 1971, Dance Theatre of Harlem made its first European tour. The first series of concerts were scheduled at the Teatro Nuovo in Spoleto, Italy, from June 25 to July 11. The concerts were part of the *Festival dei Due Mondi*, organized annually by the Italian composer Gian Carlo Menotti (1911–2007). The Juilliard Orchestra was scheduled to play with the company.[1] However, Dance Theatre of Harlem had never danced to a live orchestra, always having used recorded music in their performances. Arthur Mitchell and Menotti discussed what they should do. They agreed that it was better to have live music for the concerts, but there was nobody who knew the music and the company's stylistic choreographic nuances. They decided that León, being the company's *répétiteur*, was the best candidate to lead the orchestra. "[Mitchell and Menotti] threw me in the orchestral pit and told me, 'You'll conduct it,'" recalls León. "And I said, 'But I do not [know how to] conduct!' 'You'll do it. You know [all the music] by heart.'"[2] Given the company's working style—León reveals that "at Dance Theatre of Harlem everybody did everything. If I wiped the floor or painted the walls and put the nails [sic] [or] wrote a ballet, okay, now I conduct an orchestra. It was not a big deal"[3]—Mitchell and Menotti's request did not seem completely arbitrary. Thus, León's first time holding a baton in front of an orchestra fulfilled her "chosen responsibilities" as the company's music director. She had to rise to the challenge. As she explains, "I never thought that it would become such an endeavor in my life."[4]

Back in the United States, León resumed her studies, kept playing the piano, and continued to serve as music director at Dance Theatre of Harlem. Nevertheless, so many professional commitments inevitably ended up taking a toll on her piano technique. It was at that time that she began to seriously consider a change of career, from pianist to conductor.[5] A few years after her experience in Spoleto, León decided to study conducting in a more formal way. She began taking lessons with Laszlo Halasz (1905–2001), a Hungarian-born conductor who settled in the United States in the 1930s. Halasz made a name for himself as an opera conductor, especially as founding director of what would become the New York City Opera. He was known for his interest in modern operatic repertory—he collaborated on several projects with Gian Carlo Menotti among other living composers—his eye for new talent, and his defiance and contempt of racist practices in the operatic world. When he hired Camilla Williams (1919–2012) for the New York City Opera in 1946, she became the first African American to receive a regular contract at a major U.S. opera house, which led to assassination threats and plenty of hate mail for him.[6] He promptly took the talented León under his wing.

As a conductor, Halasz was interested in precision and unobtrusive expressivity. His students remember him as "a martinet who demanded attention to detail [. . .], perfect ensemble [. . .], [and who was able to draw] from his players a higher level of performance than they could draw from themselves."[7] Although some remember Halasz as a harsh critic, he could certainly be very generous, too. In the 1970s, he was the conductor of the Concert Orchestra and Choir of Long Island, an orchestra he would let his more advanced students conduct on occasion. "[Halasz] got to like me a lot," León remembers:

> [H]e had this orchestra in Long Island and he gave it to me so I could conduct some concerts . . . I remember concerts with Pepita Embil—Plácido Domingo's mother—and with Manuel Barrueco, playing [Joaquín Rodrigo's] *Concierto de Aranjuez*. I conducted all of that.[8]

After working with Halasz, León studied with Vincent La Selva (1929–2017), another frequent collaborator of Menotti's and the founder of the New York Grand Opera Company, who taught conducting at the Juilliard School. It was around that time, in the mid-to-late 1970s, that her career as conductor coalesced.

León's big break into the conducting scene came in 1976. During the third season of the PBS series *Great Performances*, the show's producers introduced a series called "Dance in America." León was invited to conduct the Brooklyn Philharmonia for a recording session for one of its episodes.[9] Maurice Edwards,

FIGURE 4.1. Tania León conducting Joaquín Rodrigo's *Concierto de Aranjuez* with the Concert Orchestra of Long Island and Manuel Barrueco as soloist. Photograph by Marbeth, courtesy of Tania León.

then manager of the orchestra, noticed her conducting. Recalling the occasion, León says, "to be frank, [the performance] was phenomenal. Whenever I listen to that recording I am like 'Oh my God! That was so good.'"[10] Edwards told Lukas Foss about her and Foss invited her to help put together a series to promote the music of composers of color. Although the Community Concert Series (as the program was called) ended after Foss retired in 1990, León continued collaborating with Dennis Russell Davies when he took over the orchestra. Her long tenure at the series enabled her to use her art to fulfill an urgent social mission: to present the music of nonwhite composers to a new audience.

In 1978, León joined the Broadway production of *The Wiz* as conductor. This was an intense experience that truly propelled her professionally. León said that she

> learned a lot [doing the musical], because at Broadway you mechanize yourself in such a way that you become a clock. Every night I'd check everything, from beginning to end. I would check with the stage manager and all the crew behind [the stage] . . . you memorize everything, the tempi, everything. I learned a lot but I almost [went] crazy, too. There were eight shows a week![11]

In as much as Broadway taught her many practical things about conducting, it also made her aware of the technical limitations that she still had. She

FIGURE 4.2. Tania León and Leonard Bernstein in Tanglewood. Photograph by Marbeth, courtesy of Tania León.

remembered what Orestes Urfé, her neighbor in Havana, told her when she was young: "Go and study in Tanglewood as soon as you have a chance."[12] Urfé had attended the Berkshire Festival back in 1948, where he studied with Serge Koussevitzky (1874–1951). León packed her things as soon as the Broadway season was over and went directly to Tanglewood, where she had been accepted at the Berkshire Music Center's conducting workshop. There she took lessons with Leonard Bernstein (1918–1990), was coached by Seiji Ozawa (b. 1935), and attended rehearsals led by many other guest conductors, including Vladimir Ashkenazy (b. 1937). Although León continued to learn from many other conductors—including as the guest of Zubin Mehta (b. 1936) at the New York Philharmonic as well as Sergiu Comissiona (1928–2005)—she considers her time at Tanglewood as a very special moment in her development.

The workshop was the beginning of a lifelong friendship between her and Bernstein, who helped and supported her throughout her career (see figure 4.2).

León especially remembers a comment that Bernstein made at an ASCAP (American Society of Composers, Authors and Publishers) meeting. When observing what he understood to be a marginalization of her opinions, Bernstein emphatically and provokingly said that "he did not want persons like me—and you must realize that I was the only person of color at the meeting—sitting in the back of the bus."[13] Ten years later, when Tanglewood organized "Bernstein at 70!," León was invited—along with a stellar list of celebrities that included Lauren Bacall, Victor Borge, Quincy Jones, Yo-Yo Ma, Midori, Mstislav Rostropovich, and Dawn Upshaw—to celebrate the conductor and composer's life and works.

Conducting Style

León's conducting style is sober and pragmatic, yet breathtakingly precise, elegant, and communicative. Her style can be traced back to how she remembers her work at the Tanglewood Festival in 1978. From Ozawa's coaching she learned the nuances of conducting technique in a very poetic way. She remembers how he explained effective movement and hand gesture on the podium using a bouncing ball; he said:

> [W]hen the ball bounces close to the ground it does it very fast. [When you drop a] ball, it starts bouncing high and then it accelerates. And that is how conducting technique should be. I mean, when you conduct something slow the gesture is bigger; and if you conduct something fast, the gesture is very small.[14]

From Bernstein she learned about the central role of creativity and imagination when interpreting orchestral music. León explains:

> Bernstein helped me a lot. [One of the works] I had to conduct for him was Debussy's *La mer* (1905) and he made me go crazy [with his indications]. He was like, "No, no, no! That will never happen until you start feeling the water! You have to see a brave sea in front of you!" So, visualization was very important for him and I always remember that.[15]

León decided to attend Tanglewood when she was already a professional with plenty of conducting mileage under her belt. That alone speaks volumes about her work ethic, professionalism, and sense of perfectionism. Yet, it is humbling to hear someone like her—an incredibly gifted musician, both technically and artistically—speak about the importance of hard work over talent when approaching music. "When I study the most," León argues, "is when I am conducting something because I'm a total detective, and that's when you see technique. I see the technique, I see ways of coloring; I see personalities, shapes, graphics, architecture, space, culture."[16] León's description of her detective work when conducting a piece of music provides a glimpse into her working process. Technique and creativity are always intertwined, and discipline works as the reactive agent that gives them both relational meaning.

For León, the final result of working through this process and reaching a balance between technique, creativity, and discipline, is artistic communication. She compared this balancing of different elements in conducting to how electricity is generated:

> Just like a wire in which you have positive and negative currents flowing, when you put it together you get electricity. To me a conductor is that—the person that puts himself or herself in the middle of a situation where she/he can pass on communication, and the communication in this case is sound. So, I am a vehicle and make myself subservient to the sound which passes through myself.[17]

This metaphor of the conductor as a mediator or connecting interface could be read in multiple ways. In practical terms, León's statement could refer to the conductor as a mediator between the orchestral score and the actions needed from the orchestral musicians for that score to come to life. It can also be read as a declaration about the conductor as an interpretative intermediary between the composer and the audience. About this particular perspective, León comments:

> [O]ne of the things I try to do is get my own conviction of the work: the period, the style. There are so many considerations [to be made] that it would be impossible to describe all of them . . . I don't follow any specific school, but what I render represents my own esteem for what I feel about the work. It might be very similar to other interpretations, or it might be far different from other interpretations [but o]ne thing that I respect at all times and cherish is the music; whether it is ballet, opera, symphony, or musical theater, each performance calls for a specific attitude.[18]

León believes that discipline, hard work, and the conductor's intellectual capabilities should be put at the service of a larger goal: to "pass on communication" to an audience and to her musicians. Furthermore, even though she tacitly acknowledges that whatever the conductor communicates is his/her own take on what the composer's musical idea may have been (which "might be very similar to other interpretations, or it might be far different"), it is this musical idea that should prevail over the conductor's ego or musical persona. In that sense, in its search for a type of expressive objective efficiency, León's approach to conducting could be seen as in the modernist tradition of Boulez's "bracing clarity" (see figure 4.3).[19] Nevertheless, one can also see in her style much of Stravinsky's elegant *coraggio direttoriale*, as Oleg Caetani defined the Russian composer/conductor's flexibility to allow unforeseen risk and improvisation within an otherwise painstaking preparation.[20]

As with her own compositions, communicating the intricacies of rhythmical syntax efficiently is very important for León as a conductor. But she lets the musicians discover these intricacies as they perform each work:

FIGURE 4.3. Tania León conducting. Photograph by Marbeth, courtesy of Tania León.

When I do the polyrhythmia, I don't subdivide anything, and I tell the conductors don't subdivide, because then you break the flow. Musicians are very intelligent, and specifically if you repeat something, they understand all of a sudden where the groove is. So let the musician do it; trust the musician. Just give them the flow of how it goes and the musician[s] will get it."[21]

As a conductor, León doesn't try to impose her way dictatorially on the orchestra members. However, this does not mean that she does not have a clear idea of what she wants to get out of her musicians; she achieves her goal by giving the musicians agency, enabling them to be musical, and taking advantage of the skills they already have. León is able to channel their sense of pride to guide them into doing what she wants.

Music to the People:
Tania León and the Brooklyn Philharmonic

At the beginning of the Brooklyn Philharmonia's twenty-third season in 1976–1977, Lukas Foss' long-standing dream finally became a reality: it was announced that the orchestra would be offering a community concert series devoted to the music of black composers. The funding for the project came from Con Edison and Philip Morris, and the orchestra's board of directors approved it as long as the main funding for the orchestra was not affected.[22] The goal of the program was "to reach out into the community by bringing the orchestra to the people, in the hope that, in time, those who attended such concerts would be stimulated to eventually come to the academy to hear that same orchestra at its home base."[23]

In order to coordinate the project, Foss gathered three very different rising stars in the new music scene: composers Julius Eastman (1940–1990), Talib Rasul Hakim (1940–1988), and Tania León. Although the original idea was to develop programs featuring black composers, Eastman, Hakim, and León "took a 'think-tank' approach for the project. Beginning with a roster of black composers exclusively, the program expanded to include women composers and, finally, all composers [of non-European extraction]."[24] They thought of bringing small units of the Brooklyn Philharmonia to churches, gymnasiums, museums, prisons, and hospitals.[25] It was a pioneering concept because orchestras at the time did not have outreach programs.

In 1977, under the label Community Concert Series, the first season presented four different programs at several venues.[26] Especially noteworthy was the programming of an eclectic and stylistically diverse selection of short pieces by some of the most prominent African American composers on the New York scene, including Omar Clay (1935–2008), Arthur Cunningham (1928–1997), Noel Da Costa (1929–2002), Oliver Lake (b. 1942), Carman Moore (b. 1936), Dorothy Rudd Moore (b. 1940), Hale Smith (1925–2009), and Howard Swanson (1907–1978), as well as Eastman's *Conceptual Music for Piano* (1977), Hakim's *Music for Nine Players and Soprano Voice* (1977), and León's *Spiritual Suite* (1976).

Music critic and singer Raoul Abdul reviewed one of the season's concerts given on February 27, 1977; originally published in the black press, his review applauded this program and the orchestra's new initiative:

> I doubt if anyone in the large audience had a dull moment all afternoon . . . [T]he program included music representing a wide variety of composing styles. And, all of it was played by an ensemble of an exceptionally high caliber . . . [The] Brooklyn Philharmonic's [*sic*] aim [with this series] is to provide a forum for Black composers and to encourage Black participation in the orchestra's activities. This is a project which deserves your support."[27]

Most of the composers featured in the first season of the Community Concert Series were active members of the Society of Black Composers (see figure 4.4).

FIGURE 4.4. Gathering at Noel Da Costa's apartment. Standing: Talib Rasul Hakim, Hale Smith, Oliver Lake, and Carman Moore. Seated: Arthur Cunningham, Noel Da Costa, Tania León, Julius Eastman, and Dorothy Rudd Moore, 1977. Photograph by Marbeth, courtesy of Tania León.

One of the organization's aims was to challenge the downtown and uptown divisions in New York's musical world. Instead, the organization hoped to "show a more flexible community less concerned with the discursive, stylistic, and geographical categories of white downtown musicians."[28] This also became a signature of the Brooklyn Philharmonia's new series.

Although her collaboration with the Brooklyn Philharmonia started as a part-time job, León's responsibilities quickly grew and she eventually became its sole curator, after Eastman and Hakim left the project.[29] She was also in demand as a collaborator with several other of the orchestra's initiatives. By the second season of the Community Concert Series, León was serving as its chief musical advisor and principal conductor.[30] With the first Brooklyn performance of Sam Rivers' (1923–2011) improvisational opera *Solomon and Sheba* (1973), the series began to diversify its musical offerings to include not only classical music but also jazz and jazz-influenced musics.[31] Although still predominantly African American, the inclusion of composers from Japan, China, and America from a wide variety of ethnic backgrounds, as well as classical and jazz musicians and popular-music songwriters, reflected León's ecumenical take on ethnicity and musical styles as a curator.[32]

León's involvement with the orchestra increased during its 1980–1981 seasons. In June 1980, León served as pianist and assistant conductor to Foss for the orchestra's tour of Mexico before resuming her role as leader of the Community Concert Series with a summer concert at the Brooklyn campus of Long Island University.[33] Grants from the Ford Foundation and the National Endowment for the Arts, along with municipal and state support—given to support programming of Latin American music—allowed the Community Concert Series to present more ambitious programs during this season. As part of this expansion, the orchestra, under León's baton, appeared for the first time at the Lincoln Center Out of Doors Festival with a program of music by African American and Latin American composers, including Adolphus Hailstorck (b. 1941), Ed Bland (1926–2013), Francisco Zumaque (b. 1945), and León herself.[34]

During the 1981–1982 season, León was a more active collaborator with other programs offered by the orchestra.[35] She also was appointed music director and principal conductor for the newly refashioned Community Concert Series, which resulted from its merger with the Family Subscription Series.[36] For this season, the series focused on opera. For its first program, the orchestra collaborated with the Harlem School of the Arts to premiere two one-act operas by Noel Da Costa: *The Singing Tortoise* (1982), conducted by León, and *Babu's Juju* (1982), conducted by Ronald Isaac.[37] This concert was positively reviewed by Edward Rothstein, who wrote that the

> origins of opera lie in the folk tradition; music was connected to myth and story, to community sharing of sensations and senses. The Brooklyn Philharmonia Community Concert Series . . . had something of this aura when presenting two music theater pieces by Noel Da Costa . . . [T]hese were self-consciously "community" presentations. The works . . . were meant to strike resonant chords in the children who attended, affirming a heritage that included traditions of Africa and Haiti.[38]

The remaining eight programs of the series presented three more operas and orchestral works by mostly Latin American and African American composers.[39]

The 1982–1983 season brought the end of the Ford Foundation grant for the series, which limited the project's budget. However, León was still able to put together a hefty season program, which included collaborations with the Western Wind Vocal Sextet, the Charles Moore Dance Theater, and the Nicolo Marionettes, as well as a concert of Chinese music and a concert to celebrate

Martin Luther King's birthday. (King's birthday celebration would become a regular feature of the series.) In order to allow local high school students to join the orchestra in the last concert of the season, León also organized a series of clinics and workshops during the winter.[40]

Only seven concerts were presented in the series' 1983–1984 season. León conducted two programs of contemporary orchestral music.[41] The final concert of the season was a celebration of jazz featuring singer Betty Carter (1930–1998), saxophonist Paquito D'Rivera—León's old friend and classmate from the García Caturla Conservatory in Havana—and trombonist Janice Robinson (b. 1951).[42]

The 1984–1985 series focused on composers from three traditions, including music by Latin American composers, featuring the Annabella Gonzalez Dance Theater;[43] Asian and Asian-American composers, in collaboration with the Asian-American Dance Theater;[44] and African American composers, including Dinizulu and his African Dancers, Drummers and Singers.[45]

In February 1985, León and the Brooklyn Philharmonic Chamber Ensemble were unexpectedly invited by Puerto Rico–based composer Francis Schwartz for a week-long residency at the University of Puerto Rico to present a series of concerts and seminars. Although in artistic and educational terms the trip was a success, the orchestra's board of directors failed to see its potential "in building an audience within the considerable Hispanic community in Brooklyn,"[46] and remained indifferent to León's outstanding achievement in coordinating the residency on such short notice.

The most important event of León's collaboration with the Brooklyn Philharmonic in the 1985–1986 season was a program entitled Three Hundred Years of Black Classical Music. The program was curated by Kermit Moore (1929–2013); conducted jointly by Moore, Foss, and León; and financed by a Creative Program Grant from the National Endowment for the Arts. It was planned to be a culmination of León's efforts to promote the music of composers of color at a moment when the series' difficult financial situation put its existence in jeopardy.[47] Music critic John Rockwell noted the series' importance: "Starting in 1977, the orchestra has played more than 60 works by black, Latin and other ethnic composers and mostly under the direction of Tania León." He called the concert "a stirring occasion."[48] The concert featured works by Ignacio Neves (1730–1792), Chevalier de St. George (1739–1799), José White (1833–1920), Noel Da Costa, and Undine Smith Moore (1904–1989).

The Community Concert Series had been suffering serious financial difficulties for several years, and its next three seasons saw continuing cutbacks. It finally came to an end during the 1989–1990 season, which coincided with Lukas

Foss' resignation from the orchestra. As her work as director of the series was reduced, León received more opportunities to participate in other orchestral activities, especially the curation of a symphonic jazz program as part of the Free Summer Park Concert Series.

León spent over thirteen years as the leader of the orchestra's Community Concert Series and as its Latin American music and jazz advisor. And although the sheer excitement and experimental attitude that characterized the early years of her collaboration with the Brooklyn Philharmonic slowly changed to a sense of duty, the series remained true to its mission to challenge highbrow and lowbrow archetypes as well as the divisions in the contemporary music world that characterized the 1970s New York music scene. León has fond memories of how the series allowed her to engage with the community where she lived:

> Mayor [Ed] Koch congratulated us for the amount of concerts we did through New York City . . . and above all, for promoting the music of [composers of] color and jazz. We really gave jazz a push. There was always some [jazz] in the series [. . .] We did concerts with Betty Carter, the famous jazz singer; we did concerts with Tito Puente. We did all of that at Prospect Park and the place was always full. And, because they were in the community, people knew us. So, whenever I was on stage they would yell at me, "Hey, Tania!" You know? It was a very popular thing.[49]

Certainly, the amount of premieres played, the number of young composers supported, the frequent commissions of new works, the performance of many pieces by female composers and composers of color, the continuous crossing of cultural and social boundaries (in terms of race, class, and gender), and the sustained engagement of young black and Latinx audiences throughout the city of New York are accomplishments that would make any music entrepreneur proud.

A Bittersweet Achievement: Residency with the New York Philharmonic

In January 1993, Tania León was selected to be Charles H. Revson Composer Fellow at the New York Philharmonic. This was a three-year fellowship managed by Meet the Composer, a prestigious program designed to give composers exposure to the workings of major U.S. orchestras and new ways of interaction with a variety of music communities. The selection was made directly by John Duffy (1926–2015), president and director of Meet the Composer, and Kurt Masur

(1927–2015), music director of the orchestra. León remembers her first meeting with Masur to interview for the residency:

> Mr. Masur asked me what did I think of the stage of contemporary music right now. I said, "Well, I think that this is one of the most vital moments [. . .] Composers are writing whatever they feel like writing. And they are not asking academia or anyone for permission to say whatever they want to say." . . . The next thing I know, I had a call from Deborah Borda [Executive Director of the New York Philharmonic], telling me that they would like me to serve on a residency for three years.[50]

By 1993, young U.S. composers were challenging the modernist, logical, and positivist dogmas that had led serialist and post-serialist composers (especially on the East Coast) to seek refuge and intellectual validation in the academy.[51] Although León had been teaching at Brooklyn College since 1985, she was never a spokesperson for any particular school of composition and did not see academia as the natural outlet for contemporary music to stay culturally and socially relevant. For composers like her, who had never felt at home within the restrictive modes of any specific compositional creed, the growing pluralism in the contemporary music scene of the early 1990s was something to highlight and celebrate. Apparently, Masur and Duffy found León's stance a plus when making a decision about the Revson Fellowship (see figure 4.5).

FIGURE 4.5. Tania León and John Duffy, founder of Meet the Composer. Photograph by Marbeth, courtesy of Tania León.

The original Meet the Composer program was designed in 1982 as a ten-year-long endeavor that would "place composers in residence with major American orchestras and raised the money to make the idea a reality. . . . Through the program, composers gained a foothold in the American orchestral world and began to sense new opportunities."[52] The idea was to generate enough of an interest so that when the program's funds ended orchestras would include composers in residency in their own budgets. However, when the program ended in 1992, some orchestras retained the position, others retired it, while others redefined it according to their own needs. One of the orchestras where the position was redefined was the New York Philharmonic, which retitled the role as "new-music advisor."[53]

The New York Philharmonic's press release when León was announced as its 1993–1995 fellow outlined her main activities: to "advise Mr. Masur on American music, review scores submitted to the Philharmonic, introduce visiting composers during Pre-Concert Lectures, and work with the Orchestra, the staff, and the composer community."[54] Masur was quoted in the release as stating: "I am committed to seeking out the best in new music, especially the work of American composers. An advisor of Ms. León's abilities and great talent as a composer will be a help to me and a wonderful asset to our artistic staff."[55] The press release ended by reiterating the mission of Meet the Composer, "to increase the opportunities for American composers to write, perform, and record their works, and to increase audiences for contemporary music."[56]

When León accepted the residency with the New York Philharmonic, she thought she would continue doing the kind of work she had done for the Brooklyn Philharmonic: curating programs, conducting concerts, and pitching in new ideas. Nevertheless, she spent the first year of her tenure assessing and cataloguing a room full of music scores and tapes that the orchestra had commissioned or that composers had sent independently over the last several years. Most of the materials and letters went back to the period when Zubin Mehta was musical director of the orchestra and David del Tredici (b. 1937) was composer in residence (1988–1990). Only by the beginning of her second year was León invited to participate in the coordination of a festival of U.S. music called The American Eccentrics. It presented orchestral music by Charles Ives (1874–1954), Carl Ruggles, Henry Brant (1913–2008), and Wallingford Riegger (1885–1961), and a chamber concert of music by Henry Cowell (1897–1965), John Cage (1912–1992), Conlon Nancarrow (1912–1997), and Terry Riley (1935).[57]

In retrospect, León believes that Nancarrow, who was flown in from Mexico City to participate in the festival, should have been "celebrated like royalty" by the orchestra, but that did not happen. "I even asked Kurt Masur to come [to the concert]," she explains, "and he did not show up."[58] She also was making suggestions that were not being seriously considered by Masur or the board of the orchestra. This made her realize that there was something strange about how her residency was unfolding.[59] The second year of her tenure came to an end without her having conducted the orchestra, having none of her works performed, without any of her ideas coming to fruition, and without the board and Masur accepting any of her suggestions about programing or commissioning works from composers of color.

During the third year, Masur finally gave León a concert. Although it was not presented in New York and did not feature her conducting the New York Philharmonic, it was a very important opportunity: to travel to Leipzig, Germany, to conduct the prestigious *Gewandhausorchester*. The plan was to present her orchestral arrangement of *Seven Spirituals* (1995), sung by the African American bass-baritone Simon Estes (b. 1938). León went to Leipzig in advance to rehearse the orchestra, but at the very last minute, Estes canceled. She had to reorganize everything at the eleventh hour, change the program, and find a singer able to do the concert on short notice. León speculates:

> At the time, there was this whole thing with O. J. Simpson and the famous policeman who used the "n" word. The piece that Simon Estes had to sing had the "n" word because it was based on poetry by Langston Hughes, and Estes started saying that he was not going to sing that movement of the piece because it had the "n" word, and blah-blah-blah. . . . To tell you the truth, I think that Simon Estes . . . what he felt was that this program I was doing there was very problematic. The thing is that Masur called me to the office and told me: "Look, I want you to go and do a program at the Gewandhaus, and I want this program to be with a lot of rhythm and things, I don't want you to think I'm sending you there to do a black concert." But in a way, that's what I did.[60]

Yet, at the time, Léon was still willing to accept promises from Masur and the orchestra, especially when, after the residency came to an end in December 1995, she was asked to stay in her role for an extra year. She kept pushing for a new music festival or commissioning short pieces from young composers for the orchestra's regular children's concerts to no avail. Nevertheless, she was finally given a chance to lead the orchestra for a Young People's Concert as part of its tribute to Manuel de Falla. On February 11, 1996, she conducted a chamber orchestra concert with Falla's Concerto for Harpsichord (1923–1926), selections from *Siete canciones populares españolas* (1914), and *El amor brujo*

(1915). She also was able to squeeze in *Sentado sobre un golfo de sombra* (1993), a brand-new work by the young Spanish composer Xavier de Paz López-Novoa (b. 1963). The event was an audience success, but the logistics of both the concert and the dress rehearsal were marred by problems that, looking back, can only be interpreted as expressing a profound lack of respect for León. Among other slights, the orchestra manager did not send anyone to set up the stage and she had to do that herself before the rehearsal.

The opportunities to conduct both the Gewandhausorchester and the New York Philharmonic were indeed exceptional. However, the way that these events unfolded and the problems they generated were important red flags that León was no longer willing to let go unnoticed. The situation reached a crisis when her own community—the African American community that had nurtured her as an artist and that she had championed as a curator of the Brooklyn Philharmonic's Community Concert Series—started to harshly criticize her. During a concert with the Boys Choir of Harlem, Dorothy Rudd Moore, with whom León had collaborated at the beginning of her tenure with the Brooklyn Philharmonic, publicly confronted her. León remembers that

> all of a sudden Dorothy Rudd Moore stood up in the audience and [said], "Tania, what a shame you're doing this. How can you do this when you know that the Philharmonic does not play any of our music, not even yours?!" . . . And the head of the [orchestra's] education department . . . she was standing right there. She was livid.[61]

León also received letters from her African American colleagues who saw her tenure at the Philharmonic as a missed opportunity for the U.S. music mainstream to reevaluate works by composers of color. She brought the missives to the attention of the orchestra's management and received no answer. This continuous neglect finally pushed her to confront Masur and the administration:

> I started complaining that I was not really doing anything related to my interests there. . . . That's when I realized I did not want to be there. . . . What would I be there for? To be a [type of] cosmetic [change]? That is the impression I had, that I was the politically correct person to have. The face of . . . You understand me, right? Having a Latin woman of color may have looked very nice, but the fact is that I was not satisfied as an artist.[62]

The problems between León and the orchestra became public when K. Robert Schwarz published "Is There a Composer in the House? Not Always" in the *New York Times*. This article focused on the role of composers in residency at U.S.

orchestras, particularly on León's mistreatment by the New York Philharmonic. John Duffy declared that when León was hired:

> it was my understanding in conversation with the management and the music director that they were going to perform Tania's work, and that she would play a central role in advising Kurt Masur. . . . Now they have an outstanding composer who has very little input.[63]

At the end of 1996, as one of her last acts as composer in residence, León wrote a letter to Masur detailing her concerns and feelings. After four years with the New York Philharmonic, León left with the bittersweet sensation that, regardless of the prestige of having been associated with this institution, she had been prevented from doing what she could have done there. She believed she could have accomplished important things if the surrounding conditions had been more favorable and if its management had been more willing to take artistic and social chances.

The American Composers Orchestra and the Sonidos de las Américas Festival

If León's 1990s tenure with the New York Philharmonic was looked upon with suspicion by many of her colleagues, her collaboration with the American Composers Orchestra in the creation of the multi-annual Sonidos de las Américas Festival was seen as a major accomplishment locally, nationally, and internationally.[64] Before this project, León had collaborated with Dennis Russell Davies, the music director of the American Composers Orchestra, for several years. Their paths first crossed when León was interviewed for a position as composer in residence for the group in 1988. She did not get the position, but Davies ended up commissioning her to write a work for piano and orchestra. The result was *Kabiosile* (1988), which premiered at Carnegie Hall with Ursula Oppens as soloist in December 1988.[65] Soon after, Davies invited León to be one of three composers in residence at the 1990 Cabrillo Festival of Contemporary Music.[66] León curated a chamber music concert for the festival, which included two classic Latin American modernist scores, *Energía* (1925) by Carlos Chávez (1899–1978) and *Homenaje a Federico García Lorca* (1936) by Silvestre Revueltas. The concert also featured the U.S. premiere of *Trio mit Stabpandeira* (1983) by Nicolaus Huber (b. 1939) and a performance of León's *Parajota delaté* (1988).[67]

The idea for Sonidos de las Américas was born out of this curated concert. "After that concert," León says:

[Dennis] and I were talking about Latin America and I mentioned that there are no links [between the United States and] Latin America. We [in the United States] did not know much of what was going on in Latin America.[68]

Davies was particularly intrigued by the fact that there was a larger presence of Latin American composers in Europe than in the United States. León continues:

We decided to suggest to the board the idea of a kind of Latin American festival where we could promote and create links between the composer communities in the United States and Latin America. We proposed it to the board but the board was not interested in it.[69]

It took a couple of years for León to convince the orchestra's board of the potential of the festival. The turning point came when Francis Thorne (1922–2017), founder of the orchestra, invited Thomas Buckner (b. 1941) to join the board. Buckner was a baritone and champion of new music who had recently moved to New York City from California, where he had been active as a concert promoter, philanthropist, and record label entrepreneur. He met León when he was asked to perform for the premiere of a new work by a young composer with the Brooklyn Philharmonic. León was conducting the orchestra, and her work with the musicians in getting the piece ready for performance in just a couple of rehearsals—especially given the unfavorable circumstances surrounding the concert—impressed Buckner. He explains:

This fellow [the composer] did not finish his piece until the day before the rehearsal, so [León] only had a chance to look at the music the night before. [But] she is such an outstanding musician! . . . She could sing any line of music that she looks at without thinking about it. It just makes me jealous. So, I was so impressed with her musicianship. I liked her and we got to know each other.[70]

When he arrived in New York, Buckner was doing well financially and was interested in donating funds to organizations that promoted contemporary music. León recommended two projects that needed financial support at the time, Dance Theatre of Harlem and Meet the Composer. Because Buckner and she had a common interest in increasing the musical and ethnic diversity of the American Composers Orchestra's offerings, she also shared with him her idea about a Latin American music festival. He was interested right away and their alliance became the platform to more assertively pitch the project to the orchestra's board. Buckner speaks about the board members' reticence and how León and he managed to work around it:

Tania had this idea for years; and it was at a time when I was in a position to do something. So, I [could] help with tailoring it [and giving] a little gift to them, to be used for Sonidos, because otherwise it wouldn't have happened. Tania was of course the real visionary. . . . I supported her and I also contributed towards it. It wasn't easy. There was resistance. I think a lot of people felt that their mission as American Composers Orchestra meant the United States of America. And I think it probably did. I mean, after all, when Francis [Thorne] founded it, he knew what he meant. But [Tania] wanted to expand it to include the Americas.[71]

León puts it more bluntly, "Tom showed up with $90,000 to start the festival. Thanks to him we could begin."[72] Once the initial funds were there, the board could not continue to deny the festival's feasibility. In fact, they did their own fund-raising and were able to receive support from a variety of government agencies and private institutions, most notably the Rockefeller Foundation and the National Endowment of the Humanities.

In 1994, after years of logistical planning and coordination among musicians in New York and in several Latin American countries, the American Composers Orchestra presented Sonidos de las Américas. The project ultimately led to six annual, individual, weeklong festivals devoted to Mexico, Venezuela, Brazil, Puerto Rico, Argentina, and Cuba, presented in collaboration with Carnegie Hall, as well as several institutions of higher education.[73] With this generous funding, León was able to expand the idea of the festival beyond a simple series of concerts to truly build bridges and provide spaces for an intellectual and artistic dialogue between composers and musicians in the United States and in Latin America. León states that:

We were able to bring a delegation of musicians from different countries to initiate conversations with a delegation of musicians from the United States. Thus, we had composer-to-composer sessions, and brought soloists from each of those countries to perform the music according to the style and cultural influences in the [programmed] pieces. Jesse Rosen, who was the Executive Director of the American Composers Orchestra, and I went to Mexico, Venezuela, Argentina, Brazil, [and Puerto Rico] to interview the composers, discuss the idea, and [to ask them] to send us scores so we could make a selection and form a delegation.[74]

Although the final word was always León's, the selection of the music as well as the composition of the delegations of composers and performers from each country was arranged through conversations. Each festival consisted of orchestral and chamber music concerts, lectures, master classes, preconference discussions, and composer-to-composer sessions.

The six editions of the festival featured over 60 concerts and close to 200 compositions by a long list of established as well as younger Latin American composers.[75] Following the tradition that she had established at the Brooklyn Philharmonic, León programed concerts of popular, folk, and jazz musicians along with classical music events, making the festival a success in commercial, artistic, intellectual, and political terms.[76]

By the time Sonidos de las Américas started, León was already a Composer in Residence with the New York Philharmonic. While Masur and his team failed to take full advantage of León's creative energy, the American Composers Orchestra took her seriously. The venture paid the orchestra back in an impressive way. In December 1994, when reviewing the second edition of the festival, Alex Ross stated that

> the Sonidos project is performing a vital service . . . Since Latin America is the scene of some of the most vital and independent new activity, listeners should stay closely tuned to "Sonidos" in the next few years.[77]

Many fellow musicians and audience members couldn't top "the sense of wonder and the excitement of discovery"[78] provided by Sonidos de las Américas from 1994–1999, even in a musical scene as diverse as New York City's.

Connecting Networks: Composers Now

If leading an orchestra for the first time was the result of León accepting her artistic responsibilities, then serving on boards of major arts organizations, speaking up, and challenging people has been her way to fulfill her social responsibilities. For León, social responsibility is an extension of artistic responsibility; or maybe they are one and the same. It is only natural for her to address social issues by using the tools she has developed as an artist. Championing causes that are close and dear to her is not something she has ever shied away from. Promoting diversity and inclusion, supporting composers and artists from social and cultural groups that have been systematically oppressed, neglected, or rendered invisible, and providing opportunities to connect to low-income communities have always been important to her.

Throughout her career, León has worked for many contemporary-music organizations. In addition to the positions we have already noted, she was music director of the contemporary music series at the Whitney Museum, and was on the boards of Meet the Composer and Composer's Forum, Inc. She has also been a very active member of ASCAP. In all of these posts, León has been a very strong advocate of young composers as well as gender and racial equality in music programming and access to education, grants, commissions, and performance venues. Nevertheless, through her work with these organizations, she has also learned of the difficulties of achieving these goals.

Composers Now was born in response to the systematic inequality León witnessed through her involvement with other groups. Its mission is to empower "all living composers, celebrate the diversity of their voices and honor the significance of their contributions to society."[79] Although vague in explaining how it intends to accomplish those goals, the ecumenical attitude that has characterized León's community work is clearly central to the organization's mission statement. However, launching the project took almost ten years. Multiple budgetary problems prevented it from taking off sooner. León remembers:

> James Jordan, who was in charge of the music section of the New York Council on the Arts, gave me a five thousand dollar grant to put together a narrative for the project. [Georgiana Pickett] wrote the document but it did not work because there were no ways to generate more funds. Not until I talked to Laura Kaminsky about it [in 2008].[80]

Kaminsky had been recently named artistic director of New York's multidisciplinary performance center Symphony Space, and León thought her project would be the kind of venture that would appeal to her. It took some work to convince Kaminsky, but eventually Cynthia Elliott, CEO of Symphony Space, decided to support the project. After three years of incubation, the first Composers Now Festival was launched in 2010.

Many of New York's cultural organizations focus on promoting the work of a single ethnic group. Although they often share similar strategic goals, they had rarely worked together. One of León's goals for Composers Now was to facilitate collaboration among these groups. She says that she wanted:

> Symphony Space to have a link with Harlem Stage, and for Harlem Stage to have a link with Jazzmobile. I mean, this institution is here, in the middle of the city, but it is not connected to what is happening in the neighborhoods and to the organizations in those neighborhoods. This is how I see it. Many of these organizations are minority-based institutions with a minority-based leadership. In white institutions the leadership is white while institutions of color have a leadership of color. In sum, we are still isolated, there is no inclusion, there is no diversity. So, that's the reason why we wanted to link all of these different organizations together. But it was me who had the connections [because of my work with all of them]; it was not them [Symphony Space].[81]

León's promotion of inclusion is at the center of Composers Now's many differ-ent projects and initiatives, especially its festival. Cosponsored by organizations across New York City, Composers Now presents an annual month-long festival that programs concerts of classical music (from Western and non-Western tradi-tions), jazz, sound art, electronic music, and indie-rock. The organization also offers annual composition residencies, a performance series that includes public conversations with composers, and an award to celebrate the work of living com-posers who have made a lasting and positive impact on contemporary culture.

Carlos Carrillo, one of León's former students, highlights that "she has achieved her [personal] goals but keeps helping her students and those around her. That is what she is doing with Composers Now. She is helping others."[82] In a way, Composers Now is an extension of Tania León. One could see the organization as a cyber device, a mechanism that allows her to continue to en-ergize, enhance, maximize, and better channel the community-oriented efforts for which she has been widely recognized throughout her career.

Teaching and Mentorship as Conducting

If the idea of conductivity as transmission—or as the capacity to enable the flow of ideas among different constituencies—is essential to understand León's work as an organizer and cultural broker, it is also one of the most important principles behind her work as a mentor. In 1985, after watching her conduct one of the Brooklyn Philharmonic's community concerts, Dorothy Klotzman (1937–2014), then chair of Brooklyn College's Conservatory of Music, invited León to join the faculty. León recalls that

> [Klotzman] asked me to teach some classes as an adjunct. So, that's what I did. But it looks like she was thinking about bringing me [full time] to Brooklyn Col-lege because she called me later and told me they were conducting a search . . . [that] they were looking for someone who could conduct and teach [composi-tion] lessons. . . . They interviewed me. The only thing I remember is that I said I did not know if I could do it because I was not going to stop my conducting career. I did not want to stop conducting and composing to become a professor. But they said there was no problem. So, that's how it started. They hired me as an associate professor.[83]

León's arrival at Brooklyn College caused quite a stir among both faculty and students. Although located in a very diverse borough of New York City, for decades the faculty at Brooklyn College's Conservatory of Music had failed to reflect that diversity. Carol Oja describes the situation at the time León joined the faculty, "unless I am missing someone, I think the entire music conservatory faculty was white. She was the only person of color. . . . So, Tania's presence stood out."[84] About the issue of representation, León says:

> [W]hen I arrived [at the conservatory] there were very few women. There were some but not in the percentage that [there] should have been. . . . But regarding race, it has always been dreadful. . . . There has always been [a] minimal [presence of people of color]. Unfortunately, that has been one of the main criticisms [against the college].[85]

Yet, Oja affirms that, although rather fluid in terms of composition, the conservatory's student body had instead a "wild range of kids in terms of capacities, race, and ethnicity."[86] It should not come as a surprise that, if León's arrival at Brooklyn College was questioned by some faculty members,[87] students found her presence nothing short of a blessing.

Ellie Hisama, one of León's colleagues at the college from 1999 to 2006, says that she got to know her well during that period. Hisama "saw just how a humane and caring person she is with students. So many composition faculty—and faculty, period—they do not really care about teaching, from my perspective. But she is someone who really did."[88] In the classroom, León's teaching style is unorthodox and continuously varies depending on the individual student. But the goal informing these changes is one and the same regardless of the student: to enable them to become more musical individuals. Jason Stanyek, one of León's first composition students, explains it this way:

> She was by far—and I would say, remains—the most musical person I had ever met. From the moment I met her, she just exuded music. Every time I saw her, whether it was in a classroom or whether it was in front of an orchestra. . . . Whether it was just walking on campus, there was a musicality that was present. I think in the lessons, she was trying to pass that [musicality] on to me in any way she could. She used every single tactic you can imagine. . . . Everything that was at her disposal she used. I think for that reason I consider her one of the best professors . . . one of the most effective professors [I ever had].[89]

Transmitting musicality is León's primary goal as a professor. To achieve it, she has developed both systematic and creative classroom strategies. She believes in the corporeality of knowledge, an idea that privileges the body as much as the mind as both a producer and repository of knowledge. As such, one of her pedagogical methods is to ask students to abandon current notation technology for a while in order to copy music by hand. Angélica Negrón, who got a PhD in composition under León's supervision, describes this as a kind of initiation rite:

> She asked me to copy a page from a quartet by Bartók and a page from a quartet by Ligeti. . . . I also remember a flute piece by Ferneyhough that was super complicated . . . the rhythms were very precise and I had to go about [copying] them using a ruler, making the divisions and all by hand. That was my homework and then we would talk about the process and what I had discovered. So, it was a different way of analyzing the pieces.[90]

León clarifies that this particular assignment's goal is to return to the methods used by the old masters, before the widespread use of mass reproduction technologies. They gained musical knowledge by copying the music of their predecessors by hand. She describes this process:

> I ask many of my students about the scores they are interested in, what new composer they are interested in, what sound they are interested in. [I tell them,] "Look for the score you are interested in and search for a couple of pages you do not understand. Then sit down and copy them using pencil and staff paper. And I want you to do it perfectly aligned." Because when they are doing that they are entering the mind of the composer. So, I want them to come to my class and tell me what technique [the composer] used, how different things were connected. You see? They have to teach that [music] to me.[91]

León is also concerned with finding ways to get her students out of the embodied habits that they have developed through years of musical training. She is particularly interested in having them move away from the type of digital memory created by repetitive practice on their instrument. "Pianists have a digital memory," León explains:

> [T]hey play a lot of Chopin and get that memory [in their hands]. It is the memory of the chords, the harmonies. How can you get out of that memory? You have to do it consciously. You have to sit down and look for things that have nothing to do with that memory.[92]

Polina Nazaykinzkaya, another of León's doctoral students, experienced this challenge when León asked her to improvise on the piano during her lessons:

> I am a violinist and it is not customary for violinists to play the piano, but because I was trained at the Moscow Conservatory, and everybody plays the piano very well there, I was able to do it. . . . But at the same time, [this conservatory] strict education is limiting in some ways, because it all should be very proper. [So],

she tried to pull me out of this super-academic approach to music. She always pushed me to try something crazy, something out there. . . . I was just very shy about it. I would never improvise in front of anyone. That was something that was deeply personal. So that was great, you know? To try to improvise in front of her, but to be honest, it was very scary because she is such a great improviser.[93]

León says that some students are intellectually interested in using nontraditional musical elements, including sounds or rhythms that they can hear but, because of their strict academic training, often cannot feel through their bodies and thus have a hard time incorporating into their music. She uses improvisation as a tool to allow them to start understanding more corporeally than intellectually. "For me it is a little bit of mind [theory] and a lot of heart. I cannot write without intuition," León affirms, "and my intuition is very improvisatory. . . . So, sometimes I just tell my students, 'start a piece by improvising. Just sit at the piano and improvise.'"[94]

León spends a lot of time in her lessons encouraging her students to become more musical individuals by pushing them out of their comfort zone and to avoid reproducing conventions. But as much as this is a central tenet of her relationship with them, she also often goes out of her way to advise them on career-related issues and life in general. When asked about their relationship to León, many of her current and former students refer to her as a second or surrogate mother of sorts. Unlike many professors for whom the mentor-mentee relationship ends when the students leave their classroom or their office, León's concerns with her students' well-being often follows them beyond the walls of academia.

León acknowledges this relationship herself:

My students are like my family. They are like my children. I give them a lot of advice. They tell me about their lives [and] I try to give them encouragement towards success. I use failure as a step in the experience [towards success].[95]

It is not rare to find León late at night on the phone talking to her students, helping them overcome bureaucratic snags, letting them know about possible commissions or funding sources, consoling them over unforeseen family crises, or simply giving them and their families positive feedback about their future as musicians. In the words of Jason Stanyek, these actions "reveal something very important about Tania's personality. She was like family. She didn't separate music and the familial. I felt like she was part of my family and I think she felt the same way."[96] Carlos Carrillo's relationship with León exemplifies this type of bond:

I met [Tania's] mother. . . . [Tania] knows my wife and my son. We have been to her place. To me she has been much more than a mentor or a teacher one meets once and then disappears. She establishes this incredible personal connection with you. . . . So, she basically put me on this [academic and professional] track and has been with me throughout the years. I am eternally grateful to her. . . . And it is not just me; I know plenty of people who have said exactly the same, that they owe their careers to Tania. . . . She is a true mentor. She uses her position to help other people. To me she is a role model.[97]

Community and family have always been a central part of León's life. She grew up in Havana supported by a strong—if unconventional—family network. She was a part of a matriarchal household, where Mamota and Mima provided the space for her to flourish through rough financial and political times. In the United States, alone and away from her immediate family, León found in Arthur Mitchell, Dance Theatre of Harlem, and other African American and Latin theater networks a community not only conducive to her blossoming as an artist, but also a family that supported her through the bumpy road of acclimating to her new U.S. life and becoming a cultural citizen. Once she found her footing in the United States, she was able to return to Cuba and help her relatives there—not by imposing her vision of how things should be, but enabling their dreams on their own terms. Her work with the Brooklyn Philharmonic, fueled by a desire to create a support network, is not unlike her approach to mentoring. It is an *ava raris* in a cultural and social system that privileges individualism over collective accomplishment. She did not forget her community when she achieved success; rather, she understands success and community as indubitably intertwined. Having been raised in Mamota and Mima's matriarchy, she has taken up their torch to become a conducive woman, a conductor, an enabler and a guide, through her work on the podium, as an organizer, and as an educator. For Tania León, leading in music is but a small part of leading in life.

Tania León's (third from the left) high school graduation at Academia Bravo. Courtesy of Tania León.

Pepita Embil (singing), Zenaida Manfugás (at the piano), and Tania León. Photograph by Marbeth, courtesy of Tania León.

Tania León conducting. Photograph by Marbeth, courtesy of Tania León.

Leonard Bernstein and Tania León. Photograph by Marbeth, courtesy of Tania León.

Composers Pauline Oliveros, Tania León, and Joan Tower after an American Samples concert. Photograph by Marbeth, courtesy of Tania León.

Harry Belafonte, Tania León, and Tito Puente. Photograph by Marbeth, courtesy of Tania León.

Queen Elizabeth The Queen Mother, Anthony Armstrong-Jones (1st Earl of Snowdon), Karel Shook, Tania León, and Arthur Mitchell. Photograph by Marbeth, courtesy of Tania León.

John Corigliano and Tania León. Photograph by Marbeth,
courtesy of Tania León.

Tania León and poet Rita Dove. Courtesy of Tania León.

Tania León conducting *Permutations Seven*. Photograph by Marbeth, courtesy of Tania León.

5

VOICE
Style and Idea in the Music of Tania León

I met Tania León in person for the first time on Thursday March 6, 2014, when, as composer in residence at Cornell University, she led a discussion of her music for the student Contrapunkt forum. Although we had never met before, Robin Moore and I had written about her music in our book *Danzón: Circum-Caribbean Dialogues in Music and Dance* (2013). We focused on León's *Toque* (2006), a dense and complex work for chamber ensemble that uses the *montuno* from "Almendra" (1938), the classic Cuban danzón by Abelardo Valdés (1911–1958), as the structural basis for the unfolding of its musical discourse.[1] But León does not simply quote Valdés' danzón; that would have been the easy way to recycle it. Instead, she shreds it to pieces, turns the fragments around and upside down, and puts them back together in new and creative kaleidoscopic ways.[2] When Moore and I conducted our analysis of *Toque*, it took a lot of time to come to a shared interpretation of how she uses the danzón's montuno. León read and enjoyed our analysis, but never said whether we were right or wrong; she was clearly respectful of how we listened to and made sense of her music.

When I heard she was coming to Cornell, I was excited about meeting her in person and hearing her speak about her compositional process. I looked forward to bouncing ideas back and forth about how our listenings of her music—mine and hers—could be similar or different. The most fascinating aspect of seeing her speak about her music that evening was the way she explained her conception of rhythm to an audience of undergraduate and graduate students. Some of the students had specific questions about the most prominent rhythmic figures and patterns in a particular section of *Batá*. She answered their questions, but then went on to draw a big imaginary circle with her arms around her head and upper body. "This is how I understand rhythm," she said. Some of the students seemed a bit baffled. "It is a non-Western understanding of rhythm," she continued, and repeated the gesture. As Zen as this explanation may seem, it made perfect sense to me in the context of having studied her music in such painstaking detail years before.

In this chapter, I explore the development of Tania León's compositional voice and how different individuals make sense of it, tracing it through a selection of representative works that were composed from 1965 to 2002. My intention is not to provide thorough analytical descriptions of her major works, but rather to trace the technical and stylistic elements that could lead an attentive listener to identify her music as her own. I had the privilege of being able to speak to León, who was able and willing to describe and explain her music in her own voice. However, understanding that we all listen to music in different ways—responding to our own previous musical experiences in order to draw meaning when listening to new compositions—I use her voice as the basis of a polyphonic conversation between her, musicians who have played her music, and critics and scholars who have written about the particular works I focus on here. This includes myself and composer Sergio Cote-Barco who was in residence at Cornell University while I was writing this book. My understanding of León's music was profoundly affected by my conversations with him. By bringing together all of these voices I wanted to explore how different listeners unavoidably pay attention to different things when hearing the same compositions. The exercise was intended as a kind of communal "contrapuntal listening."

Each piece is discussed following a similar format: my interviews with León in which she describes how she worked on a particular piece of music are followed by an analytical discussion that summarizes my conversations with Cote-Barco in which we have bounced ideas off each other about what we hear in those works. These discussions are necessarily mediated by my authorial voice as I summarize them and integrate them into the chapter's prose. Nevertheless, I want to clarify from the outset that the ideas presented there are the result of those conversations; they are not my sole analytical voice even if the format suggests it. Finally, each section closes with an assessment in which I tie together the ideas discussed in the different conversations. My goal is to imagine ways that these works may both connect with one another to provide stylistic continuity and depart from one another in order to open new creative and aesthetic windows. My intention is not to assign preconceived categories or trademarks to León's compositions, but rather to track down how her artistic voice may have developed in the process of thinking about and composing these works. I consider León's scores and her ideas about her music as traces of a larger process of performative composition, a creative practice by which the composer fashions her musical persona in the act of "working out the details of . . . particular composition[s]."[3]

The idea of an individual musical voice is ambiguous. Composer John Corigliano has argued that this individuality refers to unconscious rather than conscious choices (which he considers techniques) in a composer's practice:

> If I want to use a twelve-tone technique in the building of a piece I do, if I want to use tonal techniques or anything else I can do it because they are available to me, but they have nothing to do with my personal style. My personal style is the chords, the pitches, the sonorities that I come to just because I like them . . . and I do not question that.[4]

In my study of León's voice, I follow Corigliano's belief that technique is separate from personal style. I focus on identifying both the techniques that link León's music to larger musical practices at specific historical moments, and the recurring sonorities, gestures, and ideas that provide these larger techniques with a particular imprint in her music. It is only in this dialogue between shared trends and techniques and their individual articulation that any discussion of style and voice is culturally and socially meaningful.

The Compositional Process

I begin this exploration of León's musical voice with a broad assessment, largely in the composer's own voice, about the particular idiosyncrasies that mark her approach to composition. This should provide a general gateway into León's compositional craft and practice that will illuminate the later discussion of specific works.

León does not compose at the piano, but she often uses the instrument at the beginning of the creative process to formulate ideas through improvisation. She notes that "[Improvisation] is a part of my compositional process because it is a natural part of the human experience. We are always improvising."[5] As these ideas begin to take shape, she writes them down as sketches:

> Whenever I get an idea, I create a sketch of that idea. By the time I get ready to put the entire puzzle together, I may have 100 or 150 sketches. So, it takes me a great deal of time to begin the piece, but that's how I begin.[6]

León stresses that these ideas do not always come to her while improvising at the piano. Sometimes they arise at unexpected moments and places because "[o]nce I settle into a piece, my mind centers on it, and I start collecting materials. If you focus on what you want to do, you are always writing."[7] She explains that:

> I usually travel around with a pad, and wherever I am when I get an idea, I'll write it down. That flash can come anywhere and at any time, and it might be a really important idea for the piece, so I like to be prepared to write it down.[8]

Once the sketches are ready, she works directly on the staff paper:

> I sometimes post [the sketches] on the wall in my studio. After examining them, I formulate a concept of the piece as a whole, and then my approach to assembling the work is largely intuitive. I write what I feel.[9]

In this intuitive process of putting the work together, León balances notions of rhythm, direction, and form. While many musicians, critics, and audiences highlight the rhythmic vitality of her music, León feels that

> *motion*, not rhythm, is the most important element of my compositional style. It is much like riding a bicycle: in order to sit on a bicycle without falling, one must be in motion, and it is necessary to create forward momentum before riding. So I am endeavoring to maintain constant motion. . . . For me, form isn't as important as motion, as the pieces having a sense of moving somewhere.[10]

The intuitive, almost mystical character of her compositional process is often in evidence when the composer tries to consciously describe how she developed some of the specific traits in her pieces:

> [S]ometimes I'll come back to a score days after finishing a piece and there are whole sections that I cannot identify or remember writing. I seriously wonder, "Who wrote that?" I don't know. It feels like someone else came in at just that moment and wrote that passage, or that entire section.[11]

Although León clearly explains that her compositional process combines intuitive and systematic techniques, there have been times in which the more mysterious aspect of the process takes over, allowing her to sometimes write pieces very quickly. When a piece comes to her in such a way, fully composed in a quick flash, she notes that

> I almost feel like I am in contact with something. It's hard to define, but *something* that is driving *me*, rather than me driving *it*. . . . Sometimes as humans, I think we are working on many planes, some that we do not understand so well yet.[12]

In discussing her music, she often says that she does not know how she composed a specific passage or even a complete piece. The process of listening together to her music was always a fascinating one; it frequently entailed witnessing how she marveled at discovering herself by working through these many mysterious moments in her scores.

Composing before Being a Composer

Tania León began to come up with songs when she was a child. Composing was nothing serious for her at the time; it was just another playful activity in her repertory of childhood games. As a teenager, she continued writing songs and started rearranging the classical European repertory that she was working on for her piano lessons: syncopating the melodies, changing the rhythmic patterns, and making variations out of the main themes.[13] She also joined in fun, improvisatory jam sessions with her fellow conservatory classmates. It was only when she started taking postgraduate music-theory lessons with Alfredo Diez Nieto and Harold Gramatges at the *Seminario de Música Popular* in the mid-1960s that she started taking composition more seriously. While there, León composed the earliest pieces that have made it into her catalog: the song "Ciego reto," as well as the solo piano pieces *Homenaje a Prokofiev* (1965), Two Preludes ("Sorpresa" ["Surprise"] and "Pecera" ["Fishbowl"], 1965), and *Rondó a la criolla* (1965).

León describes the work that she did before emigrating from Cuba as "the music I composed before I was a composer."[14] These pieces were not part of her catalog until recently, when she decided to include them—as samples of her first attempts at composition—in Adam Kent's recording of her complete works for solo piano. León says that these pieces were

> three harmony homework assignments I made. I was not trying to invent anything, but they somehow caught the attention of Diez Nieto, Edmundo López and Harold Gramatges. [They] said, "Let's put this girl in one of the [Hermanos Saíz] programs." And that's how it happened."[15]

Although meant as music-theory assignments, the technical and musical complexity of the *Homenaje a Prokofiev*, Two Preludes, and *Rondó a la criolla* surpasses what one may expect from typical student work. They reflect the Havana musical world that nurtured León in the late 1950s and early 1960s. Neither Diez Nieto nor Gramatges were part of the experimental avant-garde music scene that took Havana by storm in the early 1960s. Their work was a continuation of the neoclassical practices inherited by their own teachers, ideas that were popular throughout Latin America since the 1930s. Diez Nieto studied with Amadeo Roldán (1900–1939) in Cuba and with the Dutch-American composer Bernard Wagenaar (1894–1971) at the Juilliard School in New York. Gramatges also studied in Cuba with Roldán as well as with José Ardévol (1911–1981)—the founder of *Grupo de Renovación Musical*, one of the strongest neoclassical forces in the musical world of pre-1959 Cuba—and, later, with Aaron Copland (1900–1990) at the Berkshire Center in Tanglewood.

It should come as no surprise that, having been written under Diez Nieto's and Gramatges' influence, these early pieces by León feature the neoclassical aesthetic that dominated the Cuban music scene before the revolution and that remained influential, if slowly fading, through the 1960s. *Homenaje a Prokofiev*, the shortest piece in this group, is a waltz that proficiently and playfully imitates the Russian composer's mildly dissonant yet accessible harmonic style in works like the three so-called *War Sonatas* (1940–1944).

The Two Preludes, also short, are more personal pieces. "Sorpresa" is a lively work based on rhythmic and motivic repetition, and contrapuntal writing that unfolds over a rich, dissonance-peppered chordal sonority that resembles both Prokofiev's and Ravel's music. Within this framework, the prelude's harmonic motion is largely tonal and predictably progresses through a cadence in D major, that nevertheless is unexpectedly interrupted. "Pecera" is a more meditative piece that starts with the unfolding of a whole-tone sonority (F sharp-C-A sharp-G sharp-D) disturbed by the presence of an E flat. This ambiguity sets into motion a more homophonic section based on a mildly dissonant, repetitive motive in the bass line and a melodic line based on unfolding motives that emphasizes B flat over the chromatic motion in the bass line. This section leads into a final harmonic cadence that briefly highlights G as a tonal center but quickly reverts to B flat major. The overall harmonic sensation at the end of the piece is a quirky ambiguity between G minor and B flat major. The use of the altered whole-tone sonority at the beginning of this prelude forecasts the kinds of modal or harmonic disturbances that became a feature of León's mature musical style.

Rondó a la criolla is an energetic exploration of harmonic suspensions and resolutions based on a compound duple-meter pattern that gives the piece an almost folklike feel. In the second part of the piece, León presents a contrasting theme (slow and in triple meter) that alternates with the original one as the returning rondo refrain. This provides the piece with a sense of formal ambiguity that is further emphasized by the introduction of fragments of the first theme during the presentation of the slow refrain at the end of the piece. This piece is as much a study of form as it is an investigation of harmony. Although there are no actual quotations of popular or Cuban folk music in the rondo, León acknowledges that it does "reflect the melodic contour of traditional Cuban music, things that [she] used to hear in old songs and even *guajira* songs,"[16] a type of music she still enjoys. Two Preludes and *Rondó a la criolla* are the pieces that moved Edmundo López, León's childhood piano teacher, to prophetically announce, "we may lose a pianist but we will gain a composer."[17]

Tones: A Modernist Ballet for Arthur Mitchell

Tones, a ballet in three movements scored for two flutes, two oboes, clarinet, horn, trombone, tuba, timpani, percussion, piano, and strings, is Tania León's first major work. For many years, it was considered her first composition. Written for Arthur Mitchell and Dance Theatre Harlem over a two-year period (1970–1971), this ballet was born out of creative necessity. The specific constraints that gave birth to it influenced the work's deep and superficial structural levels. Its rather disjointed, nonorganic, three-movement structure is the result of an overly long period of composition, in which improvisation in the dance studio rather than systematic motivic development at the composer's desk was the main agent behind the compositional process. This resulted in a stylistically heterogeneous work across the movements. For example, the use of distinct melodic gestures in the third movement provide a musical flow that is very different from the more rhythmically unrelenting, less motivic movement in the first movement.

Tones' rhythmic and metrical surface developed out of the pragmatic need to negotiate between counting dance steps and counting musical beats.[18] This allowed León to make the kinds of choreographic syncopations across the music that allow the different counting systems to promote the central feature behind the unfolding of the piece. Nevertheless, one can already observe in this early piece that—although rhythm and polyrhythm are very important aspects at the surface level of León's music—what is really at stake here is motion. It is the idea of bodily motion that activates and informs the stylistic features of the piece.

In Conversation with Léon

> Tania León: I truly do not know how I composed [*Tones*]. It was basically a thing of inspiration. I went to the library and checked out music-theory and orchestration books. So, I did it on my own. Nobody told me how to do it.
>
> Alejandro L. Madrid: But what were you thinking about in terms of harmony?
>
> T.L.: My own harmony. Harmony that comes out of all the experience I had as a pianist. . . . What I had in my ear was what I have always had, a jambalaya of

sounds and information. And rhythmically it was inspired by Arturo [Mitchell] and his [counting] numbers [for dancers]. So, I was always paying attention to how the choreography was in conversation with his counting.

A.M.: And what do you hear when you listen to *Tones* today?

T.T.: I discover many things that have to do with me today: some cadences, ways to modulate from one tonal center to another. . . . I also notice the use of triplets, which is so stuck on . . .

A.M.: The counting for the dancers . . .

T.L.: Yes. It is always ti-ki-ti-ki [sixteenth notes] tan-tan [quarter notes]. It is very mechanical, right? But I also have the triplet. So, up to a certain point it is four against three. I can see that I was already doing polyrhythms . . . although very simple ones.

A.M.: What about the use of these rhythmic cells? Ti-tan-ti [sixteenth note-eight note-sixteenth note] tan-tan [two eight notes]. It is almost like ragtime, no?

T.L.: To me it is very interesting to look at; and to ask, "Where did I get this from?" I will not lie to you: I do not know.

A.M.: And how were you thinking in terms of timbre and orchestration?

T.L.: I believe this was just what happens to me today. I hear things . . . I mean, I can have this instrumental base [the piano] and then, all of a sudden, my mind starts to fantasize . . . sound fantasies . . . and I like them and I start just grabbing them. For example, [in *Tones*] the strings are very formal. They are always there but accompanying; they do not have an individual identity. The piano calls my attention, though.

A.M.: Do you think the piano dominates throughout the piece?

T.L.: I do. The piano is the main actor . . . [Referring to the score, mm. 16–17 from the second movement; see example 5.1] I find these [gestures] interesting [the piano imitating the violin runs behind a melodic gesture played by flutes and oboes].

EXAMPLE 5.1. Tania León, *Tones* (1970–1971), second movement, mm. 16–17, piano reduction.

A.M.: They are almost chromatic, right?

T.L.: Yes. Let me remind you that what really impressed me when I was [a student] in Cuba, was Bartók. Maybe that was the influence there.

A.M.: And harmonically too? Were you interested in quartal harmonies?

T.L.: Well . . . in my music there are a lot of seconds, ninths, fourths, and fifths.

A.M.: [Going back to some of the work's rhythmic features], in the third movement you have these changes from simple to compound duple meter.

T.L.: That is what I was telling you. I can see similar things there [to what I do now]. I can see where things started . . . of course, I was a baby back then. But these are metric changes I use [in my music today]. They also have a lot to do with our [Latin American] music. We are always playing these two-against-three or three-against-two games. And here [mm. 20–23 from the third movement; see example 5.2], I am going from ti-ki-ti-ki [eight sixteenth notes] to um-pah-pah [triplets]. So instead of writing it down like a waltz, [I did it in 6]: 1–2–3 4–5–6.

EXAMPLE 5.2. León, *Tones*, third movement, mm. 20–23, piano reduction.

A.M.: So, were you consciously thinking about those kinds of Latin American folk-music metric systems?

T.L.: No. I did not start thinking about that until the 1980s. After my father died.

A.M.: What can you tell me about your use of percussion instruments.

T.L.: Very classical. This work is completely square. Percussion here is insignificant [in terms of style]; it is [used to provide] color. [Looking through the score] One day I will sit down and try to really understand where all of this came from. Look at this [rhythmic patterns on mm. 33–36 of the third movement]. Prokofiev! I am not talking about harmony or melody but about the rhythmic [gesture].

A.M.: When I talked to [Arthur] Mitchell he said that, when he asked you to write this ballet, he wanted something neoclassical. He used that word. What did he mean?

T.L.: I do not know. I just followed him. I was trying to respond musically to his movements.

A.M.: OK. Here, at the end you have this cadence to a C major chord with that added C sharp [final measure of the third movement; see example 5.3].

EXAMPLE 5.3. León, *Tones*, third movement, mm. 162–163, piano reduction.

T.L.: That is my own invention. My harmony is never based on [what you find in] harmony books. It is always a practical response to my way of hearing.

A.M.: So, do you think at all in terms of tension and resolution?

T.L.: No, I cannot deal with that! The issue is that this is how I hear [the harmonies]. I hear these things; and when I hear them, I do not question them. What I hear creates in me a sensation and I [immediately] know that that is how it should be.[19]

Analytical Discussion

Most works by Tania León evade systematic analytical approaches. One cannot really make sense of them through thorough applications of set theory or post-Schenkerian methods. Nevertheless, these analytical approaches can be helpful in analyzing specific idiosyncrasies in many of her latest works, including pitch selection or large-scale structural transformations. However, *Tones* is probably one of León's most enigmatic works precisely because it completely evades a systematic analytical approach.

Keeping in mind León's admonishment about intuition and improvisation as being truly at the core of this composition, one can find certain stylistic and idiomatic peculiarities that truly challenge conventionally tonal forms of scalar and intervallic organization. These features not only provide *Tones* with a sense of mystifying coherence, they also signal stylistic habits uniting León's early and later compositional outputs in unforeseen ways. The harmonies are largely the product of nontonal contrapuntal motion that produces highly chromatic and often dissonant chords (although major sonorities with added sevenths or ninths as well as quartal harmonies also appear sporadically within the nontonal context). This harmonic texture unfolds through the interplay of modes that move back and forth between major and minor sonorities; it does not seem to be the result of thinking in terms of harmonies or harmonic motion (see example 5.4).

EXAMPLE 5.4. León, *Tones*, first movement, mm. 113–115, piano reduction.

These modes are also often altered in order to provide fleeting whole-tone and octatonic references. Many of these happen so quickly or within sections that are densely dissonant that it is easier to identify them by looking at the score than by listening to the music.[20] This often results in rather harmonically static moments regardless of the presence of evident tonal centers (F and D are very prominent in the first and second movements, respectively). Nevertheless, these centers are never emphasized through voice leading or harmonic direction. Instead, it is through repetition (as the beginning or end of certain scalar passages or as the pitches where octave displacement happens) that they remain in the listener's ear. In terms of form, *Tones* is a very eclectic. The through-composed character of the first two movements reflects the improvisational practices at the core of the work's inception and stand in stark contrast to the somehow more conventional formal practices of the third movement. There, the recurrence of a motive in 6/8 (see example 5.2) infuses the music with a rondo-like quality of an almost neoclassical charm.[21]

Assessment

As already noted, the melodic gestures, harmonic motion, and intervallic practices in *Tones* seem on the surface to be a bit arbitrary. Nevertheless, a closer look shows that there are certain recurring ideas in terms of intervallic and harmonic organization. One of them is the atypical use of conventional scales, modes, or chords. The sudden appearance of triadic chords in the middle of chromatic dissonant passages is one example of this technique, as is the systematic and increasing insertion of chromatic pitches within otherwise largely diatonic textures in the first movement, giving the uneducated ear an impression of a certain randomness. León does the same when it comes to breaking scalar expectations, where the composer breaks the chromatic sequence by inserting major seconds (see example 5.1). Her use of a C sharp in the C major chord at the end of the piece (example 5.3) is another good example of this tendency to create ambiguity or shock by inserting unexpected pitches. (This is foreshadowed in her use of whole-tone sonorities in "Pecera.") A tendency to generate tonal centers based on repeated intervallic sequences (thirds in the case of *Tones*) is also something that will become a signature of her more mature compositional style.

In a way, *Tones* allowed León to revisit some of the influences evident in her early piano pieces (the quartal harmonies of Bartók, the rhythmic drive of Prokofiev, and the references to sonorities often heard in Debussy) in order to reinvent them in a new cultural and creative setting. An important connection between *Tones* and those early pieces is the centrality of the piano to the score, including the musical turns and gestures that León discovered through the physicality of improvising on the instrument. *Tones* was composed at the piano before it was orchestrated, and as such, the sonorities in the music could have entered León's musical rhetoric precisely through her training as a pianist. After all, León herself admonishes her students to consciously move away from the digital memory that their musical upbringing instills in their bodies.[22]

In general, *Tones* offers an insight into the practice of a composer at the outset of her career, showing that there are a series of perhaps unconscious concerns that inform her compositional choices. These would eventually develop into more systematic processes to generate musical material and structure in her later works.

Haiku: Flirting with the Avant-Garde

After completing *Tones*, Tania León became more serious about composition and pursued a degree at New York University. There, she studied composition with Ursula Mamlok (1923–2016):

> [I had] one-on-one lessons [with her]. She taught me structure, twelve-tone technique, serialism, and pointillism. These are procedures I still use in my music. There are things I do [today] that come out of all of that.[23]

León studied with Mamlok until 1975, when she graduated with a Master of Arts in composition from NYU. Thus, this was the academic and intellectual world in which she was immersed when she composed her second ballet, *Haiku*, which was commissioned by the American Dance Festival in 1973. The ballet is based on seventeen traditional Japanese haikus selected by the composer and choreographed by Walter Raines.

Scored for flute, bassoon, cello, bass, guitar, two kotos (one prepared and one unprepared), percussion, narrator, and tape, *Haiku* departs considerably from the neoclassical aesthetic of León's earlier works. For the first time, León engages some of the techniques and idioms favored by the avant-garde and experimental composers she became acquainted with largely through her presence on the New York new-music scene of the early 1970s and her work with Mamlok.

In Conversation with Léon

> **Alejandro L. Madrid:** *Haiku* starts in a very diatonic fashion and slowly becomes more chromatic. And then you have these scales that are very clearly defined; you even write them down in the score. I imagine it may be because the koto is tuned that way but I am not sure. They are scales that are almost octatonic . . . but there is always a pitch or something that breaks the octatonicism.
>
> **Tania León:** I do not know. I hear this piece a lot and I always marvel at it. . . . I ask myself, "How did you compose that?"
>
> **A.M.:** Is that a Moog synthesizer?
>
> **T.L.:** Yes. I created [the tape part] myself. I remember I was [at the music lab] and connected this to that and started with the oscillator; and I was like "Ah! This is a flute that comes from another planet." Because it has this eerie quality. I did it all; even the voices, [which I transformed] with the oscillator.[24] That was something in composition I wished I could have continued, electroacoustic music.
>
> **A.M.:** And the synthesizer, was it NYU's?
>
> **T.L.:** Yes. Professor Gilbert gave me permission to use it.
>
> **A.M.:** Something that I find unique about this work—that is not as evident in some of your later work—is a world of chance and improvisation. For example, there are a few things in the score that are not actually played in the [commercially available] recording [of *Haiku*]. It comes across as if these were decisions made by the performers. Some modules they decided to play and some others not. So, it is a much more open work than any of your other pieces.
>
> **T.L.:** It is a completely intuitive work. I tell you, sometimes I write and I do not know who is writing. It is as if I am in trance, hearing things and [writing them down].
>
> **A.M.:** Is there a relation between the words in the haikus and anything in the music? Is there something in the structure of the poems that translates into the structure of the music?
>
> **T.L.:** I used the poems in a very simple way. They gave me the sonic images that I identified with each [poetic] thought.
>
> **A.M.:** I was also interested in their [musical] duration. Some of the haikus are very short, only a couple of bars, while others are very long.
>
> **T.L.:** That relates to Walter [Raines]'s choreography. [Their duration depends on] what we were going to do for that [particular haiku].
>
> **A.M.:** How did you decide the instruments for the orchestration? Why did you choose a guitar?

T.L.: I thought the contrast between the strings of the guitar and the strings of the koto was interesting. So, I thought I could play with these timbres, which were sometimes similar. I always like colors. I work with colors without realizing [it]. In all of my works, there is something that has colors. I do not work in terms of instrumental families. I combine colors in an unconventional manner. I do not follow [orchestration] treatises.

A.M.: Many of your works have long pointillistic sections.

T.L.: I understand pointillism as a manifestation of color and light. It is like when you put a light [behind a kaleidoscope] and you get all these reflections. That is how I use it. And it could be a melody. When you take all those [scattered] pitches and organize them in the same range you realize it is a melody, but I throw [the pitches] to different [registers]. . . . Even though this is a Japanese-inspired work, it has a lot of my grandfather's mystery. A lot of space . . . often when you asked [my grandfather] something, he would not answer immediately.

A.M.: I notice some things in this work that I also hear in your later music. Like your tendency to break the octave or the use of [harmonies based on] clusters separated by a fifth or a fourth.

T.L.: Yes, I use [those intervals] a lot in my writing. I love those sonorities.[25]

Analytical Discussion

This discussion of *Haiku* attempts to determine its overall harmonic or intervallic sonorities and the way that Léon derives new pitch material from conventional pitch collections. *Haiku* starts with very open harmonies, using intervals of perfect fourths and major seconds played in harmonics by the bass and cello. These evoke the type of transparent imagery from the poem by Konishi Raizan that opens the piece ("There in the water color of the water moves . . . translucent fishes"). These intervals are used to create a sonic carpet upon which León starts to slowly fill out the gamut. At the beginning of the piece she introduces the pitches from the pentatonic scale and, toward the end of "Haiku I," all the diatonic pitches. In "Haiku II," the largely diatonic texture shifts with the introduction of a series of minor seconds. This generates largely whole-tone sonorities that León expands with the introduction of pitches outside of the collection. In this case, she uses a whole-tone collection on C but breaks the intervallic sequence, first with the addition of an F, and later with the addition of an A (see example 5.5).

EXAMPLE 5.5. Tania León, *Haiku* (1973), "Haiku I" and "Haiku II," harmonic reduction.

A similar process happens with León's use of octatonic sonorities, which she also expands by adding extra pitches in order to derive different modes and pitch material. The solo flute in "Haiku VIII" provides a good example; it also shows the type of octave displacement in melodic contours that León will continue to use throughout her career (see example 5.6).[26]

EXAMPLE 5.6. León, *Haiku*, "Haiku VIII," for solo flute.

Assessment

In *Haiku*, León combines instruments from a wide variety of musical cultures (kalimba, clay drum, African harp, bongos, temple bell, mamola, Chinese cymbal, African maracas, guitar, and koto). She also attempts to evoke a poetic atmosphere of open spaces and silence through the manipulation of "eerie" sounds. As such, this work is both León's response to the Zen-influenced avant-garde developments that had shaped the New York music scene since the late 1950s, as well as her contribution to the changes that were taking place there in the early 1970s. At the time, Tom Johnson characterized these transformations as triggered by

> the infiltration of non-Western ideas. . . . In one way or another, all the current experimentation with static non-developmental forms must be influenced by non-Western cultures. . . . The "climax" has been one of our most fundamental assumptions ever since Aristotle. Only Asians, Africans, American Indians, and current Western composers have been satisfied with unclimactic music.[27]

In *Haiku*, León generates a musical language that responds to the motivic, intervallic ideas that occupied post-serial composers, while also developing a texture and a structure that responds to the concerns of 1970s New York composers with indeterminacy, openness, static forms, and multiculturalism. The former is evident in her tendency to use pitch collections or pitch sets that refer to specific scales (such as the whole-tone scale, the octatonic scale, or the diatonic gamut), only to systematically disrupt them with the addition of alien pitches in the generation of new musical material. This is clear in example 5.7, where the initial octatonic pitch set is chromatically altered in a harmonic prolongation that leads to a diatonic harmony that in time is also altered with the incorporation of dissonant intervals of major and minor seconds.

EXAMPLE 5.7. León, *Haiku*, "Haiku IV," harmonic reduction.

However, rather than following a strict system of intervallic derivation, León generates material through a more intuitive process that often provides the freedom to choose apparently random pivot pitches to lead through new tonal and harmonic excursions (as the harmonic reduction in example 5.5 shows).

Overall, *Haiku* provides a window into the mind of a composer negotiating a variety of very tough experiences in her life—working for Dance Theatre Harlem, struggling to make ends meet, dealing with critical familial and personal circumstances, completing a graduate degree in composition, discovering the avant-garde musical legacy of her adoptive city—who, in the process, is able to produce a work of ineffable beauty.

Four Pieces for Violoncello: *El tumbao de papá*

Tania León had engaged with elements from a variety of African and Afro-Caribbean drumming traditions in some of her works before she composed *Four Pieces for Violoncello* in 1981, including *Dougla* and *Spiritual Suite*. However, it was only with *Four Pieces*—composed after returning to Cuba for the first time in twelve years in 1979 and the passing of her father in 1980—that León began to consciously incorporate elements from Cuban music in her works. "During the 1970s," León recalls, "I was very keen to conceal my background. . . . Perhaps I was looking for an entry into the mainstream."[28] However, after the emotional reencounter with her father,[29] she argues that "I felt an explosion inside me. I realized that there were very cherished things in me that I was denying. And I felt the sounds of my environment, the sounds of my childhood, starting to come back to me."[30]

Four Pieces for Violoncello is a technically demanding work. The first movement, "Allegro," presents "a declamatory motive based on the whole-tone collection [that] sets the tone for the work, both in character and melodic language"[31] (see example 5.8).

EXAMPLE 5.8. Tania León, *Four Pieces for Violoncello* (1981), "Allegro," m. 5.

The second movement, "Lento doloroso, sempre cantabile," "is a beautiful and quiet meditation [with] [d]elicate dynamic shadings ranging from *ppp* to *mf* [that] will challenge the performer's command of nuance to bring a convincing performance to an audience."[32] The third movement, "Montuno," "functions as a scherzo [with a] dancelike quality,"[33] and features "foot-stamping on main beats to set off the syncopated and jagged lines played by the cello"[34] (see example 5.9). The final movement, "Vivo," "is a tour de force that displays the virtuosity of both composer and performer."[35]

In Conversation with Léon

Tania León: This is where I started experimenting with the cello as percussion and with a little bit of the Cuban [*son*] clave [see examples 5.9 and 5.10].[36] The second and third movements are dedicated to my father. The second [movement] is a prayer and the third one is his *tumbao* [groove], his walking style.

EXAMPLE 5.9. León, *Four Pieces for Violoncello*, "Montuno," mm. 5–7.

EXAMPLE 5.10. Cuban son clave rhythmic pattern.

Alejandro L. Madrid: Can you tell me something about the writing style?

T.L.: Many musicians tell me, "This music is so hard!" Then I look at it and for me it is very easy. I do not find anything strange in the writing. I think the accentuation is different from how people [are used] to accentuate. For example, when I write in 6/8 it is not the typical **1**-2-3 **4**-5-6, instead it could be **1**-2-**3** **4**-5-**6**.

A.M.: What about the materials used in the piece?

T.L.: The first and fourth pieces are the most neoclassical. I thought about them that way and did not imagine that the second and third pieces would musically become what they became. I composed the first and the fourth pieces first. But, because this was the first piece I composed after my father's death, and I was so tormented by the conversation I had with him [when I last saw him in Cuba], out of my sadness I decided to make the second movement into a prayer. And then, what happens afterward has to do with my character. You see, I can be suffering for three minutes but after three minutes I say, "Enough!" I do not make those three minutes into three hours or thirty days; instead, I just drop it and keep moving. That's how I understand the contrast between the second and third movements. The second movement is very sad and the third movement is *joie de vivre*.

A.M.: Can you tell me more about the first and second movements?

T.L.: The first one is an exploration of the cello register [with] large intervallic leaps; the second one too, just in a slower tempo. In the second movement, I use natural harmonics because it is a sound that elevates . . . it is present but it is not present. . . . You hear the sound but it leaves [immediately]. The first three measures are the source of everything [see example 5.11]. They are all the same pitches but in different registers.

EXAMPLE 5.11. León, *Four Pieces for Violoncello*, "Lento doloroso, sempre cantabile," mm. 1–4.

A.M: And the fourth movement?

T.L.: That is a matter of instrumental virtuosity. That is why I have all these scales. This is a lot of what I do now, breaking [the melody] in different octaves. I just tweak things around . . . and the pitches [the C sharp] act as tonal centers (see example 5.12).[37]

EXAMPLE 5.12. León, *Four Pieces for Violoncello*, "Vivo," mm. 7–8.

Analytical Discussion

Instead of focusing on its Cuban rhythmic elements, which feature prominently in my conversation with Léon, this discussion centers on the ways in which the composer creates formal and tonal structure throughout the work. This is especially significant to understanding how León approaches structure when she is not working with a ballet's choreographic and narrative plots.

The first movement, "Allegro," is divided in three sections (A-B-Codetta). The beginning of each of these sections is marked by gestures that make clear references to whole-tone collections and augmented sonorities. Each section is differentiated by character and tempo, with the more lyrical middle section framed by two fast ones. The tonal center at the beginning of the piece is established by repetition and by melodic and chordal gestures that move back and forth between F and F sharp, giving its tonal center modal ambiguity. The middle section starts with an emphasis on D but soon moves to E and E flat as alternate tonal centers. The last part feels like a brief codetta that borrows the gestures and intervallic material from the beginning; it closes with an ambiguous movement toward the fifth degree.

Formally, the second movement, "Lento doloroso, sempre cantabile," flows more freely than the first movement. Its three parts are differentiated primarily by harmonic texture, which is diatonic at the beginning and the end and more chromatically ambiguous in the middle of the movement. Nevertheless, the overall impression is more diatonic than in the other movements. Tonally, the movement starts with an emphasis on D and moves toward F in the middle section, featuring a dramatic gesture outlining a B minor chord with major seventh played in *sforzato*. This minor sonority stands out from the rest of the material in terms of pitch choice, dynamic range, and meter; it is the only instance in which the internal subdivision of the beat changes from 3 to 2, thus creating a moment that feels like an expanded hemiola.[38] Because this work is dedicated to the memory of León's father, one could easily interpret it in a semi-programmatic way: this harmonic and metric disruption may represent the moment of death. It is followed by an attempt to return to light as represented by the more diatonic harmonies and the harmonics that close the movement.

The third movement is the montuno. This is the first time in León's music that she consciously used Cuban dance rhythms. The music is driven by clave rhythmic patterns and syncopations typical of *son cubano*. The physicality of the dance is further emphasized by the score's request to have the cellist stamp their feet on the floor, knock on the soundboard, and play Bartók pizzicati at several moments throughout the piece. The pitch choices also are very different from the previous two movements. Instead of referring to the whole-tone collection, León takes a chromatic collection as the basis for modal derivation that creates a new sonic character. Tonal centers are also less clear than in the previous movements. This section seems to move more freely through the gamut, although C is emphasized frequently toward the end of the piece through accentuation and the use of Bartók pizzicati.

In contrast, C sharp is clearly the most prominent pitch throughout the last movement, "Vivo." This pitch is especially important because it marks the beginning and end of the movement's characteristic virtuosic, toccata-like sequences as well as its larger structural sections. For the most part, the texture is diatonic; it becomes more chromatic only toward the end of the piece, which contrasts with the character of the third movement. Léon may have selected C sharp to be the prominent pitch for this movement because it is the lowest pitch of the cello that can be played with vibrato. This allows the performer to have some expressive control over the different sections of the piece.[39]

Assessment

Besides the programmatic character of some of its sections, one of the most interesting features of *Four Pieces for Violoncello* is its corporeality. Just as the *tumbao* of León's father is taken as both a literal evocation of his personal walking style and a metaphor of the ways he carried himself through life, corporeality in *Four Pieces* is used to generate structures at different levels of composition. Probably the most obvious is at the performatic level: the composer indicates that the performer take a series of physical actions beyond the traditional conventions of cello playing. This not only provides the performance with a unique visual component but also makes a connection between the style and idea of the composition by linking together the piece's foreground and structural rhythmic levels. Nevertheless, this is not the only way in which the composer takes advantage of the performer's corporeality. She also takes the different ways in which the performing body interacts with the instrument in order to generate sound to create different articulation layers. This is a feature that composers like Milton Babbitt (1916–2011) also found crucial in the structuring of their most complex serialist works.

When observing these performance practices in relation to León's recurrent harmonic and melodic stylistic tendencies—the way she obscures conventional pitch collections by inserting alien sounds; her tendency to privilege certain intervallic collections; the type of motivic organicism she explores in these pieces; and the novel use of traditional Cuban rhythmic practices not as an expression of local color but as an attempt to generate texture and structure—we discover a composer whose artistic voice unfolds as the improbable blending of multiple and contrasting emotional and aesthetic experiences. The technical and aesthetic practices behind these pieces represent the kind of "motile, kinetic [and] active" ways in which, as Jason Stanyek suggests, León's music sounds "a vast number of interlocking cultures and histories."[40]

Batá: Embracing the Past, Looking into the Future

In 1985, León received a commission to write an orchestral piece for the Bay Area Women's Philharmonic. The result was *Batá*, a short, one-movement work that "recreates the rhythms and texture of the ritual batá drumming"[41] from the

Yoruba people of West Africa. The title of León's composition also "draws on the rhythms played on the double-headed, hourglass-shaped drums of the same name, traditionally played in a set of three to accompany the Cuban religion variously called Santería and Regla de Ochá."[42] Because León's father took her to a Santería session when she visited Cuba in 1979, it makes sense that *Batá* is dedicated to him. In fact, the opening gesture of the work, played by the piccolo, is an exact transcription of León's father whistling to signal his arrival back home when she was a child.[43] It not only reappears in different iterations throughout the composition, but also organically generates the work's musical material.

In Conversation with Léon

> **Alejandro L. Madrid:** I see *Batá* as a more organic piece than some of your previous work. All of the materials in the piece are derived from the motivic cell at the beginning (see example 5.13); and at the end, the material comes back to bring the piece to an end.

EXAMPLE 5.13. Tania León, *Batá* (1985), mm. 1–2, piccolo.

> **Tania León:** There is no return . . . what happens is, that is the moment when [my father] leaves! He leaves again! [Laughing].[44] Of course, he leaves in a different way. He had been dead for five years [when I composed this piece]. My father always left and you never knew when he was going to come back. So, every time [the motive] passes by, you have a different trait of him. That is what helped me structure the piece, his leaving and coming back.
>
> **A.M.:** You also have these contrasting sections; sometimes very pointillistic and other times using the instruments in more [melodic] dialogues. And then you have these Cuban *cinquillos* playing very consonant harmonies.
>
> **T.L.:** Yes, that is related to what I do with *Indígena*. I consider this piece [*Batá*] something a bit crazy. You never know what to look at.
>
> **A.M.:** It also feels like you were in G and then moved to G sharp as the tonal center. And again, you have these very consonant, triadic chords but in an atonal context.
>
> **T.L.:** Yes. It is for contrast. . . . The end [of the piece] is just completely batá [drumming, m. 137; see example 5.14, especially the cowbell part]. Every person who listens to this piece asks me why I do not expand [the last] part. But something I always do is, once I finish a piece, that's it. That is the piece. I do not like to interfere and go back to the past.[45]

EXAMPLE 5.14. León, *Batá*, mm. 137–141, reduction: violin and cowbell parts.

Analytical Discussion

Batá is more analytically accessible than some of León's previous compositions, perhaps because by this point of her career she had already solidified a personal voice, making it is easier to trace patterns and conventions across works. This analytical discussion focuses on León's intervallic relations, the way she emphasizes tonal centers, and the relationship between the overall tonal plan of the piece in the background level and the materials that appear in the foreground.

In *Batá*, León uses the melodic gesture that informs the generation of pitch material throughout the piece (see example 5.13) as a way to also explore the instrumental register of the orchestra. Every iteration of the generative motive by a different family of instruments is also accompanied by pitch and intervallic variations and an expansion of this motivic cell. This motive's presentation not only allows León to generate material and explore its timbral possibilities in the orchestra, it also generates structure.[46]

Assessment

Organic construction is central to understanding *Batá*. As noted, León generates most of her musical materials out of the intervallic relations in the opening gesture played by the piccolo. However, she also uses the intervallic clash between G and G sharp—which is first introduced by the trumpet at the very beginning of the piece—to generate ambiguity at cadential moments, as well as to mark the larger tonal center structure of the piece. More generally, *Batá* is a work that expands the ideas and stylistic procedures that León featured in *Four Pieces for Violoncello*, including the organicist generation of material and also the semi-programmatic character of the structure. This would become more evident in some of her later works.

Although through-composed, *Batá* presents an overall structure based on three sections: a presentation of the material; its expansion; and its recapitulation. The novelty here is that between the second and third parts León introduces the batá section. This could be understood, in a very traditionalist and formalist way, as a virtuoso cadence of sorts before the recapitulation. In this sense, *Batá* is a hybrid exploration between the conventions of traditional structures like the sonata-allegro form and the formal inventiveness allowed by the open programmatic character of the piece itself.

Carabalí: A Spirit that Cannot Be Broken

Carabalí is an orchestral piece composed in 1991 as a result of a commission from the Cincinnati Symphony Orchestra. It is a single-movement, densely dissonant, and complex composition that shows a different facet of León's compositional style. Although she borrows from a number of African musical traditions, the way she uses them here is less transparent and more difficult to identify than in previous works. The title of the work refers to an African group from the coast of Calabar in southern Nigeria, members of which were enslaved and brought to the Americas during the slave-trade era. According to León, *Carabalí* is a celebration of "a type of spirit that cannot be broken."[47] Upon its premiere, the work was described as "[a] kaleidoscope of color and pattern, it is a chain of tonal and atonal events and moods; rhythm is the life blood that provides continuity. . . . Highly intellectual and a demanding piece for both orchestra and conductor, *Carabalí* is both accessible and powerful."[48]

In Conversation with León

Alejandro L. Madrid: It looks to me like you are playing with the complete chromatic gamut in *Carabalí*, but there is always one missing or delayed pitch. This occurs within a very dense, yet pointillistic, texture. Because of this scattered texture, it is not easy to hear the African rhythmic elements. But, sometimes they do stick out, like when the winds play this repeated dissonant chord over a rhythmically undetermined gesture of the strings in mm. 61–69 (see example 5.15).

EXAMPLE 5.15. Tania León, *Carabalí* (1991), mm. 61–69, reduction: wind section.

T.L: You know? One of the American composers who has inspired me and who I still like is Charles Ives.

A.M.: I find *Carabalí* to be a bit Ivesian . . .

T.L.: Yes. That [idea] just crossed my mind. I like that he is very cultural. I mean, he has [works] where you are listening, in the background, to very powerful cultural statements about the [United States].

A.M.: *Carabalí* is very dense in the sense that there are many things happening at the same time. Maybe it is Ivesian in that sense . . . Is there a relationship between the title and the music?

T.L: I dedicated this piece to [my niece], Yordanka. I helped her [to travel] abroad and [to move into] a different environment[49] . . . I just heard something there that is related to *Toque*. In *Toque*, I use [the danzón] "Almendra," and I just heard it come through in *Carabalí* [see examples 5.16 and 5.17] . . . So, it may have a lot to do with breaking away from Cuba.[50]

EXAMPLE 5.16. León, *Carabalí*, mm. 188–190, reduction: horns, trumpets, and trombone parts.

EXAMPLE 5.17. Abelardo Valdés, "Almendra" (1938), riff from the montuno section.

Analytical Discussion

Carabalí is one of León's most harmonically complex and dense pieces. This analytical discussion therefore focuses on the organization of the clusters that appear throughout the densest sections of the piece, and the use of orchestration to color these harmonies and other intervallic features of the piece.

Although *Carabalí* is a long and dense piece, its form is rather simple, juxtaposing rhythmically dense and slower sections. León's interest in infusing her compositions with multicultural influences is reflected in this work's harmonic vocabulary. Chromatic clusters, octatonic sonorities, and the superimposition of different whole-tone scales on different instruments are combined with triadic chords with chromatic aggregates that refer to the world of jazz. Color is very important for understanding the ways that León uses these intervallic collections. She often orchestrates these clusters in different instrumental families. This timbre and octave displacement allows her to reorganize the gamut through the orchestral register and lessen the prominence of cluster-like dissonances. This can be heard in example 5.18, where the cluster is scattered throughout the woodwinds and brass sections.

EXAMPLE 5.18. León, *Carabalí*, mm. 12–14, reduction: piccolo, flute, oboe, clarinet, contrabassoon, and horn parts.

Another way in which León uses orchestration to provide tonal clarity, as well as to generate structure, is the presence of expressive instrumental solos that break the dense texture of the orchestral tutti. This feature predicts the type of orchestration practices she will later use in *Horizons*. Finally, another interesting orchestration feature in *Carabalí* is the use of timbre melodies in the tradition of Schoenberg's *klangfarbenmelodie*. They can be heard in a few places in the piece, for example in mm. 101–114. However, the most personal use of this technique appears in the quotation from "Almendra" (example 5.16), where it is as if the ghost of Abelardo Valdés suddenly shows up to temporarily stop the intricate and busy flow of dense musical material.[51]

Assessment

Carabalí occupies a very important place in León's catalog. It is a work that, stylistically and ideologically, sets the tone for much of her later compositional output. The use of soli alternating dense orchestral sections, the spreading of the clusters in its orchestration, the privileging of specific solo or lead instruments (such as the trumpet), the decontextualized quotation of features or elements from Cuban popular music all forecast techniques found in works like *Indígena*, *Horizons* (1999), *Desde* . . . (2001), or *Toque*.

The idea behind *Carabalí* is quite simple: the juxtaposition, overlapping, and simultaneous presentation of contrasting musical material embedded throughout the composition. There are also disguised and distorted references to Cuban musical traditions: the hidden quotations of Cuban popular music; the distorted batá rhythmic patterns (see example 5.15); and the cinquillo timeline (the danzón's basic rhythmic pattern) buried under busy orchestral textures.

How can we reconcile these references to Cuban music with the composer's statement that this piece represented her breaking away from her native country? Rather than understanding these sounds as being simplistically nostalgic, they should be read against Yordanka's dreams to leave her native country and study abroad, which reverberated with León's own desire to do so when she was a young woman. One could interpret these decontextualized cultural references as the "spirit that cannot be broken," the cultural sources that—instead of bleakly rooting you to a specific locality—become the substance for something novel and more cosmopolitan to develop elsewhere. León's reference to Ives as an influence on this work is not gratuitous; it invokes the type of palimpsestic textures that characterize the work of the composer from New England and that León evidently engages in her search for complexity and vernacular cosmopolitanism.[52]

Indígena: Of Accent and Identity

Tania León composed *Indígena* for Ransom Wilson's Solisti New York Chamber Orchestra, through a commission from New York City's Town Hall. In a way, *Indígena* is a smaller sibling of *Carabalí*: they were composed the same year; unfold out of a similar musical idea; share a number of stylistic features as well as a palimpsestic character; and are dedicated to Alain and Yordanka León, respectively, the composer's nephew and niece. However, the texture of *Indígena*, scored for a chamber ensemble of thirteen musicians, is more transparent, simpler, and more direct and accessible than *Carabalí's*.

When León traveled back to Cuba for the first time in 1979, Alain León was only three years old. However, when he heard what he felt was her strange accent, he questioned the loss of her Cuban identity.[53] Alain's comments confronted León with questions of identity that she had put on hold during the years she was unable to return to her native country. *Indígena* was her musical response to those concerns. Nevertheless, León has stated that this work seeks to capture not only her nephew's expressive and wild character as a child, it also attempts to encapsulate "the sounds of my neighborhood, the conversations I used to listen to."[54]

In Conversation with León

Tania León: There is a montuno [m.21], it is just that it is all disfigured . . . and then I come out of this world of salsa and into the world of Santería [m. 26] . . . And all of this section [mm. 40–73], it is all conversations I had with my neighbors. When I talk to someone I hear the rhythmic structure of that person['s speech]. So, I took that memory from my conversations with people I had not seen in twelve years . . . This is the entrance to the Havana bay [m. 79].

Alejandro L. Madrid: What about that G major chord in measure 85?

T.L.: [Laughing] Yes, it is there . . . It marks the entrance of Cuban folk music. And [this trumpet] is a fusion of the trumpet player in the Cuban *comparsa* and the trumpet player in jazz [m. 91–93]. What I am interested in when I am composing is the question of handling the length of things; how to handle, within a given work, how long should an event last.

A. M.: And where is this quotation from that is played by the trumpet and imitated by the horns and winds? (mm. 115–120)

T.L.: It is from a *comparsa*, a comparsa that used to rehearse by my house.[55]

A.M.: What about the piano part at the very end?

T.L.: It is a *guajira*. [And the end] is the plane leaving Cuba.[56]

Figure 5.1 provides a map through the programmatic elements in *Indígena* based on León's description of this work.

Program	Tonal centricity	Instruments	Measure
Disfigured montuno	D	piano and strings	21
World of Santería	none	hn., tpt., pno., strings	26
Conversations	B	several instrumental duets	40-73
Havana bay	A	ob., cl., bsn., hn, vla.	79
Entrance of Cuban folk music	G	winds and strings	85
Comparsa and jazz fusion	E	trumpet	91-94
Latin jazz	G	tutti	95-102
Cuban comparsa	G	trumpet + winds	115 and after
Guajira	C#	piano	165 onwards
Plane leaving Cuba	G #	winds + brass	165 onwards

FIGURE 5.1. Programmatic Chart of *Indígena*.

Analytical Discussion

In discussing *Indígena*, this analysis focuses on issues of orchestration in relation to the presentation of specific modes and intervallic collections as well as in relation to Cuban popular music practices. Like in *Carabalí*, the form of *Indígena* is punctuated by the juxtaposition of orchestral and instrumental solo sections. The presentation of the solos follows the order of instruments in the orchestral score, beginning with the flute and moving down to the trumpet.

One could say that the drama in the orchestration reaches its climax with the arrival of the trumpet solo toward the end of the piece. When it first appears, the trumpet's intervallic collection is almost octatonic. The composer uses this feature to move back and forth between the worlds of Cuban popular music, U.S. jazz, and contemporary art music. The octatonic collection's combination of sequences of major and minor thirds can be used to pivot into a world of modal sonorities. In this particular case, it becomes the Phrygian mode (example 5.19).

EXAMPLE 5.19. Tania León, *Indígena* (1991), mm. 91–93, trumpet part.

León uses the octatonic collection as a cultural pivot point that allows her to enter effortlessly into the sonic world of Hispanic music. The trumpet's solo transforms the musical texture into a Cuban party with its quotation of the comparsa "*La jardinera*" throughout the last section of the piece (example 5.20). The party leads to another Cuban reference, when the piano gesture at the end of the piece, based again on octatonic fragments, evokes the guajira, especially through the accenting of the last sixteenth note of the group (example 5.21).[57]

EXAMPLE 5.20. León, *Indígena*, mm. 114–117, trumpet part.

EXAMPLE 5.21. León, *Indígena*, mm. 165, piano part.

Assessment

James Spinazzola has also noted the importance of octatonicism in *Indígena*, not only in terms of the scales and pitch sets used at the foreground level but also in relation to the generation of the larger, structural harmonic motion of the piece. Spinazzola determined that most of the work centers around G, but noticed that it ends in C sharp (a C sharp major chord with major sixth), which highlights a tritone relationship, the symmetric axis of an octatonic collection. He explained that

> [t]he relationship is further clarified by examining the G [major with major sixth] chord that begins Section B (m. 86) and the C [sharp major with major sixth] chord that concludes the piece (m. 165). A major triad with an added sixth degree (0358) in prime form is an octatonic subset; it follows that because these chords are separated by a tritone, when joined together they produce [an octatonic scale (c sharp, d, e, e sharp, g, g sharp, a sharp, b)], the predominant collection of the work.[58]

Listening to *Indígena* with knowledge of its programmatic features is an illuminating experience. It provides new meaning to the relationship between style, accent, and identity at the center of the composition, which León has acknowledged publicly on many occasions. However, listening to the Cuban references in relation to the move away from G into C sharp (the plane leaving Cuba) reveals that they are not an attempt to reclaim roots as fixed conditions that determine one's identity, but rather are a way to emphasize routes and an attempt to show how culture is re-signified by the encounters that traveling those routes facilitates. As Kevin Salfen sensibly puts it, "*Indígena* seems to ask the listener to consider how we all come to create our sense of belonging in a world when we're made of so many fragments, disconnected from their original context."[59]

Horizons: Episode in the Life of a Flying Composer

Horizons is an orchestral work that was composed in 1999 as a commission from the *Hammoniale Festival der Frauen*, a women's arts festival in Hamburg, Germany, founded by Irmgard Schleier, to whom the work is dedicated. This piece was written in memory of Philippa Schulyer, a child prodigy and pianist, and the product of a rich interracial couple. After being a celebrity of sorts in the 1930s and 1940s, racial prejudices eventually prevented Schluyer from having a music career in the United States.[60] León has stated that, like most of her music, *Horizons* has a descriptive or programmatic concept behind it:

> When I was a teenager I used to sit on the *Malecón* and stare at the sunsets. If you live on an island, you do a lot of staring at the horizon! . . . [S]o that was very normal for me, to stare at the sea, always wondering what was on the other side. That inspired the title and design of the piece.[61]

In Conversation with León

> **Tania León:** What I like the most about *Horizons* is the beginning, which is related to the mystical [character] of *Haiku*. It is like it is out of time. You don't feel the [pulse].
>
> **Alejandro L. Madrid:** [At the beginning] I hear a big contrast between the declamatory character of the winds and the static quality of the strings.
>
> **T.L.:** [The strings] are the forest; and what I am doing with the flute are the birds . . . there's one that is leaping upward, it is taking off; that is me. This piece is autobiographic. It is about my trips around the world, where I am like a bird flying through storms and typhoons.

A.M.: There is a pentatonic quality to the sustained chords in the strings (mm. 117–125).

T.L.: It is very eclectic. Those [dissonant gestures in the piano] represent Latin American indigenous people. It is my vision of the Mayas and the [Mexicans] interrupting the tranquility of the [tropical forest]. This piece is more about visions and imagination than technical aspects. . . . The D is coming in here [m. 171 in the strings plus the brass in m. 175]. I love that sonority. I do not know why. Some people say that D is the strongest vibration at the center of the Earth . . . as if it was the Earth's womb.

A.M.: Do you have that in mind when you use the D?

T.L.: I do not know, because I learned that later. But it is a pitch that captivates me. For some time in my life, it was the B flat. I had a great affinity for B flat, but then I changed to D, and I do not know how I got stuck there.[62]

Combining this description of *Horizons* with a similar depiction León offered James Spinazzola about this piece,[63] I have put together a programmatic chart of the work (figure 5.2).

Program	Tonal centricity	Instruments	Measure
Tropical Forest	B	strings	1-18
Flock over the forest	B/D	winds	1-18
One bird flies away	B	piccolo and flute	30-35
Storms	D/B flat	tutti	39-74
Staring at the sea from above	B flat	strings + winds	76-88
Hurricanes	E	trumpet + tutti	91-116
Staring at the forest from above	pentatonic-sounding	strings	117-140
Latin American indigenous people	clusters	sporadic piano	117-140
Transformation	D	strings + horn	171 onwards
Struggle (the seagull morphs into a condor)	D	clarinet	171-175
Landing in the Yucatan	D	harp	194 onwards
The bird's final song	D	clarinet	204-207

FIGURE 5.2. Programmatic Chart of *Horizons*.

EXAMPLE 5.22. Tania León, *Horizons* (1999), mm. 110–122.

EXAMPLE 5.22. (continued)

Analytical Discussion

In *Horizons*, León organizes tension and release in relation to the work's texture. There is a clear relation between structure, texture, and orchestration that makes it a unique work. At moments of structural climax, the musical material is always placed close together in terms of instrumental range; it is also more chromatically dense. This creates a certain sense of enclosure that recedes once the climax is left behind and the orchestration opens again. Example 5.22 shows how the instrumentation focuses on the brass section at the most rhythmically and chromatically dense moments, only to disperse through the strings and woodwinds afterward.

León's choice of pitch and intervals follows some of the techniques she used in earlier pieces: mainly, the presentation of largely conventional non-tonal collections with extra pitches to obscure them, which provides a path for the derivation of new modes and intervallic material. The string arpeggios and runs in measures 37–38 are a good example of how León takes a fragment of the octatonic collection (G-A-B flat-C-D flat-E) and expands it with the addition of extra pitches (D and B).

The piece also features a few references to Cuban musical culture. Nevertheless, they are never as blatant as they are in *Four Pieces for Violoncello, Carabalí*, or *Indígena*. In *Horizons*, these references are concealed and somehow estranged so as to make them almost imperceptible. Example 5.23 shows an intervallic cell made of minor seconds that is spread over several octaves played on the piano in the traditional habanera rhythmic pattern. Just as the octave separation masks the dissonant character of the cluster, it also prevents the habanera pattern to be perceived as such.[64]

EXAMPLE 5.23. León, *Horizons*, m. 76, piano part.

Assessment

In several ways, *Horizons* can be thought of as a sequel to *Indígena*. This is most evident in its programmatic aspect, which focuses on Tania León's experiences after leaving her native country, almost as if beginning where *Indígena* ended (with her flying out of Cuba). However, it is also clear in the relationship between the work's style and idea. *Horizons* shows the recurrence of a number of technical traits she had used in previous works: octave displacement; the simultaneous use of contrasting musical material; the estrangement of conventional pitch collections; spreading clusters throughout the orchestral register; the use of repeated figures; and the decontextualization of features from Cuban popular music. Nevertheless, as Jason Stanyek argues, *Horizons*, like all of León's music, cannot be reduced to the presence of these features; instead, it would be more productive to listen to it as "built out of breaks, fissures, and ruptures of flow"[65] that brings us to unexpected sonic places.

In writing about León's compositional trajectory, Will Robin acknowledges that works such as *Four Pieces for Violoncello, Batá*, and *Indígena* were explorations in which the composer's "angular and pointillistic gestures undergirded by kinetic, perpetual motion" show an artist developing "a forceful, bustling modernis[t]" voice.[66] However, in *Horizons*, León is no longer coming to terms with her palimpsestic accent, but is using it to tell us a very personal story of freedom, struggle, and transcendental transformation.

Axon: Making New Sounds Out of Old Sounds

Axon is a piece for solo violin and interactive computer written and dedicated to violin virtuoso Mari Kimura, who commissioned it for a concert at the 2002 ISCM World Music Days in Hong Kong. Kimura had wanted to commission a piece from Tania León for a long time. However, the ideal situation did not present itself until she was invited to play a concert at the World Music Days:

> They invited me to do a recital, [and] I get this bunch of music from them. . . . Among all these submissions I was supposed to come up with a recital program . . . but it was mostly [composers from] Western European countries. So, I thought to myself; is this World Music Days or World European Days?! . . . I actually reached out to the organizers saying, "Would you consider me bringing my own commission?"[67]

When the organizers agreed, Kimura invited León to write a piece for violin and live electronics. She created the original MaxMSP program for the work using sound samples from two of the composer's earlier works, *A la par* (1986) and *Batéy*—especially from the a capella sections composed by León. The work gets its title from the axons, the nerve fibers that transmit information among neurons and between neurons and body organs through electrical impulses. It is a metaphor for the type of information flows that characterize this piece at the technical, artistic, and expressive levels. *Axon* unfolds and acquires a form through a number of impulses that take place during its live performance, in conversation through the computerized samples with the composer's memories.

Other than her work with a Moog synthesizer for *Haiku*, León did not have experience composing electronic or electroacoustic music, let alone music for live computer interaction. Nevertheless, working closely with and trusting Kimura guaranteed that the project could be done smoothly and efficiently. Kimura reports:

> I told her, "Just think of anything that you want to do, just come up with a score or things that you want to do. And I will figure out how to do it." . . . She came and said, "I want to use some of my old pieces . . . an orchestra piece . . ., a chorus piece, and some pieces using Cuban drumming." Noah Creshevsky helped her gather the sound materials from her CDs and to make a sort of bank of sounds, and then she went over those samples with me; I asked her, "What would you like to do with them?" She actually came to me with a full score [to our] next meeting. . . . I had the violin notes and everything, and then she had a very clear idea. "Oh, here I want to have a voice accompanying it." And then she also said I want some effects to multiply this or transform that . . . she just described [them] to me. . . . So, after I laid out some effects she said, "I want this to be multiplied" or whatever, and I would do that and then go back to her and . . . she would direct me, as a kind of [conductor]. "Can you make more of this?" It was a very funny thing![68]

Axon was a successful piece. Eventually more violinists started to play it and record it, leading León to repeat the experience with the composition of *Abanico* (2007), a second piece for violin and interactive computer.

In Conversation with León

Tania León: *Axon* is made with scraps from some of my pieces. There are fragments from *A la par* and *Batéy* embedded in [the MaxMSP program]. They are filtered and manipulated. With Mari, we worked in such a way that the player controls the computer and the computer follows the player.

Alejandro L. Madrid: How did you think about the computer part in relation to the violin?

T.L.: It was easy for me because it was my own material and I knew where I wanted it to make an interjection.

A.M.: Was there a close collaboration with Mari while composing the piece other than the computer part?

T.L.: Yes. I always kept in mind her technique, especially the subharmonics, which is something that called my attention and [I] wanted to include.[69]

A.M.: Why did you choose the samples you chose from your previous work?

T.L.: Because I wanted to have a contrast between the urban and the classical. I chose the traditional drum and the voices [from *Batéy*] doing harmonies that had nothing to do with the aesthetics [in the violin part]. It was a matter of surprise. I always like to have surprises . . . but if you know *Batéy* well you can identify where the [samples] come from. . . . If you compare this piece to my other pieces, it is like another person made it. When I composed this piece I never thought it was going to become such an enigma within my catalogue.[70]

Analytical Discussion

The form of *Axon* is based on a recurring motive that works almost like a cadential gesture (see example 5.24). It divides the piece into a series of bursts of different length.

EXAMPLE 5.24. Tania León, *Axon* (2002), m. 7.

Each of these bursts is a creative exploration of the ways in which the violin can be expanded, as a kaleidoscopic transformation of itself, an eerie reflection of some of the traditional ways to play it, or a complete mutation into percussive or vocal echoes. The instrumental writing is very idiomatic and practical, providing a sense of virtuosic display by making full use of open strings, double stops, arpeggios across the complete violin range, glissandi, harmonics, and extended techniques like subharmonics. It is the combination of these extended techniques and the electronics that give *Axon* its quasi-phantasmatic character.

Regardless of the novelty of the musical setting, some of León's recurring stylistic features are still present. These include, in the chords in m. 76, the recurring intervals often found in León's music, G and the G sharp, the G and the F sharp, the A and the G sharp (example 5.25).[71]

EXAMPLE 5.25. León, *Axon*, m. 76.

Assessment

Axon is a sonic illusion that is firmly grounded on tradition (the Cuban rumba drumming and African American vocality sampled and embedded in the Max-MSP). It uses León's personal musical vocabulary and her talent for imaginatively transforming tradition into something new. The sole presence of this piece in León's catalogue—an exploration of cutting-edge technology when the composer was close to being sixty years old—speaks volumes about her strong sense of exploration and the spirit of curiosity that informs her musical output.

Its technological requirements make *Axon* something of an oddity in León's catalogue. Nevertheless, León makes a statement about renovation that reverberates with the ideas that she had long pursued. By using the sounds of her previous work and consciously transforming them to create a new one, while maintaining her trademark stylistic features, León shows a commitment to renovation and the organic ways in which this process takes place, not as rupture but as seamless continuity. Jason Stanyek considers *Axon* a metaphor of the kind of "processes that are at the center of León's music: transmission, connection, interdependence, linkage."[72] This fluidity and connectivity between continuity and change is fundamental in understanding León's voice. It developed through decades of give and take between tradition and innovation, community and individualism, and highbrow and lowbrow culture.

E pluribus unum: A Voice that Contains Many Voices

Tania León's music traverses so many different modes of expression and styles that to make a fair assessment of the development of her compositional voice would require a systematic analysis of many more works. Nevertheless, the works that are selected here provide a good idea of how her compositional voice has developed and how she has used different styles and modes of expression to highlight the ideas that give meaning to her music. These works make clear that León's artistic voice sounds loud and clear, regardless of the multiplicity of accents and styles her music may adopt. Diversity and concomitance are intrinsic characteristics of that expression—that hers is a voice where many voices fit.

E pluribus unum [Of Many, One] is the ideal of unity in diversity behind León's daring musical statements that gives meaning to their palimpsestic character. Listening in detail to her compositional output reveals how these voices coexist, sometimes in conflict and sometimes in harmony, but always as a result of artistic and social sincerity and responsibility. If stylistic fluidity is a feature of León's music, so is the consistency of her musical ideas (palimpsest, hybridity, simultaneity, motion), which remain constant through the years and the diversity of her compositional output.

To put it in terms of Corigiliano's statement about personal style and technique: if pointillism, intervallic derivation, aleatorism, octave displacement, and polyrhythm are some of the recurrent techniques in León's music, then certain expanded octatonic and whole-tone gestures, pandiatonic harmonies, and melodies that constantly evade the octave are the sonorities that Léon often uses because she likes them. These sonorities may determine a personal style, as Corigliano argues, but they do not define León's compositional voice by themselves. León's voice comes out of what she does with these recurring sonorities, how she makes them hers and uses them to illustrate the prevalent ideas that inform her music. León's use of *klangfarbenmelodie* through her manipulation of the montuno of "Almendra," a popular song that she returns to more than once in her catalogue, is one example. Nevertheless, what is truly remarkable about her personal use of technique is how she uses it within a larger palimpsestic texture to speak about resilience and hybridity based on her unique life experiences. It is at that intersection of style and idea that Tania León's compositional voice emerges clear, recognizable, and unique.

When I met León at Cornell University, she baffled a few students with her corporeal description of rhythm in her music. Drawing a big, imaginary circle with her arms around her head and upper body was a perfect metaphor for the cyclic character of rhythm informing her music, where small rhythmic units and patterns interlock in the development of larger circular structural sequences that contain them and give them meaning. It also stands for the circularity behind her understanding of life itself. Everything moves in circles, everything comes back; from the musical motives in her music to her moving back and forth between her native island, her new country, and the world. But these returns happen always in renewed ways. It is not the idea of roots that give meaning to diasporic individuals, but the routes they travel and the transformations they experience through those trips.

It would be unfair to pretend that the works analyzed here define León as an artist. Nevertheless, besides providing an insight into the technical ideas that the composer constantly reinvents to develop a variety of musical styles, these works show the consistency of the idea behind León's musical transformations. As this idea continues to feed León's musical imagination, audiences should expect more compelling musical works that revamp and reaffirm her concern with diversity, fluidity, openness, and nonconformity.

6
CANON
Representation, Identity, and Legacy

On April 28, 2018, the Hostos Center for the Arts and Culture in the Bronx presented an event called "I Am in Constant Transit!," a two-hour-long series of community activities. After a resource fair and visual arts workshop hosted by Ivory Nunez-Medrano at the center's gym, the event concluded with a concert by The Dream Unfinished dedicated to the music of Tania León. The Dream Unfinished is an activist orchestra whose mission is to use classical music to open spaces for community conversations about racial and social justice.[1] The event was part of the Lincoln Center Education's Boro-Linc series, which is devoted to the presentation of "free world-class performances, family workshops, and exhibitions"[2] in the neighborhoods of the five boroughs of New York City.

The concert portion of the event was billed as "an interactive exploration of the colorful music and groundbreaking career of composer and conductor Tania León."[3] It began with Eun Lee, The Dream Unfinished's founder and executive producer, distributing pieces of paper to the audience and asking them to write down how they describe or identify themselves. The answers were varied: some people chose to label themselves in relation to ethnicity as Latinxs or blacks; others preferred to talk about themselves in relation to other people as daughters, husbands, or friends; others decided to use their nationality as a label of identification. A discussion followed of how we label ourselves always relationally: in relation to other people or certain social expectations.

This was the preamble to a conversation about Tania León's choice not to use labels to describe herself (see figure 6.1). Lee spoke about how, throughout her

FIGURE 6.1. Tania León, Eun Lee, and Ivory Nunez-Medrano (lower right corner) at the Hostos Center for the Arts and Culture. Courtesy of Ekaterina Pirozhenko.

career, León has rejected terms such as "black composer," "woman composer," or even "Afro-Cuban music," in favor of more fluid and strategic ways to highlight the impermanence and transitivity of the human experience.

When I asked Lee about her decision to host an event dedicated to Tania León, she responded:

> This event is part of a larger series we have called "Sanctuary," where all of the composers we are featuring this year are either immigrant composers themselves or first-generation Americans. . . . We are using their music to talk about the current and historic immigration crisis that's really been impacting communities of color around the United States. Tania is really one of the preeminent composers of our day. She also happens to be a Cuban-American. And so [the] criteria for the season was music of the utmost quality, but also music of composers who fit these parameters. . . . In doing my research about her and her music I notice[d] that [the idea of rejecting labels] was a theme that came up quite frequently [with her]. . . . [And] the idea of our work, The Dream Unfinished, is that we don't use these kinds of labels any longer to talk about musicians and music composers, that we can be stripped free of all of that and that the music can just be appreciated for what it is.[4]

It is telling that Tania León was the dedicatee of this event. She is an artist who started her career in Harlem and Brooklyn, who came out of these communities but has always returned to give back to them. And she is a champion of artists and musicians who struggle in the margins of the U.S. mainstream; she is always willing to use her artistic and academic prominence to help shift the spotlight to them. In sum, Tania León is a role model, a leader of community work, an unrelenting critic of boxes and labels, and a composer going through the process of canonization (as the discussion of historiography in the next section shows). This performance, its dedication to her, and the conversations it generated provide an entry into discussing three issues that are very important for León: representation, identity, and legacy.

Representation: Mapping Tania León in U.S. Music Historiography

Being part of any canonic narrative is significant, because it is the result of the recognition of someone's accomplishments and artistic and professional influence on a particular cultural world. However, the meaning of being a "canonic figure" may be less certain. The circumstances in which some individuals enter canonic narratives are key to understanding why, how, and in which context it may be important or relevant. As narratives that embody aesthetic, social, and political values, canonic formations reveal how communities with the power to shape the representation of the world—and those who embrace those representations—give meaning to their cultural environment and the human relations that make it possible.

In this section, I examine the different ways in which Tania León appears in Western art music history narratives. I will discuss the significance of her insertion into these formations, as well as the importance of her support of change in representation and inclusion. Ultimately, I am interested in asking not only whether León is a canonic composer—or one in the process of being canonized—but also in considering who, and under which conditions, can make this claim. Finally, I question why it would be interesting or useful to even think about her and her work in those terms.

The first books that pay attention to León's musical activities presented her as African American—or at least as heavily involved in African American networks—many years before she was described as "Cuban" or "Latin." Two of these early books were published in 1977. The first one, *Notable Americans of 1976–77*, is not about musicians, and León's entry is one of more than one thousand brief biographical articles.[5] Because the entries in this book are comprised simply of a list of basic information without a descriptive narrative, it is difficult to discern any particular agenda behind her inclusion, other than providing a wide spectrum of U.S. cultural life for that period. If anything, the fact that she was considered worth including in a book that intended to report on the United States' most prominent personalities at a moment when the country celebrated its bicentennial speaks about how her musical activities may have struck a chord in the imaginary of U.S. identity. By the time this book was published, she had been working professionally for only ten years, but the impact on the African American community of some of her work—the entry highlights *Spiritual Suite* as well as her conducting for Dance Theatre of Harlem locally and internationally—made her presence a must when describing the New York dance and music scene of the early 1970s.

The second book is Raoul Abdul's *Blacks in Classical Music: A Personal History*, a collection of mini-reviews written over a period of twenty years for the black press. Abdul mentions Tania León in a review about a concert of new music by black composers presented as part of the Brooklyn Philharmonia's Community Concert Series on February 27, 1977.[6] León's name is mentioned only in passing as the cocurator of the event. However, the fact that she appears in relation to another initiative connected to African American music is a good indication of the impression critics and cultural brokers had of her and her early work.

A decade later, in 1988, Anne Lundy included León in an article that presents conversations with three "minority conductors wielding the symphonic baton ... who have earned the title of Maestro or Maestra in a field dominated by while male conductors."[7] Lundy posed the same questions to the three conductors featured in the article (Dennis DeCoteau, Jon Robinson, and Tania León). Although her last question asks for their reaction to being labeled "black conductors," the overall conversations do not dwell on issues of race. Nevertheless, given that the title of the journal publishing the article was *"Black Perspective in Music"* and the three interviewees were black, it is clear that the unstated topic running through each of these conversations is connected to their particular experiences in the world of classical music as musicians of color.

Nevertheless, behind the rather transparent agenda informing the publication, it is interesting to note that all of the interviewees rejected the labels "black conductor" or "women conductor," arguing instead that they were simply "conductors" who also happened to be black or women.[8] León answered the question emphatically, "I am not a feminist, am not a black conductor, and am not a woman conductor. I am nothing that people want to call me. They do not know me."[9] This is one of León's earliest assertions regarding her discomfort with identity labels. It reflects her concern with how the public's impressions might shape her representation in ways with which she disagrees.

Three years later, J. Michele Edwards devoted a few lines to León in her chapter, "North America since 1920," in Karin Pendle's edited volume *Women & Music: A History* (1991). Edwards first mentions León as one of nine women holding conducting positions at professional orchestras in the United States and Canada. She later provides a very brief biography of León in a subsection of the chapter entitled "Neighbors to the South: Mexico and Latin America."[10] Edwards includes her alongside two other Cuban musicians, Cecilia Aritzi and Olga de Blanck, who according to her must all be mentioned as distinguished artists from that country. The biography states that León, "of African descent (her grandmother was a slave in Cuba), was trained in Cuba as a musician and an accountant."[11] Every time Edwards mentions León in the text, she does so in relation to her activities in the United States. However, she chooses to refer to León not as a U.S. composer but rather as a Cuban composer, notwithstanding that, by 1991, with the exception of the short piano pieces she composed as a young student in Havana, her music had not been played in Cuba.

Pendle's book was republished in a revised edition in 2001. For the second edition, Edwards expanded León's biographical entry. Although she still described her as a Cuban composer, she revised her earlier ethnic characterization to describe her family background as "French, Spanish, Chinese, and African."[12] It is telling that Edwards refused to speak about León as an "American" even though she was already a U.S. citizen, and her complete professional musical career had unfolded in the United States when the first edition of the book was published. This is especially problematic because Edwards wrote about other immigrant musicians (for example, Ethel Leginska and Antonia Brisco) not as foreign but as American. Whether this oversight was conscious or unconscious, the fact that white Europeans like Leginska and Brisco are able to inconsequentially transition from being foreign to nationals, while people of color have more problems going through this transfiguration, stresses the problematic, entrenched racial and ethnic overtones that mar the transparency of such discourse.

This race-based discursive neglect provides another argument in favor of understanding León's transition into the cultural life of her new country through her experience of African American culture and its marginality. As her body and accent are seen and heard with suspicion by the white U.S. mainstream, it is by becoming African American—in representation as well as in personal and human embodied experiences that move beyond the superficial labels that the composer rightly rejects—that León becomes a cultural citizen of the United States. Nevertheless, the perceived contradiction between León's own identification statements and her life experience have made it difficult for people who adhere to more rigid interpretations of identity to understand her and her work. This misperception informs how scholars continue to use her in telling stories about U.S. music that, regardless of having inclusivity as their main goal, keep reproducing problematic race- and gender-based dichotomies.

Although Anne Gray's *Popular Guide to Classical Music* (1993) amends Edwards' problematic excision of León from the body of U.S. music, it reproduces previous categorizations by including her and other black women composers in a section called "Talent and Triumph—Black Women."[13] Regardless of the good intentions behind Gray's strategy for inclusiveness, she tacitly reproduces the idea that composers who happen to be women or who happen to be black can occupy only a marginal space in the imagined male- and white-centric history of U.S. music. In 2007, Gray published *The World of Women in Classical Music*, a book that continues to reproduce this problematic characterization even within the already fragmented field of "women composers." Here, Gray includes León in a chapter entitled "Women of Color—Triumph and Tragedy."[14] The author's decision to write a separate chapter on women of color may be understandable as a strategy to focus on the particular challenges that these artists have to face in a blatantly racist and sexist society. However, the text's descriptive character does not lend itself to an analysis of how these composers' race or gender made their experience in and passage through the world of classical music particularly difficult. It is never explained what is the "triumph" and the "tragedy" in the experience of these composers or whether one could even think of their sharing a collective experience. The chapter creates an arbitrary categorization that further reproduces racial dichotomies that a more critical take on the place of women in music could have also challenged.

Within a period of five years, León was featured in two projects that responded to similar concerns about the systematic absence of women and their music in historical surveys of classical music: James R. Briscoe's *Contemporary Anthology of Music by Women* (1997), which includes music scores by 33 female composers from a wide variety of styles and instrumental combinations; and Kristine H. Burns' *Women and Music in America since 1900: An Encyclopedia* (2002), which offers over 400 topical and biographical articles. Briscoe's choice for his collection, León's *Momentum* (1986), an intensely modernist solo piano piece dedicated to fellow composer Joan Tower, and Burns' decision to commission Cuban-American composer Orlando Jacinto García to write León's lengthy encyclopedia entry, both signaled the preeminent position that León had attained in the U.S. music mainstream by the turn of the century.[15] Nevertheless, as much as the reformist mission of female visibility behind these two projects is successfully achieved, they also further reinforce one of the labels León refuses to be categorized into ("women/female musicians").

At the same time, she appeared in the third brief edition of Joseph Kerman's *Listen* (1996), a major music appreciation text used in colleges and universities throughout the United States. In this text, her piano and orchestra piece, *Kabiosile*, is discussed in the context of music at the end of the twentieth century without pigeonholing her as a "black" or "female" composer.[16] In 2002, León made a brief appearance in the fourth edition of Roger Kamien's widely popular textbook *Music: An Appreciation*. León's mention in this book, like her presence in Joseph Kerman's *Listen*, broadly circulated her name among college students in the United States given these textbooks' pervasiveness through the U.S. music-education system at the turn of the twenty-first century.[17] Sadly, while Kerman had taken León seriously as a subject of study, Kamien used her name as a typical tokenistic gesture to simply flesh out a list of African American composers active in the twentieth century, without bothering to say anything in depth about any of them or their music.[18]

Helen Walker-Hill's *From Spirituals to Symphonies* was also published in 2002.[19] Even though León is not featured in the book, her attitude toward labels seems to inform both positively and negatively several of the conversations in the volume. Addressing the double marginalization of African American female composers in mainstream musical narratives is very important; but for León, producing a book that separates and labels those who have already been sidelined is a strategy that necessarily invokes the very demons it tries to exorcize.

In 2003, three more books dedicate lines or pages to León and her music. Two of those books are similarly gender-based reform projects about women in music: Sylvia Glickman and Martha Furman Schleifer's edited volume *From Convent to Concert Hall* (2003), which includes a brief biography of León as part of a chapter entitled "The Twentieth Century," written by Adeline Mueller; and Pilar Ramos López's *Feminismo y música. Introducción crítica* (2003), which mentions her as part of a list of contemporary female conductors. López also includes León in a discussion of the anxieties mainstream audiences experience when they realize that the composer of a work they have just heard is black or a woman.[20]

On the other hand, Mark Evan Bonds' popular music-history textbook, *A History of Music in Western Culture* (2003), departs from the strategies we have seen so far when writing about León. Instead of including her as part of a narrative about women or black composers, Bonds chooses to include an analysis of a solo piano piece, *Ritual* (1987), to illustrate a discussion about "the tendency of music in the late twentieth century toward a synthesis of diverse styles and traditions."[21] Bonds follows Kerman in discussing León without labeling her a "black" or "female" composer.

Two textbooks published in 2005—Ellen Koskoff's edited volume *Music Cultures in the United States* and Adelaida Reyes' *Music in America*—cover León's music. In *Music Cultures in the United States*, Josephine R. B. Wright includes León in a chapter section about contemporary concert music entitled "African-American Concert Music in the Twentieth Century."[22] Wright's is a commendable effort that tries to bring marginalized African American composers into the light; however, it misses the opportunity to develop a narrative in which African American composers could be discussed in equal terms as other musicians regardless of their ethnic background. On the other hand, although Reyes' *Music in America* speaks about León's music in relation to Afro-Caribbean rhythmic practices in León/Camilo's *Batéy*, it does so as part of an argument in favor of cultural and ethnic diversity, instead of as an attempt to label León or her music as Afro-Cuban or Afro-Caribbean.[23]

A year later, in 2006, Josephine R. B. Wright was in charge of writing a chapter about classical/art music in Mellonee V. Burnim and Portia K. Maultsby's edited volume, *African American Music: An Introduction*. Wright includes León in a chronological overview of twentieth-century African American composers. Here, the author is sensitive enough to inform readers that the composer "has rejected the application of ethnic, racial, or gender labels to her work because she believes that such labels limit the boundaries of an individual." Nevertheless, Wright follows that sentence by noting that: "[y]et her compositions draw heavily upon syncretic sounds of her native Cuba, where Afro-Cuban, Yoruban, Congolese, and Creole Spanish culture comingle."[24] Wright implies that León's refusal to be pigeonholed and her use of the musical traditions that have nurtured her throughout her life were a contradiction, indicating that she may not have truly understood the reasons why León refuses to be labeled in terms of race, ethnicity, or gender. However, Wright's willingness to at least mention León's concerns was a departure from previous texts in which racialized or gendered representations of the composer, indifferent to her self-identifying concerns, were used solely with the purpose of advancing their specific agendas.

In 2011, James Spinazzola wrote a lengthy article about Tania León for Michael K. Slayton's edited volume, *Women of Influence in Contemporary Music*.[25] Spinazzola's article combines oral testimony, archival research, and music analysis. It gives León the opportunity to move beyond the book's agenda of gender inclusiveness, not only to express her ideas and her experience about being a woman in a male-dominated field but also to highlight her rejection of identity politics.

Also, in 2011, Daisy Rubiera Castillo and Inés María Martiatu Terry published in Cuba the edited volume *Afrocubanas. Historia, pensamiento y prácticas culturales*, which includes a chapter by María Elena Mendiola entitled "Dar vida a los sueños, que no es lo mismo que soñar" ["To Give Life to Her Dreams, Which Is Not the Same as Dreaming"]. This chapter is a detailed assessment of Tania León's life in a book devoted to celebrating the legacy of women of African heritage in Cuba. León's presence in this book is particularly significant because, regardless of the fact that in agreement with the book's specific agenda, she was described as a "black woman of great talent"[26] (against León's own rejection of labels), this was the first time that she was featured prominently in a Cuban publication. Within Cuban intellectual life, this book signals a shift in the understanding of Cuban identity by opening it to include the Cuban diaspora. In a way, this book is a response to the changes that allowed for the official invitation to have León's music performed in Cuba at the Festival de Música de Cámara Leo Brouwer in 2010 (which occurred just one year before the book was published; see Chapter 2) and a precursor of the official invitation she would receive to conduct Cuba's National Symphony Orchestra in 2016 (see the opening vignette in Chapter 1).

The last two texts are books about Latin American music published in 2012 and 2018. Walter Aaron Clark's "Latin American Impact on Contemporary Classical Music," Chapter 9 in Robin Moore and Clark's edited volume *Musics of Latin America* (2012), deals with León's music in great detail in the context of both contemporary Latin American composers in general and "The Rise of Women Composers"[27] in particular. Clark offers a meticulous listening guide to León's *Horizons* and an assessment of the composer's career in the United States within a chapter that otherwise organizes composers according to aesthetics and the uses of their music rather than by heritage.[28] Carol Hess' *Experiencing Latin American Music* (2018) is an innovative book that largely organizes materials according to shared histories and experiences instead of national or ethnic origins. Nevertheless, it mentions León only in passing in a brief subsection called "Latin American Women in Classical Music over Time" in a chapter devoted to aesthetic concerns in classical music from Latin America.

There is clearly an essentialist problem at the core of how both of these textbooks represent Tania León as a "Latin American" simply because of where she was born and raised, even though she does not share any professional networks or experiences with her colleagues active in Cuba in particular and Latin America in general. Clark seems to be moved by an undeclared desire to expand the notion of "Latin America" to include the experience of Latinxs in the United States. His discussion of León along with Gabriela Lena Frank (b. 1972), Mario Davidovsky (1934–2019), Paulo Chagas (b. 1953), and Gustavo Santaolalla (b. 1951)—who were either born in the United States or have developed careers away from their native Latin American countries (all of them live or lived in the United States)—seems to point in that direction. Nevertheless, the diverse nuances of the Latinx experience are lost in Clark's description of stylistic musical features. No Latin American is ever a Latinx in their country of origin; that label is applied only once they migrate to the United States. In other words, the identification or representation as "Latinx" is only a side effect of becoming the "Other" in the racial discourse of the United States. None of these pressing issues, which have been central in the development of León's musical career, are discussed in Clark's textbook.[29] Hess' passing reference to León is even more problematic not only due to the essentialist understanding of Latin American identity informing her inclusion but also because doing it as part of a brief section about female musicians that provides no other information about her music or her activities comes across as a tokenist gesture at best.

This brief overview shows that Tania León has a long presence in U.S. music writings, having appeared in books and textbooks about American music, African American music, Latin music, and Latin American music as early as 1977. She has been characterized as African American, Afro-Cuban, Latina, Latin American, and Cuban, as well as a black or woman composer. Each of those characterizations dwells on a particular aspect of her life, musical production, and networks of belonging; but mostly, her presence in these texts betrays deeply ingrained aspects of racial desire in the American imagination. By co-opting, racializing, and reducing León's life experience in the name of identity politics, these characterizations not only do violence to the composer's vision of herself as a complete subject, their repetition in the musical and social networks in which they circulate—even if in the name of representation—perpetuates and further reinscribes in the professional sphere the type of violence she has experienced in her everyday life as an immigrant woman of color in contemporary U.S. society.

Identity: "Labels [Are] Selling Short What the Whole Thing Is About"

Discourses of representation may coincide or stand in stark contrast with discourses of self-identification.[30] With few exceptions, most textbooks have found a way to place León within the Western art-music canon, but only as an individual marked by gender, racial, national, or ethnic considerations. However, León has often rejected these labels, and although her critique has occasionally been taken into consideration, most often it has been ignored.[31] In reacting to these representations, León has stated that

> [i]t's a question of identity. What is my identity to other people? How do they see me? Do they see me? Do they hear me? Do they watch me? Every time I read a different article, I [am classified under] a different category.[32]

One of León's main concerns with identity labels is that, since by definition identity works through difference and exclusion, accepting any of these labels would mean to deny the identities that any particular label excludes. For an individual who embraces gender, racial, ethnic, and cultural fluidity instead of fixity, who sees herself as being in constant transit—as the title of the concert celebrating her and her music at the Hostos Center put it—and who understands life, culture, and humanity as ontologically creole or *mestizo*, identity labels are restrictive, incomplete, and misleading in their essentialist nature. While labels may be meaningful within larger universalist and ethnocentric discourses, León believes that they work to further marginalize individuals or cultural expressions that do not fit this normalized speech. She questions the conventional practice of describing the music of non-European composers as "nationalist" or "folk-influenced," while refusing to give similar labels to the music of classical European composers like Bach, Beethoven, or Brahms, who also borrow from their own folk music and dance traditions. By stressing this point, León highlights the dynamics of othering that inform the marginalization of non-European composers. This is precisely the type of cultural work that the labels she rejects continuously do. Thus, the seeming contradiction of rejecting identity labels while relying on local sounds and rhythms is only an expression of the cultural upbringing that informs the individuality of a composer regardless of his/her ethnic background.

León has been particularly adamant about the irrelevance of one of the most recurrent labels regarding Cuban music, the notion of "Afro-Cuban" music—which has often been invoked to label her an "Afro-Cuban" composer. She states that

> the music of Cuba is not Afro-Cuban or is not Chinese-Cuban or is not Spanish-Cuban. It's Cuban music. . . . Cuban music is comprised of many influences—Amerindians . . . [t]hen the entire Spanish conquest and all the Spanish people that come to Cuba from different regions of Spain. . . . You have different regional

situations, with different rhythmical emphasis, with different melodic contours. . . . All of that comes to Cuba. Then . . . the forced labor that is imported from Africa. . . . All of these different people come from different regions of Africa, too, with their different inflections—rhythmical inflections also [of] language, music, traditions. . . . So, therefore, they're coming with all of these, too. This mélange, this minestrone [soup] begins. Then you have the importation of all this migration that comes from the east part of the hemisphere. I'm talking about the Caribbean, with the migrations of the Haitians [who] come to Cuba because they're fleeing their own revolutions. These Haitians have been dominated or conquered, or whatever you want to call it, by the French, so they're coming with a French influence into Cuba. The last migration that arrived in Cuba at the turn of the [twentieth] century is the Chinese, who are coming with all of these aspects of the five-tone scale. That is the Cuban music. You can find all of that in the music.[33]

Robin Moore and I have also noted the problematic racial dynamics that inform conventional categorizations of Cuban music, especially the dichotomy "Cuban music/Afro-Cuban music" within a discourse in which other labels such as "Hispano-Cuban music" are absent. These dynamics de facto mark Cuban music—as used in this dichotomic complex—as white or European and tacitly separates Afro-Cuban heritage from national heritage.[34] This contradiction is central to how identity politics validate discourses about mainstream and marginal culture. It informs León's aversion to labels and her privileging ideas about culture as something in constant flux and transition that help her define herself as well as her musical craft. The composer's use of analogies from food and cooking—minestrone soup here, but also jambalaya, *moros con cristianos* (rice and beans), and other mixed cuisines—as metaphors of cultural and ethnic mixing in music as well as people is a recurring trope for her. León describes her music, her family, and herself in these terms. Her definition of Cuban music as a transcultural formation could perfectly be used as a definition of herself as a transcultural individual for whom labels are also irrelevant.

Sensitive toward her beliefs and ideas, Marc Gidal has interpreted León's aversion to labels as an expression of vernacular cosmopolitanism where culturally specific loyalties coexist with transnational and universalist ones.[35] Gidal explains that, early in her career, León utilized a rhetoric of aesthetic universalism in order to counter the dynamics of marginalization that nonwhite and female composers used to face in the art-music environment before the multicultural turn of the late 1970s and early 1980s.[36] However, after her first trip back to Cuba at the end of the 1970s,[37] she started to consciously incorporate elements from her native Cuba's musical traditions in her music, which created a divide between her earlier universalist discourse and her new musical praxis. León began to realize that the raceless and ethnic-free rhetoric about white European composers masked the same type of dynamics of borrowing from local music traditions that often generate the ghettoizing of nonwhite composers. Gidal argues that by interpreting this shift in León's music—and I would also argue, in her rhetoric—through the lens of vernacular cosmopolitanism, one can make sense of the apparent contradiction between universalism and locality that still informs the work of many music scholars.[38] I believe that León's move also underscores the shortcomings of identity politics that inform not only the use of labels regarding female and nonwhite composers, but also the exceptionalist and tacit white supremacist values behind the universalist rhetoric about white male European composers. In emphasizing the transitivity and fluidity of real human experience over the fixity of identity labels, León's discourse resonates with Paul Gilroy's call to move away from "race" toward an emphasis on "diaspora" as an interpretative and political way out of essentialist concepts of identity that inform both identity politics and fascist ideology.[39]

Legacy: A Polyrhythmic Life

In 1999, Frank J. Oteri asked Tania León if she considered herself an American composer. Surprisingly, León answered positively, "I consider myself an American. Do you know why? Because I was born in the Americas."[40] Although her answer may seem at first a provocative reaction against the U.S. tendency to monopolize the name of the continent, in the balance of the interview it becomes clear that there is something else behind her response. León goes on to speak about the shared history of colonization that characterizes the experience of the people from the Americas. Although she is careful not to romanticize the experience of violence and genocide of the encounters that gave birth to the current human societies on the continent, she emphasizes that this history of displacement, conquest, cultural imposition, relocation, diaspora, and forced migration generated new hybrid cultures. It is this encounter of civilizations and the melting pot that they generate, that she considers quintessentially American. In other words, America is the experience of violent transculturation and cultural overlapping shared by the people of North America, Central America, South America, and the Caribbean. For León, America is a cultural palimpsest. Americanness is not about being but rather about becoming. It is about the transformations one experiences as one takes the physical and emotional journeys of life. In acknowledging both the utopian promise of the U.S. experiment to allow individuals to become something new, as well as the nightmarish history of violence and oppression that makes that promise possible, León recognizes a fundamental contradiction of U.S. identity. Historian Edmund Morgan termed this as the "American paradox," whereby the existence of U.S. freedom requires the existence of U.S. slavery and oppression.[41]

Embracing the emergence of a palimpsestic artistic voice—one that reflects on and responds to the painfully contradictory process of coming to terms with a multiethnic, diasporic, and gender-fluid experience in a new country—was a crucial rite of passage in becoming an American for León. Her clash with Cuban musicians during her 2016 visit to conduct the National Symphony Orchestra bears witness to the fact that such a move—the exploration, adoption and adaptation, translation, incorporation, and development of a new accent—could not have happened in the way it did if she had not migrated from her native country. As a woman of color, staying in Cuba would not have been conducive to becoming what she had dreamed of since childhood or what following that dream allowed her to become. As María Elena Mendiola poetically puts it, leaving is what allowed her "to give life to her dreams, which is not the same as dreaming."[42] In that sense, and in relation to the experiences of her Cuban colleagues, León's life, experience, work, and art can be understood only in the context of the United States and what moving to this country allowed her to become.

The Merriam-Webster dictionary defines "legacy" as "something transmitted by or received from an ancestor or predecessor or from the past."[43] Tania León is still busy composing, conducting, teaching, and organizing, so we can't be certain what her final artistic legacy will be. Nevertheless, a look at how she has chosen to live her life and approached teaching and mentorship, as well as what she has chosen to express through her artistic voice and to do for those who are less privileged than she is, clearly shows that her legacy will be more than her artistic output.

León's legacy is primarily about the lessons we can learn by understanding her polyrhythmic process of becoming. To truly appreciate León's music and what her art offers, one needs to understand her journeys. Arthur Mitchell once said that he understood what Tania León was fighting for throughout her life because they were both battling for the same thing.[44] If violence is about the perpetuation of current structures of inequality, as Frantz Fanon has argued,[45] then León's work toward countering the real and symbolic violence against herself, as well as other women, people of color, and immigrants, speaks about a radical legacy of love as hermeneutics of social change.[46] León's art, work, and love of people is expressed through a "'breaking' through whatever controls in order to find 'understanding and community.'"[47]

Tania León's music is more than the wonderful aesthetic beauty she has created; it is her deeply personal statements about tolerance, openness, fluidity, and the power of freedom and dreams. The story of her life is an example of love, integrity, determination, independence, and struggle to succeed against all odds. Her work as a cultural broker and role model for young people of color are lessons about how to lead with passion, assertiveness, and selflessness. This is what she has chosen to leave behind and transmit to those coming after her. As she has repeatedly stated and implied in her personal rejection of identity politics, there is only one label that does justice to her palimpsestic voice, as well as her multiethnic, diasporic, and gender-fluid experience. That label is not African American, Cuban, Cuban-American, Latina, Latin American, or black or female composer, the label is simply, but polyrhythmically, Tania León.

EPILOGUE

Tania León's Stride: An Echo that Reaches Our Ears

On February 13, 2020, over 23 years after León left her position as New Music Advisor with the New York Philharmonic, she walked on the stage of the David Geffen Hall to address this orchestra's audience before the premier of *Stride* (2020). As she stepped on the stage, the audience erupted in a long and loud ovation. Standing by León's side was Jaap van Zweden, Music Director of the New York Philharmonic since 2018, who waited until the applause was over to simply state: "Evidently, Tania León needs no introduction."

Stride was commissioned and premiered as part of Project 19, the New York Philharmonic's initiative to present works by nineteen female composers in celebration of the centennial of the 19th Amendment, which granted women the right to vote when it was ratified in 1920. Project 19 was a program developed by van Zweden and Deborah Borda, who returned to the New York Philharmonic as President and CEO in 2017, after seventeen years at the Los Angeles Philharmonic. León stated that *Stride* was dedicated in honor of Susan B. Anthony and her determination in the women's suffrage movement, and in honor of two visionaries, Borda and van Zweden, "for having the audacity to commission nineteen works from nineteen composers who happen to be women."[1] Nevertheless, León reminded the audience that although the 19th Amendment was passed in 1920, in practice, women of color encountered restrictions and discrimination that severely hindered their ability to exercise their right to vote until the passing of the Voting Rights Act of 1965.

When León was approached to participate in Project 19, she thought about it as a "reparations gesture"[2] for the many creative women who have been ignored by or left behind in the shades of the world of classical orchestral music. As she mulled over the project and its significance, she immediately thought of Mamota, her grandmother, that progressive woman of action whose decisive steps and strong guiding hand set León on a path that would lead her to things the older woman could not have even dreamed of for herself. Then she thought of Susan B. Anthony and her struggle to accomplish her vision toward a future of political equality for women.[3] Suddenly, she realized what the link between these two women was: it was their attitude toward obstacles; they were both relentless forces moving forward to overcome the hurdles in their lives. It was this vision of women walking forward with decisive steps toward their goal, regardless of whether those around them believe they could do it or not, that led León to call her piece *Stride*.[4] It is the gravitas of that walk and its repercussions that the piece both solemnly reflects upon and joyfully celebrates.

Stride is organized as a series of sonically poetic episodes alternatively performed by brass, percussion, and woodwinds, which are kept together by the presence of the strings. With their continuous intercession, which disrupts these episodes, the strings propel them forward and give them direction. The musical dynamic between the strings and the rest of the orchestra is a reflection of how the courageous work and steady determination of women like Susan B. Anthony brought progress to the life of many. The climax of León's work is marked by a brass fanfare-like motive leading into a loud passage with the tubular bells celebrating the historical achievement of the women's suffrage movement. Nevertheless, the celebration is punctuated by a quiet clave pattern in the djembe and percussion that slowly fades away, bringing the work to an end. The beautiful echo of this vanishing but persistent timeline soberly and subtly reminds us of the delays some people are forced to face before their peers are willing to truly recognize them as equals.

The successful premiere of *Stride* was followed by a nightcap concert of Latin music and jazz curated by León at the Lincoln Center's Stanley H. Kaplan Penthouse on February 15, 2020.[5] Soon after, Deborah Borda nominated León to join the Philharmonic's Board. It took African American women forty-five years to have their voices heard as full members of the American democratic process; it took the New York Philharmonic twenty-three years to listen to what Tania León's music has been expressing for over five decades. However, the way it happened—with a crowded concert hall loudly and devotedly recognizing León's artistry and a series of musical events that fully captured the diversity she has always advocated for—can only be understood as beautiful poetic justice.

Tania León's moment with the New York Philharmonic was a resounding roar that few in the U.S. classical music scene could ignore. It was an almost deafening instant in its high concentration of artistic, media, aesthetic, and political energy. But, for those willing to listen beyond the blast of the particular moment, it was also an opportunity to let the echoes of the stories that inform León's life reach their ears. Because, in a way, the story of how *Stride* came about is the story of Tania León's stride. Referring to this music provides a perfect epilogue to this account of her polyrhythmic life. It allows us to remember the stern, matriarchal family unit that nurtured her and to witness those values of perseverance and optimism reflected in her music as well as in her outlook on life. It also reminds us both of the obstacles she had to face and of the serendipitous concatenation of moments and episodes that, defined and connected by her indefatigable work ethic, have led her to where she is today.

León's stride, her determined walk through a complex, difficult, but also fulfilling and incredible life, has produced a subdued yet powerful and carrying echo that reaches our ears. It reminds us, too, that—more than the words I have written about her in this book—it is her music and its reverberations, the ideas, stories, and people it evokes and honors, that best describe who Tania León is.

Appendix A

Tania León—List of Works (June 2020)

Opera

The Little Rock Nine (in progress)
Libretto by Tulani Davis
Commissioned by the College of Fine
    Arts and Communication of the Uni-
    versity of Central Arkansas

Scourge of Hyacinths
Full Opera (1999)
Chamber Opera (1994)
Libretto by T. León, based on a radio play
    by Wole Soyinka
Commissioned by the Munich Biennale
    for New Music Theater

Ballet

Inura (2009)
For SATB voices, strings, and percussion
Commissioned by Brandon Fradd for
    Dance Brazil

Belé (with Geoffrey Holder) (1981)
For solo piano, strings, and percussion
For the Dance Theatre of Harlem

Spiritual Suite (1976)
For narrator, two sopranos, chorus, and
    amplified ensemble
For the Dance Theatre of Harlem

Dougla (with Geoffrey Holder) (1974)
For two flutes and percussion
For the Dance Theatre of Harlem

Haiku (1973)
For narrator, flute, bassoon, koto, guitar,
    cello, bass, percussion, and tape
Commissioned by the Dance Theatre of
    Harlem

The Beloved [with Judith Hamilton] (1972)
For flute, oboe, clarinet, bassoon, piano,
    cello, and bass
Arrangement and reorchestration of Ju-
    dith Hamilton's original music for the
    Dance Theatre of Harlem

Tones (1970–1971)
For chamber orchestra and piano
Commissioned by Dance Theatre of Har-
    lem

Mixed Genre

Samarkand (2005)
For speaker, SATB chorus, alto flute, saxophone, percussion, three batá drums, piano, and two cellos
Commissioned by Southern Crossroads in celebration of the opening of the Shaw Center for the Arts, Baton Rouge, Louisiana

Duende (2003)
For baritone, three batá drums, four percussionists, and Latin percussionist
Commissioned by Fest der Kontinente, Berlin, Germany in honor of the 80th birthday of György Ligeti

Drummin' (1997)
For chamber orchestra, large mixed ensemble, and percussion ensemble
Co-commissioned by Miami Light Project, Miami-Dade Community College, Arizona State University, and the New World Symphony

Orchestra

Stride (2020)
Commissioned by the New York Philharmonic as part of Project 19

Ácana (2008)
Commissioned by the Research Foundation of the State University of New York-Purchase College and Orpheus with support from the New York State Music Fund

Desde . . . (2001)
Commissioned by the American Composers Orchestra with support from the Koussevitsky Music Foundation, Inc.

Horizons (1999)
Commissioned by the NDR Sinfonie Orchester, Hamburg, and Hammoniale Festival der Frauen, Germany

Carabalí (1991)
Commissioned by the Cincinnati Symphony Orchestra

Batá (1985, rev. 1988)
Commissioned by the Bay Area Women's Philharmonic

Soloist and Orchestra

Didn't My Lord Deliver Daniel (arr. León) (2005)
For baritone and orchestra
Commissioned by the Albany Symphony Orchestra with support from Paul Underwood

Seven Spirituals (arr. Ryan, orch. Léon) (1995)
For baritone and orchestra
For the Leipzig Gewandhaus Orchestra

Para viola y orquesta (1994)
For viola and orchestra
Commissioned by Meet-the-Composer / *Reader's Digest* Commissioning Program

Kabiosile (1988)
For piano and orchestra
Commissioned by the American Composers Orchestra

Concerto criollo (1980)
For timpani, piano, and orchestra
Commissioned by the National Endowment for the Arts

Band/Wind Ensemble

Pa'lante (2016)
For flute, bassoon, saxophone, trombone, and symphonic wind ensemble
Commissioned by the Los Angeles Philharmonic and International Contemporary Ensemble

Origenes (2012)
For brass ensemble

Cumba Cumbakin (2010)
For two flutes, oboe, three bass clarinets, four saxophones, two horns, three trumpets, two trombones, tuba, timpani, three percussionists, and bass.
Commissioned by the Harvard Band Foundation

Alegre (2000)
For wind ensemble
Commissioned by the American Composers Forum for New Band Horizons

Instrumental Ensemble

Raíces (Tabla raza) (2007)
For flute, violin, voice, piano, bass, table, and percussion
Commissioned by Latin Fiesta with support from the Philadelphia Music Project, Pew Charitable Trust

Toque (2006)
For clarinet, alto sax, piano, two percussionists, violin, and bass
Commissioned by Opus 21

Caracol (2000)
For violin, viola, cello, percussion, and piano
Commissioned by the Manchester Music Festival

For four trumpets, two trombones, bass trombone, and percussion
Commissioned by The Library of Congress for the Copland Centennial Celebration

Hechizos (1995)
For flute/piccolo, oboe, clarinet (A and B-flat), bass clarinet/soprano sax/tenor sax/sop sax/ten sax, horn, trumpet, trombone, piano, percussion, guitar, and strings
Commissioned by Ensemble Modern

sin normas ajenas (1994)
For flute/piccolo, oboe, clarinet, piano, percussion, and strings
Commissioned by the U.S.-Mexico Fund for Culture

Crossings (1992)
For horn, four trumpets, four trombones, and tuba
Commissioned by the City University of New York

Indígena (1991)
For flute, oboe, clarinet, bassoon, horn, trumpet, piano, percussion, violin, viola, cello, and bass
Commissioned by New York City's Town Hall

Ascend (1983)
For four horns, four trumpets, three trombones, tuba, and percussion
Commissioned by the Queens Symphony

Permutation Seven (1981)
For flute, clarinet, trumpet, percussion, violin, and cello
Commissioned by the Lincoln Center Institute

Chamber Music

One Mo' Time (2016)
For flute, clarinet, violin, cello, and piano
Composed for the members of the Da Capo Players

Pinceladas (2016)
For bassoon and piano

Del Caribe, Soy! (2014)
For flute and piano
Commissioned by Concerts at St. Martha

Ethos (2014)
For piano and string quartet
Commissioned by NYSCA for Symphony Space; dedicated to the memory of Isaiah Sheffer

String Quartet No. 2 (2011)
Commissioned by ASCAP Foundation and Sphinx Organization

Esencia para cuarteto de cuerdas (2009)
For string quartet
Commissioned by the Fromm Music Foundation for the Del Sol Quartet

Tiempo de clave (2008)
For violin and percussion
Commissioned by Ana Milosavljevic

Alma (2007)
For flute and piano
Commissioned by the Bay Paul Foundation as part of the Flute Book for the Twenty-First Century developed through Meet the Composer's New Music, New Donors Initiative

De memorias (2000)
For wind quintet
Commissioned by The Mexico City Woodwind Quintet with support from the Mexico/US Fund for Culture

Satiné (2000)
For two pianos
Commissioned by Mirta Gomez

Entre nos (1998)
For clarinet, bassoon, and piano
Commissioned by Trio Neos

Parajota Delaté (1988)
For flute, clarinet, violin, cello, and piano
Commissioned by the Da Capo Chamber Players, 1988
Arrangement for flute, oboe, clarinet, bassoon, and piano
For the Netherlands Wind Ensemble, 1990

Saóko (1997)
For brass quintet
For the Meridian Arts Ensemble. Commissioned by the South Florida Composers Alliance/Center for Cultural Collaborations International

De color (1996–1997)
For violin and marimba
Commissioned by Marimolin

Tau (1995)
For electric oboe, electric bass, and electronic keyboards
Commissioned by First Avenue

Son Sonora (1993)
For flute and guitar
Commissioned by Duologue

Ajiaco (1992)
For electric guitar and piano
Commissioned by the Schanzer/Speach Duo

Arenas d'un tiempo (1992)
For clarinet, cello, and piano
Commissioned by the New York State Music Teachers Association

Elegia a Paul Robeson (1987)
For violin, cello, and piano

A la par (1986)
For piano and percussion
Commissioned by the Whitney Museum

Pet's Suite (1980)
For flute and piano
Commissioned by Composers' Forum

Instrumental Solo

Anima (2020)
For violin
Composed for Jennifer Koh and the
  Alone Together Project

going . . . gone (2012)
For piano
Composed for Liaisons: Reimagining
  Sondheim from the Piano

Homenatge (2011)
For piano
Commissioned by the Iberian Foundation

Abanico (2007)
For violin and interactive computer
Commissioned by the University of
  Maryland for Airi Yoshioka

Para Noah (2006)
For piano
Written in honor of Noah Creschevsky's
  sixtieth birthday

Tumbao (2005)
For piano
Commissioned by Elena Riu

Hebras d' luz (2004)
For electric viola
Commissioned and premiered by Martha
  Mooke

La Tina (2004)
For piano
Commissioned by the Lucy Moses School

Variación (2004)
For piano
Commissioned by the Gilmore Festival

Mística (2003)
For piano
Commissioned and premiered by Ursula
  Oppens

Axon (2002)
For violin and interactive computer
Commissioned by Mari Kimura for
  ISCM, Hong Kong

Bailarín (1998)
For guitar
Commissioned by David Starobin

Rituál (1987)
For piano
Commissioned by Affiliate Artists, Inc.

Momentum (1984)
For piano
Commissioned by the Women Compos-
  ers Congress (Mexico)

Paisanos semos! (1984)
For guitar

Four Pieces for Violoncello (1983)
For cello

Rondó a la criolla (1965)
For piano

Two Preludes ("Sorpresa" and "Pecera")
  (1965)
For piano

Homenaje a Prokofiev (ca. 1965)
For piano

Vocal Ensemble

Rimas tropicales (2011)
Poetry by Carlos Pintado
For girls chorus
Commissioned by Classical Movement, Inc., as part of the Eric Helms New Music Program

Ancients (2008)
For two sopranos, flute, clarinet, percussion, viola, and cello
Commissioned by Carolina Performing Arts for Terry Rhodes

Estampas (2008)
Text by Maya Islas, Iraida Iturralde, and Alina Guerrero
For SATB Chorus
Commissioned by Chicago A Cappella

Metisse (2006)
For SATB chorus and percussion
Commissioned by the Commissioning Project

A Row of Buttons (2002)
Text by Fae Myenne Ng
For SA Choir
Commissioned by the New York Treble Singers

Rezos (2001)
Text by Jamaica Kincaid
For SATB choir
Commissioned by Terry Knowles and Marshall Rutter to honor Grant Gershon, Music Director, Los Angeles Master Chorale

May the Road Be Free (1999)
Text by John Marsden
For children's chorus and percussion
Commissioned by Lincoln Center for the Tree Lighting Ceremony

Sol de doce (1997)
Text by Pedro Mir
For twelve solo voices (SSSAAATTTBBB)
Commissioned by Chamber Music America

Batéy [with Michel Camilo] (1989)
Text by T. León, M. Camilo
For two sopranos, countertenor, two tenors, and bass
Commissioned by The Western Wind Vocal Ensemble

Heart of Ours—A Piece (1988)
Texts by R. Sandecki; American Indians
For solo tenor, men's chorus, flute, four trumpets, and percussion
Commissioned by the Vietnam Veterans' Theater Company

De-Orishas (1982)
Text by Betty Neals
For two sopranos, countertenor, two tenors, and bass
Commissioned by The Western Wind Vocal Ensemble

Two Cuban Songs ("Drume Negrita" [Grenet, arr. León] and "El manisero" [Simons, arr. León])
For twelve solo voices (SSSAAATTTBBB)
Commissioned by Chanticleer

Namiac Poems (1975)
For voices and mixed ensemble
Written for NYU Contemporary Ensemble

Vocal Solo and Chamber Ensemble

Mi amor es (2015)
Text by Carlos Pintado
For baritone and piano
Commissioned by Luigi Terruso, in memory of Emory W. Harper.

Zero plus Anything (2014)
Poem by Jane Hirshfield
For baritone and piano

Atwood Songs (2007)
Poetry by Margaret Atwood
For soprano and piano
Commissioned with support from the Hanson Institute for American Music and the Syracuse University College of Arts and Sciences

Reflections (2006)
Text by Rita Dove
For soprano, piano, clarinet, alto sax, trumpet, percussion, and string quintet
Commissioned and developed by Harlem Stage for WaterWorks at The Gatehouse

Love after Love (2002)
Text by Derek Walcott
For soprano and marimba
Commissioned by Mary Sharp Cronson, Works and Process

Canto (2001)
For baritone, clarinet (B-flat/bass), marimba, cello, and piano
Commissioned by Mutable Music for Thomas Buckner

At the Fountain of Mpindelela (2000)
For vocal ensemble
Commissioned and Premiered by the National Musical Arts program, "Africa Spirit Ascending," in honor of Nelson Mandela

Ivo, Ivo (2000)
Text by Manuel Martin
For soprano, clarinet, bass clarinet, viola, cello, and double bass
Commissioned by Sequitur

Turning (2000)
For soprano, piano, and cello
Commissioned for the Ann and Richard Barshinger Center for Musical Arts in Hensel Hall, Franklin and Marshall College

Singin' Sepia (1996)
Five Songs on Poems by Rita Dove
For soprano, clarinet, violin, piano four-hand
Commissioned by the Continuum Ensemble

"Or like a . . ." (1994)
Text by John Ashbery
For baritone, cello, and percussion
Commissioned by WNYC

Journey (1990)
For high vocalist, flute, and harp
Commissioned by the Jubal Trio

To and Fro (1990)
Four Songs on Poems by Alison Knowles
For medium vocalist and piano
Commissioned by the International Society for Contemporary Music

Pueblo mulato (1987)
Three Songs on Poems by Nicolás Guillén
For soprano, oboe, guitar, double bass, percussion, and piano
Commissioned by the Cornucopia Chamber Ensemble

Musical Theater

The Golden Windows (1982)
A play in three acts. Text by Robert Wilson
For flute/piccolo/alto flute, oboe/English horn, trumpet, percussion/harpsichord/piano, and strings
Commissioned by the Byrd Hoffman Foundation

Maggie Magalita (1980)
Incidental music for the play. Text by Wendy Kesselman
For flute, clarinet, cello, percussion, piano, and guitar
Commissioned by the Kennedy Center for the Performing Arts

Carmencita (1978)
Incidental music for the play. Book and lyrics by Manuel Martín Jr.
For INTAR Theatre

La ramera de la cueva (1974)
Incidental music for Mario Peña's play
For the Duo Theatre Company

Appendix B

Tania León's Life

		Music News	Political and Cultural News
1943	Born in Havana, Cuba	Manuel M. Ponce, Violin Concerto	End of the Battle of
		Oliver Messiaen, *Visions de l'Amen*	Stalingrad (WWII)
		Anton Webern, Variations for Orchestra, Op. 30	Tehran Conference
		Duke Ellington's orchestra performs at Carnegie	
		Hall for the first time	
		Rodgers and Hammerstein, *Oklahoma*	
1945		Dmitri Shostakovich, Symphony No. 9	End of WWII
		Heitor Villa-Lobos, Piano Concerto No. 1	Potsdam Conference
		Charlie Parker, "Billie's Bounce"	
1947	Birth of Oscar León	Alberto Ginastera, Pampeana No. 1	Independence of India and
	Ferrán (brother)	André Jolivet, Concerto for Ondes Martenot and	Pakistan
		Orchestra	Creation of the C.I.A.
	Begins piano studies	Arnold Schoenberg, *A Survivor from Warsaw*,	
		op. 46	
		Milton Babbitt, Three Compositions for Piano	
		Debut of The Miles Davis All-Stars	
1957	José León	Francis Poulenc, *Dialogues des Carmélites*	The U.S.S.R. launches
	(grandfather) dies	Karlheinz Stockhausen, *Gruppen*	Sputnik I
		Toru Takemitsu, Requiem for Strings	Treaty of Rome
		Leonard Bernstein, *West Side Story*	The Little Rock Nine and
		Elvis Presley records "Jailhouse Rock"	the Little Rock crisis
1959		Elliott Carter, String Quartet No. 2	Triumph of the Cuban
		Julián Carrillo, String Quartet No. 8	Revolution
		Foundation of the Columbia-Princeton	Beginning of the Vietnam
		Electronic Music Center	War
		First Grammy Award ceremony	
		Miles Davis, *Kind of Blue*	
		Foundation of Motown Records	

		Music News	Political and Cultural News
1960	Graduates with bachelor degrees in piano and music theory from the Conservatorio Peyrellade, Havana, Cuba	Dmitri Shostakovich, String Quartet No. 8 Alberto Ginastera, *Cantata para América mágica* Krzysztof Penderecki, *Threnody for the Victims of Hiroshima* Karlheinz Stockhausen, *Kontakte* Ella Fitzgerald, *Ella in Berlin* John Coltrane, *Giant Steps*	Nationalization of U.S. companies in Cuba The Greensboro Four and the Sit-In Movement JFK elected President of the United States Olympic Games in Rome
1961	Graduates with a bachelor degree in accounting from the Escuela Profesional de Comercio de Marianao, Havana, Cuba	Carlos Chávez, *Soli II* György Ligeti, *Atmospheres* Benjamin Britten, Cello Sonata John Cage, *Silence: Lectures and Writings* The Miracles, "Shop Around" The Beach Boys, "Surfin'"	Bay of Pigs invasion Fidel Castro declares Cuba a socialist country Freedom Rides in the United States Construction of the Berlin Wall begins Assassination of Patrice Lumumba Yuri Gagarin orbits the Earth
1964	Piano lessons with Zenaida Manfugás at the Conservatorio Alejandro García Caturla, Havana, Cuba	Alberto Ginastera, *Don Rodrigo* Carlos Chávez, *Tambuco* Terry Riley, *In C* Jerry Herman, *Hello, Dolly!* Jerry Bock and Sheldon Harnick, *Fiddler on the Roof* João Gilberto and Stan Getz, *Getz/Gilberto* The Beatles, "I Want to Hold Your Hand" The Beatles' first visit to the U.S.A. Foundation of Fania Records	Leonid Brezhnev new General Secretary of the Communist Party of the U.S.S.R. Civil Rights Act abolishes segregation in the United States Olympic Games in Tokyo
1965	Preludio No. 1 and Preludio No. 2 premiered in Havana	György Ligeti, Requiem George Crumb, *Madrigals* (Books I and II) Premiere of Charles Ives' Symphony No. 4 John Coltrane, *Ascension* Mitch Leigh and Joe Darion, *Man of La Mancha* The Rolling Stones, "Satisfaction" The Beatles, "Yesterday"	Assassination of Malcolm X Selma-Montgomery March and Watts Riots Second Vatican Council closes Freedom Flights program begins
1966	Marries Eduardo Viera Collaborates with Marta Valdés and Grupo Teatro Estudio in the production of Bertolt Brecht's *El alma buena de Sechuán*	Meredith Monk, *16 Millimiter Earrings* John Kander and Fred Ebb, *Cabaret* The Beatles, *Revolver* Frank Sinatra, "Strangers in the Night" Simon and Garfunkel, "The Sound of Silence"	China's Cultural Revolution begins Black Panther Party founded Andy Warhol, Exploding Plastic Inevitable José Lezama Lima's *Paradiso* is published World Cup in England

	Music News	Political and Cultural News
1967	Emigrates to the United States	Luciano Berio, *Chemins II*	Summer of Love
	Enrolls at the New York College of Music	Steve Reich, *Piano Phase*	Six-Day War
		Toru Takemitsu, *November Steps*	Ernesto "Ché" Guevara killed in Bolivia
		The Beatles, *Sgt. Pepper's Lonely Hearts Club Band*	Gabriel García Márquez's *Cien años de soledad* is published
		The Doors, *The Doors*	
		The Velvet Underground, *The Velvet Underground & Nico*	Guillermo Cabrera Infante's *Tres tristes tigres* is published
		Pete Rodriguez, "I Like It Like That"	
1968	Meets Arthur Mitchell and starts working at Dance Theatre Harlem (DTH)	Luciano Berio, *Sinfonia*	Assassinations of Martin Luther King Jr. and Robert F. Kennedy
		George Crumb, *Songs, Drones, and Refrains of Death*	Warsaw Pact invasion of Czechoslovakia
		Per Nørgård, *Voyage into the Golden Screen*	Protests of 1968 (U.S.A., France, Poland, West Germany, Mexico, etc.)
		Carlos Chávez, *Los visitantes*	
		Gerome Ragni, James Rado and Galt MacDermont, *Hair*	Olympic Games in Mexico City
		Louis Armstrong, "What a Wonderful World"	
		The Beatles, "Hey Jude"	
1971	Rosa Julia de los Mederos "Mamota" (grandmother) dies	George Crumb, *Vox Balaenae*	Nixon removes gold backup for the U.S. dollar
		Helmut Lachenmann, *Gran Torso*	Bangladesh Liberation War
	Graduates with a Bachelor of Science from New York University (NYU)	Steve Reich, *Drumming*	Black September ends
		Iannis Xenakis, *Mikka*	Foundation of Greenpeace
		Leo Brouwer, *La espiral eterna*	
		Premiere of Heitor Villa-Lobos, *Yerma*	
	Caribbean and European tours with DTH	Andrew Lloyd Webber and Tim Rice, *Jesus Christ Superstar*	
		Ornette Coleman, *Skies of America*	
	Tones	Willie Colón, *Asalto Navideño*	
		John Lennon, "Imagine"	
		George Harrison, "My Sweet Lord"	
		Roberto Carlos, "Detalhes"	
		Jim Morrison dies	
1973	American citizenship	Alberto Ginastera, String Quartet No. 3	U.S. Supreme Court decides Roe v. Wade
	Dissolution of marriage to Eduardo Viera	Luigi Nono, *Canto per il Vietnam*	Coup d'etat in Chile
		Donald Martino, *Notturno*	Coup d'etat in Uruguay
		Julius Eastman, *Stay on It*	Yom Kippur War
	Haiku	Manuel Enríquez, *Ritual*	Skylab is launched
		Jim Jacobs and Warren Casey, *Grease*	
		Gato Barbieri, *Chapter One: Latin America*	
		Pink Floyd, *The Dark Side of The Moon*	
		Roberta Flack, "Killing Me Softly with His Song"	
1974	*Dougla*	Steve Reich, *Music for 18 Musicians*	Richard Nixon resigns the U.S. Presidency
	Music for Mario Peña's	Mario Davidovsky, *Synchronisms No. 7*	Carnation Revolution in Portugal
	La ramera de la cueva	Julius Eastman, *Femenine*	World Cup in Germany
		Celia Cruz and Johnny Pacheco, *Celia & Johnny*	
		Kiss, *Kiss*	
		Astor Piazzolla, "Libertango"	
		Carl Douglas, "Kung Fu Fighting"	

Appendix B

	Music News	Political and Cultural News
1975	Graduates with a Master of Arts (in Music Composition) from NYU	Karlheinz Stockhausen, *Harlekin* Frederic Rzewski, *The People United Will Never Be Defeated!* Claude Bolling, Suite for Flute and Jazz Piano John Kander and Fred Ebb, *Chicago*	Vietnam War ends Francisco Franco dies Cuban intervention in Angola begins
1976	*Spiritual Suite* Cofounder of the Brooklyn Philarmonia Community Concert Series	Philip Glass, *Einstein on the Beach* Henryk Górecki, Symphony No. 3 Egberto Gismonti, *Dança das Cabeças* Queen, "Bohemian Rhapsody" Chicago, "If You Leave Me Now" ABBA, "Fernando"	End of China's Cultural Revolution Mao Zedong dies Coup d'etat in Argentina The Concorde starts operating commercially Olympic Games in Montreal
1978	Music director at *The Wiz* Music for Manuel Martín Jr.'s *Carmencita* Conducting workshop with Leonard Bernstein and Seiji Ozawa at Tanglewood	György Ligeti, *Le Grand Macabre* Andrew Lloyd Webber and Tim Rice, *Evita* Willie Colón and Rubén Blades, *Siembra* Village People, "Y.M.C.A." Héctor Lavoe, "El cantante" Carlos Chávez dies	John Paul II is chosen as Pope Camp David Accords World Cup in Argentina
1979	First trip back to Cuba	John Cage, *Roaratorio* Morton Feldman, String Quartet No. 1 Steve Reich, Octet Libby Larsen, *The Silver Fox* Gloria Gaynor, "I Will Survive" The Knack, "My Sharona"	Soviet-Afghan War begins Iran hostage crisis begins Margaret Thatcher Prime Minister of the UK Nicaraguan Revolution
1980	Oscar José León (father) dies Steps down as DTH's music director Music for *Maggie Magalita* *Concierto criollo*	Sofia Gubaidulina, *Offertorium* Julios Eastman, *Gay Guerilla* Karlheinz Stockhausen, *Donnerstag aus Licht* Billy Joel, "It's Still Rock and Roll to Me" John Lennon is murdered	Founding of Solidarność in Poland Ronald Reagan elected U.S. President Iran-Iraq War begins Umberto Eco's *Il nome della rosa* is published Olympic Games in Moscow
1981	*Belé* *Permutations Seven*	Milton Babbitt, *Ars combinatoria* Alberto Ginastera, Piano Sonata No. 2, Op. 53 Leo Brouwer, *El Decamerón negro* Andrew Lloyd Webber, *Cats* John Lennon and Yoko Ono, *Double Fantasy* Phil Collins, *Face Value* Grandmaster Flash, "The Adventures of Grandmaster Flash on the Wheels of Steel" Bob Marley dies	Spanish coup d'etat attempt First recognized cases of AIDS Anwar el-Sadat is murdered
1982	*De-Orishas* Music for Robert Wilson's *The Golden Windows*	György Ligeti, Trio for violin, horn, and piano Brian Ferneyhough, *Lemma-Icon-Epigram* Mario Lavista, *Marsias* Pink Floyd — *The Wall* Thelonious Monk dies	Falklands War Yuri Andropov new General Secretary of the Communist Party of the U.S.S.R. Isabel Allende's *La casa de los espíritus* is published World Cup in Spain

		Music News	Political and Cultural News
1983	*Four Pieces for Cello Solo*	Krysztof Penderecki, Viola Concerto Morton Feldman, *String Quartet II* Jerry Herman, *La Cage aux Folles* Michael Jackson, "Billie Jean" The Police, "Every Breath You Take" Alberto Ginastera dies	Ronald Reagan announces the Strategic Defense Initiative Korean Air Lines Flight 007 is shot down by Soviet Union forces Military rule ends in Argentina with the election of Raúl Alfonsín as President Sandra Cisneros' *The House on Mango Street* is published
1984	*Momentum* *¡Paisanos semos!*	Elliott Carter, *Riconoscenza per Goffredo Petrassi* Mario Lavista, *Reflejos de la noche* Julio Estrada, *ishini'ioni* Rubén Blades, *Buscando América* Cindy Lauper, "Girls Just Want to Have Fun" Stephen Sondheim, *Sunday in the Park with George*	Konstantin Chernenko new General Secretary of the Communist Party of the U.S.S.R. Indira Gandhi is murdered Military rule ends in Uruguay with the election of Julio María Sanguinetti Olympic Games in Los Angeles
1985	*Batá* Music Director for the Alvin Ailey Dance Company Starts teaching at Brooklyn College	Pierre Boulez, *Dialogue de l'ombre double* Joan Tower, Piano Concerto Mariano Etkin, *Caminos de cornisa* Dorothy Rudd Moore, *Frederick Douglass* Madonna, "Material Girl" Rubén Blades, "Cuentas del alma" USA for Africa, "We Are the World"	Military rule ends in Brazil with the election of Tancredo Neves as President DEA agent Kiki Camarena is murdered in Mexico Mikhail Gorbachev new General Secretary of the Communist Party of the U.S.S.R. Devastating earthquake hits Mexico City
1986	*A la par* Music Director, Contemporary Music Series, Whitney Museum	Leo Brouwer, *Concierto elegiaco* Elliott Carter, String Quartet No. 4 Anthony Davies, *X, The Life and Times of Malcolm X* Roberto Sierra, *Memorias tropicales* Andrew Lloyd Weber, *The Phantom of the Opera* Afrika Bambaataa, *Planet Rock: The Album* Madonna, "Papa Don't Preach"	Space Shuttle *Challenger* disaster The U.S.S.R. launches the *Mir* space station People Power Revolution in the Philippines Mikhail Gorbachev introduces the concepts of *Glasnost* and *Perestroika* Chernobyl nuclear disaster World Cup in Mexico
1987	*Elegía a Paul Robeson* *Ritual* *Pueblo mulato* First trip to Paris	John Adams, *Nixon in China* Horacio Vaggione, *Tar* Public Enemy, *Yo! Bum Rush the Show* Los Lobos, "La bamba" Morton Feldman and Rodolfo Halffter die	Congressional investigation of the Iran-Contra affair Intermediate-Range Nuclear Forces Treaty signed Toni Morrison's *Beloved* is published

		Music News	Political and Cultural News
1988	*Kabiosile* *Parajota Delaté*	Luciano Berio, *Sequenza XI* Mario Davidovsky, *Synchronisms No. 9* Manuel Enríquez, String Quartet No. 5 Mario Lavista, *Aura* Kaija Saariaho, *Petals* Bobby McFerrin, "Don't Worry Be Happy"	Soviet-Afghan War ends Osama bin Laden forms Al-Quaeda Iran-Iraq War ends George H. W. Bush elected U.S. President Salman Rushdie published *The Satanic Verses* Olympic Games in Seoul
1989	*Batéy*	Anthony Davies, *Under the Double Moon* Claude-Michel Schönberg, *Miss Saigon* Juan Luis Guerra & 4.40, *Ojalá que llueva café* Madonna, "Like a Prayer"	Military rule ends in Chile with the election of Patricio Aylwin Tiananmen Square protests End of communism in Hungary and Rumania Fall of the Berlin Wall
1990	*Journey*	Tod Machover, *Bug Mudra* Meredith Monk, *Book of Days* John Zorn, *The Dead Man* Depeche Mode, *Violator* Public Enemy, *Fear of a Black Planet* Julius Eastman dies	Reunification of Germany Breakup of Yugoslavia Nelson Mandela released from prison Launch of the Hubble Space Telescope Creation of the World Wide Web World Cup in Italy
1991	*Carabalí* *Indígena*	Javier Álvarez, *Metro Chabacano* Daniel Catán, *La hija de Rapaccini* John Corigliano, *The Ghosts of Versailles* Meredith Monk, *Atlas* Freddie Mercury dies	Dissolution of the U.S.S.R. Gulf War Yugoslav Wars Julia Alvarez, *How the García Girls Lost Their Accents* is published
1992	*Arenas d'un tiempo* South African tour with DTH	Anthony Davies, *Tania* Brian Ferneyhough, *Terrain* Osvaldo Golijov, *Yiddishbbuk* Selena, "Como la flor" Whitney Houston, "I Will Always Love You"	Bosnian War Los Angeles riots Bill Clinton elected U.S. President Reinaldo Arenas, *Antes que anochezca* is published Olympic Games in Barcelona
1993	Begins work as Composer in Residence, New York Philharmonic	Alvin Curran, *VSTO* Marlos Nobre, *Rememórias* Karlheinz Stockhausen, *Helicopter-Streichquartett* Nirvana, *In Utero* Marc Anthony, *Otra Nota*	Waco siege World Trade Center bombing The Cuban government opens state enterprises to private investment

		Music News	Political and Cultural News
1994	*Scourge of Hyacinths* *Para viola y orquesta* Sonidos de las Américas, México	Mario Lavista, *Missa Brevis* Alvin Singleton, *Somehow We Can* Steve Reich, *City Life* Alan Menken, *Beauty and the Beast* Derrick Carter, "I'm Sorry (Clairvoyage)" Manuel Enríquez dies	NAFTA comes into force Zapatista uprising in Mexico Nelson Mandela elected President of South Africa First Chechen War begins Pursuit and arrest of O. J. Simpson World Cup in the United States
1995	*Hechizos* Sonidos de las Américas, Venezuela ASCAP Morton Gould Award	Elliott Carter, String Quartet No. 5 Gerardo Gandini, *La ciudad ausente* Gabriela Ortiz, *Altar de neón* Björk, *Post* Alanis Morrissette, *Jagged Little Pill* Los del Río, "Macarena"	Valeri Polyakov sets a record of 438 days in outer space Oklahoma City bombing NATO bombing campaign against Serbia The Unabomber manifesto is made public Yitzhak Rabin is murdered *Galileo* enters Jupiter's atmosphere
1996	*Singin' Sepia* Sonidos de las Américas, Brazil Steps down as Composer in Residence, New York Philharmonic	Sofia Gubaidulina, Viola Concerto Tristan Murail, *Le partage de eaux* Gabriela Ortiz, *Altar de muertos* Jonathan Larson, *Rent* Spice Girls, "Wannabe"	The Cuban Air Force shoots down two Brothers to the Rescue planes The Unabomber is arrested Dolly the Sheep is the first mammal cloned from an adult cell Olympic Games in Atlanta
1997	*Drummin'* *De color* Sonidos de las Américas, Puerto Rico	Anthony Davis, *Amistad* Tan Dun, *Symphony 1997: Heaven, Earth, Mankind* Julio Estrada, *yuunohui'tlapoa* Marlos Nobre, *Passacaglia para orquesta* Graciela Paraskevaídis, *Libres en el sonido, presos en el sonido* Elton John and Tim Rice, *The Lion King*	Rais Massacre The Kyoto Protocol is adopted by the United Nations Death of Diana, Princess of Wales
1998	*Bailarín* Sonidos de las Américas, Argentina Fromm Residency, American Academy of Rome	George Frederic Haas, String Quartet No. 2 Mario Davidovsky, String Quartet No. 5 Cergio Prudencio, *Uyariwaycheq* Alvin Singleton, *Ein Kleines Volkslied* Ricky Martin, "La copa de la vida"	The Cuban Five are arrested in Miami Augusto Pinochet is indicted and arrested Hugo Chávez elected President of Venezuela Impeachment of Bill Clinton World Cup in France

Appendix B

	Music News	Political and Cultural News
1999	*Horizons* *Sonidos de las* *Américas*, Cuba Honorary Doctorate, Colgate University	Samuel Adler, Viola Concerto Wolfgang Rihm, *Zwiesprache* Benny Andersson and Björn Ulvaeus, *Mamma* *Mia!* Santana, *Supernatural* Lou Bega, "Mambo No. 5"	Second Chechen War Panama gains control of the Panama Canal Elián González affair begins Boris Yeltsin resigns as President of Russia, Vladimir Putin becomes acting President
2000	*De memorias* *Ivo, Ivo* Serge Koussevitsky Award	John Adams, *El Niño* Osvaldo Golijov, *La Pasión según San Marcos* Mesías Maiguashca, *El tiempo* Kaija Saariaho, *L'Amour de loin* Britney Spears, "Oops! . . . I Did It Again"	Slobodan Milošević resigns as President of the Federal Republic of Yugoslavia George W. Bush elected U.S. President Olympic Games in Sydney
2001	*Desde . . .* *Rezos*	György Ligeti, Études, Book 3 Olga Neuwirth, *Locus . . . doublere . . . solus* Alicia Keys, *Songs in A Minor* Jennifer López, *J.Lo* Nortec Collective, *The Tijuana Sessions, Vol. 1*	The Taliban destroys the Bamiyan Buddhas Slobodan Milošević is arrested for War Crimes Terrorist attack against NY's World Trade Center and the U.S. Pentagon The United States invades Afghanistan
2002	*Axon* Honorary Doctorate, Oberlin College National Endowment for the Arts	Arvo Pärt, *Lamentate* Salvatore Sciarrino, *Altre schegge di canto* Ye Xiaogang, *Great Wall Symphony* Avril Lavigne, *Let Go* t.A.T.u, "All the Things You Said"	SARS epidemic Creation of the International Criminal Court World Cup in South Korea- Japan
2003	*Mística* *Duende* Ursula Oppens plays *Mística* in Havana	Enrico Chapela, *Íngesu* Osvaldo Golijov, *Ainadamar* Kryzstof Penderecki, *Ubu Rex* Beyoncé, *Dangerously in Love* Norah Jones, *Come Away with Me* Julieta Venegas, *Sí*	The United States invades Iraq The Human Genome Project is completed Last flight of the Concorde Roberto Bolaño's *2666* is published
2004	*Hebras d' luz*	Hans Werner Henze, *Sebastian im Traum* Dobrinka Tabakova, Concerto for Viola and Strings Gabriela Ortiz, *Únicamente la verdad* Danger Mouse, *The Gray Album* Pitbull, "Culo"	Facebook is launched Coup d'etat against Haitian President Jean-Bertrand Aristide The Orange Revolution begins Olympic Games in Athens
2005	*Tumbao* *Samarkand*	John Adams, *Dr. Atomic* Martin Matalon, *Metropolis* Cergio Prudencio, *Otra ciudad* 50 Cent, *The Massacre* Natalia Lafourcade, *Casa* Cansei de Ser Sexy, "Let's Make Love and Listen to Death from Above"	YouTube is launched Pope John Paul II dies End of the IRA's armed campaign Hurricane Katrina hits the United States Evo Morales elected President of Bolivia Angela Merkel elected Chancellor of Germany

		Music News	Political and Cultural News

2006	*Reflections*
	Toque
		Jorge Antunes, *Olga*
		Tan Dun, *The First Emperor*
		Marlos Nobre, *Toccata No. 2*
		Robert Xavier Rodriguez, *La curandera*
		Amy Winehouse, *Back to Black*
		Shakira, "Hips Don't Lie"
			Raúl Castro assumes duties
			  as President of Cuba
			Mahmoud Ahmadinejad
			  elected President of Iran
			Devastating earthquake in
			  Yogyakarta
			Saddam Hussein is
			  executed
			World Cup in Germany

2007	*Abanico*
	Alma
	Atwood Songs
	Guggenheim
	  Fellowship
	Honorary Doctorate,
	  Purchase College
		Anthony Davis, *Wakonda's Dream*
		Gabriela Lena Frank, *Compadrazgo*
		Hans Werner Herzog, *Phaedra*
		Karlheinz Stockhausen, *Cosmic Pulses*
		The Eagles, *Long Road Out of Eden*
		Beyoncé, "Déjà Vu"
			Global Financial Crisis
			Devastating earthquake
			  in Peru
			Benazir Bhutto is murdered
			Junot Díaz's *The Brief
			  Wondrous Life of Oscar
			  Wao* is published

2008	*Ácana*	Arvo Pärt, Symphony No. 4
		Tan Dun, Piano Concerto, *The Fire*
		Lady Gaga, *The Fame*
			Fidel Castro formally resigns
			  as President of Cuba
			Barack Obama is elected
			  U.S. President
			Olympic Games in Beijing

2009	*Esencia*
	Inura
	Tiempo de clave
		Elliott Carter, *Figment V*
		Sofia Gubaidulina, *Fachwerk*
		Magnus Lindberg, *Graffiti*
		The Black Eyed Peas, "I Gotta Feeling"
		Lukas Foss dies
			Gaza War ends
			Coup d'etat in Honduras
			Icelandic government and
			  banking system collapse
			End of the Sri Lankan Civil
			  War

2010	Inducted to the
	  American
	  Academy of Arts
	  and Letters
	Performances of *Alma*
	  and *Arenas d'un
	  tiempo* at the Leo
	  Brouwer Chamber
	  Music Festival in
	  Havana
		Fred Lerdahl, *Arches*
		Angélica Negrón, *Quimbombó*
		Steve Reich, *WTC 9/11*
		Kaija Saariaho, *Mirages*
		Kesha, "Tik Tok"
			Devastating earthquake in
			  Haiti
			Devastating earthquake in
			  Chile
			Eruption of Mount
			  Eyjafjallajökull in
			  Iceland
			Instagram is launched
			World Cup in South Africa

2011	String Quartet No. 2
	Homenatge
		Steven Stucky, *Silent Spring*
		Anna Thorvaldsdottir, *AERIALITY*
		Gloria Estefan, *Miss Little Havana*
		Adele, "Rolling in the Deep"
			Hosni Mubarak resigns as
			  President of Egypt
			Syrian Civil War
			Osama bin Laden is killed
			Libyan Civil War:
			  Muammar Gaddafi is
			  murdered

2012	*going . . . gone* *Orígenes*	Gabriela Lena Frank, *Requiem for a Magical America: El Día de los Muertos* Caroline Shaw, *Partita for 8 Voices* PSY, "Gangnam Style"	MERS outbreak *Curiosity* lands on Mars Olympic Games in London

	Music News	Political and Cultural News
2014	Dora Ferrán "Mima" (mother) dies *Ethos*	Chaya Czernowin, *HIDDEN* Henryk Górecki, Symphony No. 4 Julia Wolfe, *Anthracite Fields* Becky G, "Can't Stop Dancing" J Balvin, "Ay vamos"	Reestablishment of U.S.- Cuba diplomatic relations Ukrainian Revolution Russia annexes Crimea Felipe VI becomes king of Spain World Cup in Brazil
2016	*Pa'lante* Invited to conduct Cuba's National Symphony Orchestra	Marcos Balter, *Divertimento concertante* James Dillon, *The Gate* Angélica Negrón, *Las desaparecidas* Augusta Reed Thomas, *Venus Enchanted* Amara La Negra, "Se que soy"	Zika virus outbreak Barack Obama visits Cuba Impeachment of Brazilian President Dilma Rousseff Donald Trump is elected U.S. President Fidel Castro dies Olympic Games in Rio de Janeiro
2017	Commission of *Little Rock Nine* City of New York Proclamation	Chaya Czernowin, *Infinite Now* Bunita Marcus, *White Butterflies* Roberto Sierra, *La memoria* Luis Fonsi, "Despacito" Cardi B, "Bartier Cardi"	Far-Right rally in Charlottesville, VA Brexit referendum Hurricane Harvey hits the United States Cassini-Huygens enters Saturn atmosphere
2020	*Stride*	György Kurtág, *. . . concertante . . .* Bent Sørensen, *Enchantress* Nina C. Young, *Tread Softly* Roddy Ricch, "The Box" The Black Eyed Peas and J Balvin, "Ritmo (Bad Boys for Life)"	Global stock market crash COVID-19 worldwide pandemic Black Lives Matter protests

Notes

Introduction

1. "Closing Plenary Session—Joan Tower and Tania León—2019 National Conference," League of American Orchestras, online video, accessed August 21, 2019, https://www.youtube.com/watch?v=oR7lbZu69ws&t+4s.

2. See, for example, the inclusion of her compositions in popular textbooks such as Mark Evan Bonds' *A History of Music in Western Culture* (Upper Saddle River, NJ: Prentice Hall, 2003), Roger Kamien's *Music: An Appreciation* (New York: McGraw-Hill, 2002 and 2019), Robin Moore and Walter Clark's *Music of Latin America* (New York: W. W. Norton, 2012), and Adelaida Reyes' *Music in America* (New York: Oxford University Press, 2005), among others.

3. See William Safire, "People of Color," *New York Magazine*, November 20, 1988, section 6, 18.

4. For a critique of the concept "people of color" as an expression that renders invisible the experience of black slavery, see Jared Sexton, "People-of-Color-Blindness: Notes on the Afterlife of Slavery," *Social Text* 28, no. 2 (2010): 31–56; and Nadra Widatalla, "The Term 'People of Color' Erases Black People. Let's Retire It," *Los Angeles Times*, April 28, 2019, accessed online, June 5, 2020, https://www.latimes.com/opinion/op-ed/la-oe-widatalla-poc-intersectionality-race-20190428-story.html.

5. See, for example: Amia Lieblich, *Conversations with Dvora: An Experimental Biography of the First Modern Hebrew Writer* (Berkeley: University of California Press, 1997); and Carole Angier, *The Double Bond: Primo Levi, A Biography* (New York: Farrar, Straus, and Giroux, 2002). Examples of music biographies written from this perspective include: Janice Galloway, *Clara: A Novel* (New York: Simon and Schuster, 2002); Jocelyne Guilbault and Roy Cape, *Roy Cape. A Life on the Calypso and Soca Bandstand* (Durham, NC: Duke University Press, 2014); Alejandro L. Madrid, *In Search*

of Julián Carrillo and Sonido 13 (New York: Oxford University Press, 2015); and Shana Redmond, *Everything Man: The Form and Function of Paul Robeson* (Durham, NC: Duke University Press, 2020).

6. My interviews with León were conducted in Spanish. We did not plan it that way but we both gravitated naturally toward that language during our conversations. The only interview we conducted in English was our conversation with Arthur Mitchell at his apartment in Manhattan a couple of months before he died. With few exceptions, most interviews with her colleagues and mentees were also conducted in English. However, needless to say, the interviews with her relatives and acquaintances in Cuba were all conducted in Spanish.

7. The literal translation would be "a yogurt." This is a Cuban colloquialism that León used frequently in our conversations in Spanish.

8. Michelle Obama, *Becoming* (New York: Crown, 2018).

9. Tania León, "Polyrhythmia in the Music of Cuba," *Diagonal: An Ibero-American Music Review* 1, no. 2 (2016): 97.

10. For example, my colleagues María de los Angeles Torres and Maria Cristina Garcia, a political scientist and a historian of the Cuban diaspora, respectively, informally told me that many of the affective issues this text touches upon regarding León's specific Cuban-American experience were not topics historians, sociologists, or political theorists pay attention to in a systematic manner regardless of the fact that they are widely shared across the Cuban-American diasporic experience.

11. John Corigliano, interviewed by Zsolt Bognár in "Living the Classical Life," episode 60, accessed August 13, 2019, https://www.youtube.com/watch?v=Z3SCAlg3te8.

12. Dylan Robinson, *Hungry Listening: Resonant Theory for Indigenous Sound Studies* (Minneapolis: University of Minnesota Press, 2020), 144.

13. Ibid.

14. Madrid, *In Search of Julián Carrillo*, 17.

Chapter 1. Tonic

1. Comparsa is a group of singers, dancers, and musicians who participate in carnival celebrations.

2. Tania León, personal interview, Nyack, New York, December 13, 2019.

3. Tania León with Jenny Raymond, Oral History of American Music Archive, Yale University Library, OHV 292 a-e.

4. Tania León, personal interview, Nyack, New York, January 13, 2018.

5. For more about *sociedades de color* in Cuba, see Alejandro de la Fuente, *A Nation for All: Race, Inequality, and Politics in Twentieth-Century Cuba* (Chapel Hill: University of North Carolina Press, 2001); Carmen V. Montejo Arrachea, *Sociedades negras en Cuba, 1878–1960* (Havana: Editorial de Ciencias Sociales, 2004); and Elsa Pignot, "El asociacionismo negro en Cuba: una vía de integración en la sociedad republicana (1920–1960)," *Revista de Indias* 70, no. 250 (2010): 837–862.

6. Tania León, personal interview, Nyack, New York, January 13, 2018.

7. The practice of giving Spanish last names to these workers changed in the 1920s and Chinese last names became more common with newer waves of Chinese immigration

to the island. For more about Chinese coolie labor in Cuba and Cuban-Chinese communities, see Kathleen López, *Chinese Cubans: A Transnational History* (Chapel Hill: University of North Carolina Press, 2013); and Benjamin Nicolas Narvaez, "Chinese Coolies in Cuba and Peru: Race, Labor, and Immigration, 1839–1886" (PhD Dissertation, University of Texas at Austin, 2010).

8. Tania León, personal interview, Nyack, New York, June 9, 2019. León refers to the language as Chinese; most likely it was Cantonese because most of the Chinese who settled in pre-1959 Cuba were from the Guandung province. I would like to thank Maria Cristina Garcia for pointing this out to me.

9. Tania León, personal interview, Nyack, New York, January 13, 2018.

10. For more about Santería, see David H. Brown, *Santería Enthroned: Art, Ritual, and Innovation in an Afro-Cuban Religion*. Chicago: University of Chicago Press, 2003.

11. Tania León, personal interview, Nyack, New York, January 13, 2018.

12. Ibid.

13. Oscar never recognized Juan Gabriel as his legal son and never had a relationship with him. Nevertheless, Juan Gabriel remembers that on one occasion when he and his mother ran into Oscar at a party, his mother introduced him as his father. Apparently, Oscar then took Juan Gabriel to Mamota and introduced him to her as his son. Years later, Juan Gabriel became a second brother to Tania when she and Oscar José met him in the 1980s. Juan Gabriel Amoros, personal interview, Havana, Cuba, March 31, 2018.

14. In 1933, the army secured the resignation of President Gerardo Machado. Over the next few months, Cuba had two presidents, Alberto Herrera Franchi and Carlos Manuel de Céspedes, who were in charge for one day and less than a month, respectively, before the Sergeant's Revolt. For more details about this period see Jules R. Benjamin, "The Machadato and Cuban Nationalism, 1928–1932," *Hispanic American Historical Review* 55, no. 1 (1975): 66–91; and Robert Whitney, "The Architect of the Cuban State: Fulgencio Batista and Populism in Cuba, 1937–1940," *Journal of Latin American Studies* 32, no. 2 (2000): 435–459.

15. See Robert Whitney, *State and Revolution in Cuba: Mass Mobilization and Political Change, 1920–1940* (Chapel Hill: University of North Carolina Press, 2001).

16. See T. J. English, *Havana Nocturne: How the Mob Owned Cuba and Then Lost It to the Revolution* (New York: Harper, 2008).

17. León's younger brother remembers that Compay Segundo (1907–2003)—a Cuban singer and guitarist who achieved wide international recognition in the 2000s, at the end of his life, thanks to Wim Wenders' film *Buena Vista Social Club* (1999), but who was already a celebrity in the traditional Cuban *trova* scene of the 1950s—lived just around the corner. Oscar José León, phone interview, May 16, 2018.

18. See Joseph S. Roucek, "Changes in Cuban Education since Castro," *Phi Delta Kappan* 45, no. 4 (1964): 193–197.

19. Throughout Latin America, people from Spain are often called *gallegos*, regardless of whether they were born in Galicia or a different Spanish province. Marcelino was actually from Asturias.

20. Tania León in Michael Blackwood, *The Sensual Nature of Sound: 4 Composers.* Video Documentary. New York: Michael Blackwood Productions, 2005.

21. Oscar José León, phone interview, May 16, 2018.

22. Tania León, personal interview, Nyack, New York, December 13, 2019.

23. Tania León quoted in Steve Smith, "Introducing the Hildegard Series," National Sawdust Log, accessed July 25, 2019, https://nationalsawdust.org/thelog/2017/10/26/introducing-the-hildegard-series/10/.

24. Josefina Ordieres, phone interview, May 11, 2018.

25. Tania León, personal interview, Nyack, New York, December 13, 2019.

26. Tania León quoted in Ronald De Feo, "Cross-Currents and Polyrhythms: A Conversation with Tania León," *Review: Literature and Arts of the Americas* 34, no. 63 (2001): 27.

27. Tania León quoted in Frank J. Oteri, "Tania León: What It Means to Be An American Composer," *New Music USA*, August 1, 1999, accessed July 18, 2018, https://nmbx.newmusicusa.org/tania-leon-what-it-means-to-be-an-american-composer/2/.

28. For a discussion of the Americanization of Cuban culture, see Louis A. Pérez Jr., *On Becoming Cuban: Identity, Nationality and Culture* (Chapel Hill: University of North Carolina Press, 1999).

29. Tania León, personal interview, Nyack, New York, January 13, 2018.

30. Tania León, personal interview, Nyack, New York, June 1, 2017.

31. Ibid. Batá drums are double-headed percussion instruments used primarily in religious and semi-religious contexts in Yoruba and Santería ceremonies.

32. Regardless of her not being a Santería devotee, the cultural overtones of this religion have been very important in León's life. Composer, improviser, and scholar George Lewis, a friend and colleague of León, remembers that several years ago, after a meeting at Composers Now, she offered him a ride home. He was amused to notice that her license plate had a single word: OLOFI. Olofi, the Ruler of the Earth, is one of three manifestations of the Supreme God in the Yoruba and Santería pantheon. George Lewis, electronic communication, March 29, 2021.

33. Oscar José León, phone interview, May 16, 2018.

34. Ibid.

35. For more about the many songs composed to celebrate the triumph of Castro's revolution, see Robin D. Moore, *Music and Revolution. Cultural Change in Socialist Cuba* (Berkeley: University of California Press, 2006), 58–60.

36. Tania León, personal interview, Nyack, New York, June 1, 2017.

37. Tania León, personal interview, Nyack, New York, June 9, 2019.

38. Oscar José León quoted by Tania León, personal interview, Nyack, New York, January 13, 2018.

39. See Leo Brouwer, "La vanguardia en la música cubana," *Pauta. Cuadernos de Teoría y Crítica Musical* V, no. 17 (1986): 34–38. In the late 1960s, young Cuban composition students like Roberto Valera and José Loyola, acquaintances of León, took advantage of these connections and studied in Poland.

40. Joaquín Rafael Martínez, *Del verde de las palmas al rojo de la traición. Memorias de la revolución de Fidel Castro en Cuba* (Bloomington, IN: Palibrio, 2013), 115–116.

41. One exception was a yearlong period of studies in Rostock, East Germany, in the early 1970s.

42. Tania León quoted in Frank J. Oteri, "Tania León: What It Means to be an American Composer," *New Music USA*, August 1, 1999, accessed July 18, 2018, https://nmbx.newmusicusa.org/tania-leon-what-it-means-to-be-an-american-composer/3/. The details about this source are already included on footnote 27.

43. José Reyes Fortún, *Biobibliografía de Odilio Urfé* (Havana: Ediciones Museo de la Música, 2007), 17–21.

44. Tania León, quoted in Paquito D'Rivera, *My Sax Life: A Memoir* (Evanston, IL: Northwestern University Press, 2005), 74.

45. The Hermanos Saíz Brigade was a youth organization made up of writers and intellectuals that was created in 1965 by UNEAC (*Unión Nacional de Escritores y Artistas de Cuba*, the government-sponsored union of writers and artists), with the goal of promoting the artistic and literary production of young Cuban talent.

46. Federico Smith, "Música y músicos: Las Brigadas 'Hermanos Saíz,'" *Hoy*, April 7, 1965, 5.

47. Quoted by Tania León, personal interview, Nyack, New York, March 25, 2017.

48. José Loyola, personal interview, Havana, Cuba, April 4, 2018.

49. *Fílin* (from the English word "feeling") was a type of Cuban music developed at the intersection of U.S. crooning and the Cuban bolero tradition. It was very popular between the late 1940s and the early 1960s. Some people consider Marta Valdés the last songwriter in the *fílin* tradition. See Guillermo Rodríguez Rivera, *Decirlo todo: Políticas culturales (en la Revolución cubana)* (Havana: Ojalá, 2017), 84; and Guillermo Rodríguez Rivera, "La fiesta cubana, 1959–1972," in *La canción en Cuba a cinco voces*, ed. by María Elena Vinueza and Carmen Souto Anido (Havana: Ojalá, 2017), 250–331.

50. Marta Valdés, personal interview, Havana, Cuba, April 5, 2018.

51. Grupo Teatro Estudio was an iconic theater collective founded in 1958 by, among others, actors Sergio Corrieri (1939–2008), Raquel Revuelta (1925–2004), and Vicente Revuelta (1929–2012). Its mission was to help audiences develop a critical thinking regarding their social position. This critical stance helped the group successfully transition into an experimental and socially committed group during the first decade of the revolution. In the late 1960s, the group developed workshops for peasants in the countryside and became one of the forces behind the so-called Teatro Nuevo, a Latin American artistic movement that emphasized continental political solidarity. The first play produced by the group after the triumph of the revolution, in 1959, was Brecht's *El alma buena de Sechuán*, which became one of the company's signature productions. See Armando Correa, "El teatro cubano de los 80: creación versus oficialidad," *Latin American Theatre Review* 25, no. 2 (1992): 68–69; and Magaly Muguercia, *El teatro cubano en vísperas de la Revolución* (Havana: Letras Cubanas, 1988), 213.

52. Ibid.

53. Tania León, personal interview, Nyack, New York, March 25, 2017.

54. Ibid.

55. Ibid.

56. Rodríguez Rivera, *Decirlo todo*, 85–86.

57. For more about the *Quinquenio gris*, see Jorge Fornet, *El 71. Anatomía de una crisis* (Havana: Letras Cubanas, 2013).

Chapter 2. Modulation and Displacement

1. Matthew Guerrieri, "Fromm Concerts Tinge with Latin," *Boston Globe*, April 20, 2015, accessed online June 5, 2020, https://www.bostonglobe.com/arts/music/2015/04/20/fromm/Y9CeEv8TK1lSHYuyaXV74K/story.html.

2. There is plenty of anecdotal evidence about the programming shift in Cuba that de-emphasized the avant-garde music that the National Symphony Orchestra often played in the 1960s and 1970s in favor of more conventional Western art music repertory. Although this happened throughout the Cuban musical spectrum, it was particularly evident in the programs of the National Symphony Orchestra. In one of the few academic studies about this phenomenon, Nairin Rodríguez Duverger explains that these changes were already evident in the early 1980s due to budget constraints that prevented the hiring of foreign musicians, which adversely affected the level of technical proficiency of the orchestra. Performances of new music were mostly left to isolated special concerts (such as the concert celebrating the twentieth anniversary of the foundation of the orchestra). The situation worsened in the 1990s with the exodus of highly qualified Cuban musicians during the harsh economic depression that followed the collapse of the Soviet Union. Rodríguez Duverger concludes that, by the early 2000s, "the programs of the orchestra privileged traditional aesthetics and left little space for avant-garde or experimental music." See Nairin Rodríguez Duverger, "La Orquesta Sinfónica Nacional de Cuba. Trayectoria artística durante el periodo 1980–2010" (Bachelor's thesis, Instituto Superior de Arte, 2017), 59–60, 118–119.

3. Michael Cooper. "Nearly Fifty Years after Leaving, a Composer Returns to Cuba to Conduct Her Work," *New York Times*, November 1, 2016, section C, 3.

4. Ernesto "Ché" Guevara, "Crear dos, tres . . . muchos Vietnam: Mensaje a los pueblos del mundo a través de la *Tricontinental*," April 16, 1967, accessed June 6, 2020 https://www.marxists.org/espanol/guevara/04_67.htm.

5. Law 989/1961 was passed by the Cuban government on December 6, 1961. The so-called *Ley de Abandono Definitivo* (Law of Definitive Abandonment) identified migration as a treasonous act. It also enabled the state to confiscate the properties of those who left and to discretionally decide whether to authorize their return to the island or not. The law is not specific about the cancellation of citizenship or passports, but that seems to have been a shared experience among the people who left Cuba via the Vuelos de la Libertad. See Nivia Marina Brismat, "La política migratoria cubana: génesis, evolución y efectos en el proceso migratorio insular," in *Cubanos en México. Orígenes, tipologías y trayectorias migratorias (1990–2013)*, ed. Beatriz Bernal (Mexico City: IIJ-UNAM, 2011), 154–155; Armando Navarro Vega, *Cuba, el socialismo y sus éxodos* (Bloomington, IN: Palibrio, 2013), 63–64; and María de los Angeles Torres, "*El Exilio*: National Security Interests and the Origins of the Cuban Exile Enclave," in *Latino/a Thought: Culture, Politics, and Society*, ed. Francisco H. Vázquez (Lanham, MD: Rowman and Littlefield, 2009), 305–326.

6. "Lyndon Opens U.S. to Fleeing Cubans," *Clarion-Ledger*, October 4, 1965, 1.

7. Silvia Pedraza, *Political Disaffection in Cuba's Revolution and Exodus* (Cambridge: Cambridge University Press, 2007), 122.

8. Ibid. For more details about the class and race character of the first two waves of postrevolutionary migration from Cuba, see also Silvia Pedraza-Bailey, "Cuba's Exiles: Portrait of a Refugee Migration," *The International Migration Review* 19, no. 1 (1985): 9–10, 25.

9. Ibid., 23.

10. Tania León, personal interview, Nyack, New York, June 1, 2017.

11. Ibid.

12. Quoted in Oscar José León, phone interview, May 16, 2018.

13. Tania León, personal interview, Nyack, New York, March 25, 2017.

14. Martha Mooke, personal interview, Nyack, New York, April 29, 2018.

15. Ibid.

16. Yordanka León, phone interview, June 1, 2019.

17. Oscar José León, phone interview, May 16, 2018.

18. Paquito D'Rivera, phone interview, May 12, 2018.

19. José Loyola, personal interview, Havana, Cuba, April 4, 2018.

20. Guido López Gavilán, personal interview, Havana, Cuba, April 4, 2018.

21. Maria Cristina Garcia, *Havana, USA: Cuban Exiles and Cuban Americans in South Florida, 1959–1994* (Berkeley: University of California Press, 1997), 201.

22. Leonel Antonio de la Cuesta, "Perfil biográfico," in *Itinerario ideológico. Antología de Lourdes Casal*, ed. María Cristina Herrera and Leonel Antonio de la Cuesta (Miami: Instituto de Estudios Cubanos, 1982), 5–7. For more details about Casal's work and the backlash it generated from the Cuban exile community, see Maria Cristina Garcia, *Havana, USA*, 201–203.

23. Oscar José León, phone interview, May 16, 2018.

24. The fact that these individuals were rendered invisible in Cuba is well known, although scholarly literature about the processes and mechanisms by which this was achieved is not abundant. Antonio Gómez Sotolongo has touched upon these issues in relation to the reception of Julián Orbón and his music in Cuba; see Antonio Gómez Sotolongo, "Tientos y diferencias de la *Guantanamera* compuesta por Julián Orbón. Política cultural de la revolución cubana de 1959," *Cuadernos de Música, Artes Visuales y Artes Escénicas* 2, no. 2 (2006): 146–175.

25. For more about the *Quinquenio gris*, see Jorge Fornet, *El 71. Anatomía de una crisis* (Havana: Letras Cubanas, 2013).

26. Tania León, personal interview, Nyack, New York, June 1, 2017.

27. Guillermo Rodríguez Rivera, *Decirlo todo. Políticas culturales (en la Revolución cubana)* (Havana: Ojalá, 2017), 88. León's entry appears in the English version of the book published in 2004; see Helio Orovio, *Cuban Music from A to Z* (Durham, NC: Duke University Press).

28. Paquito D'Rivera, phone interview, May 12, 2018.

29. Tania León, personal interview, Nyack, New York, March 25, 2017.

30. *Danza Nacional de Cuba* was the name given to the *Conjunto Nacional de Danza Moderna* (currently *Danza Contemporánea de Cuba*) between 1971 and 1987. In 1971, the company's founder, Ramiro Guerra Suárez, was separated from the group, allegedly for creating *Decálogo del apocalipsis* (1971), a choreography that openly criticized the

problems of Cuban society at the time. Known as the Father of Cuban Modern Dance, Guerra Suárez collaborated with modernist and avant-garde composers like Argeliers León, Juan Blanco, and Leo Brouwer in the 1960s.

31. See Suki John, *Contemporary Dance in Cuba:Técnica Cubana as Revolutionary Movement* (Jefferson, NC: McFarland, 2012), 146–51.

32. A *Bembé* is a musical celebration of the Orishas, the deities in the Yoruba and Santería religions. Drumming and its underlying rhythmic patterns are central to the salutations and prayers to specific spiritual beings. For more about Bembé and drumming in Santería celebrations, see Steven Cornelius, "The Convergence of Power: Meaning and Taxonomy of the Musical Instruments of Santería in New York," PhD Dissertation, University of California at Los Angeles, 1989; and Katherine Hagedorn, *Divine Utterances: The Performance of Afro-Cuban Santería* (Washington, DC: Smithsonian Institution Press, 2001).

33. Tania León, Andrea O'Reilly Herrera, ed., *Cuba. Idea of a Nation Displaced* (Albany, NY: State University of New York Press, 2007), 227.

34. Tania León, personal interview, Nyack, New York, March 25, 2017.

35. Tania León quoted in *Cuba. Idea of a Nation Displaced*, 227.

36. Tania León, personal interview, Nyack, New York, June 1, 2017.

37. Adriana Hernandez-Reguant, "Writing the Special Period: An Introduction," in *Cuba in the Special Period: Culture and Ideology in the 1990s*, ed. Adriana Hernandez-Reguant (New York: Palgrave Macmillan, 2009), 1, 4.

38. The Cuban rafter crisis refers to the mass exodus of Cubans leaving their country on makeshift boats between April and October 1994. As a result of the economic collapse during the Special Period, many Cubans began fleeing to the United States on these kinds of rafts in the early 1990s. As a response to the increasing numbers of these attempts and a related protest that took place in in Havana on August 5, 1994, Fidel Castro announced that those who wished to leave the island could do it. Over 33,000 rafters left the island in the five months following the announcement, which also generated a diplomatic crisis between the Cuban and U.S. governments. The Clinton Administration responded with the establishment of the Wet Feet, Dry Feet policy, which allowed Cubans who made it to U.S. soil to remain in the country. For a detailed account of this moment see Holly Ackerman, "The Balsero Phenomenon, 1991–1994," *Cuban Studies* 26, no. (1996): 169–200.

39. Yordanka León, phone interview, June 1, 2019.

40. Ibid. The exit visa was a permit required by the Cuban government from all Cuban citizens who wanted to travel abroad. The requirement was put in place shortly after the Cuban revolution in 1961 and lasted until 2013.

41. For an in-depth analysis of the economic policies implemented by the Cuban government as a result of the Special Period, see Ana Julia Jatar-Hausmann, *The Cuban Way: Capitalism, Communism, and Confrontation* (West Hartford, CT: Kumarian Press, 1999).

42. Sonidos de las Américas, Cuba, accessed July 23, 2018, https://www.american-composers.org/sonidos.htm.

43. José Loyola, personal interview, Havana, Cuba, April 4, 2018.

44. Juan Piñera, personal interview, Havana, Cuba, April 5, 2018.

45. Tania León, personal interview, Nyack, New York, June 1, 2017.

46. Ibid.

47. Greg Sandow, "Tuneful Coexistence," *The Wall Street Journal*, May 27, 1999, accessed online June 5, 2020. https://www.wsj.com/articles/SB927768044144330019.

48. Tania León, personal interview, Nyack, New York, June 1, 2017.

49. Ibid.

50. "Cuba en Sonidos de las Américas," *Boletín Música*, 2 (2000): 50–51.

51. José Loyola, personal interview, Havana, Cuba, April 4, 2018. Zenaida Manfugás, Tania León's former piano teacher in Cuba, requested political asylum in 1974, after participating in the Second Festival of Cuban Art in New York organized by the Centro Cultural Cubano de Nueva York, an organization that León had supported when it first started its activities in 1973. For one of her first jobs in the country, Manfugás was hired as Dance Theatre of Harlem's piano accompanist upon León's recommendation. She died in New Jersey in 2012. See Iván Acosta, "Las cuatro estaciones del Centro Cultural Cubano de Nueva York," *Camino Real* 9, no. 12 (2017): 201, 207.

52. Sandow, "Tuneful Coexistence."

53. Juan Piñera, personal interview, Havana, Cuba, April 5, 2018.

54. When D'Rivera defected, he left his first wife and his son behind in Cuba. Since she was already able to travel back to the island, León established a connection between D'Rivera and his family. She took pictures of D'Rivera's son and brought them back for him to the United States, because he had not been able to take photos of his family with him when he left Cuba. León also invited D'Rivera to play one of his first concerts with an orchestra in the United States, with the Brooklyn Philharmonic Chamber Orchestra under her baton during a Community Concert Series event in Prospect Park on June 23, 1984. Tania León, personal interview, Nyack, New York, June 1, 2017; see also *New York Magazine* 17, no. 26 (1984): 83.

55. Ibid.

56. Leo Brouwer, phone interview, March 19, 2018.

57. Isabelle Hernández, phone interview, March 19, 2018.

58. "Despega en Cuba II Festival de Música de Cámara Leo Brouwer," *Juventud Rebelde*, October 8, 2010, accessed online June 6, 2020, http://www.juventudrebelde.cu/cultura/2010–10–08/despega-en-cuba-ii-festival-de-musica-de-camara-leo-brouwer.

59. Niurka González, personal interview, Havana, Cuba, April 2, 2018.

60. It should be mentioned that dissidents and those who challenge the legitimacy of the Castro regime are still erased regardless of the fact that family trips and the expansion of the internet makes it a more difficult task.

61. Tania León, personal interview, Nyack, New York, June 1, 2017.

62. It is a standard policy in Cuba not to allow Cubans in hotels or other areas where foreign tourists stay.

63. Timothy P. Storhoff, "Beyond the Blockade: An Ethnomusicological Study of the Policies and Aspirations for U.S.-Cuban Musical Interactions," PhD Dissertation, Florida State University, 2014, 130.

64. Tania León, personal interview, Nyack, New York, June 1, 2017.

65. Liliana González Moreno's interview with Tania León, Havana, Cuba, November 22, 2016.

66. Tania León, video of the concert at the Covarrubias Hall, recorded by Liliana González Moreno, Havana, Cuba, November 13, 2016.

67. Tania León, personal interview, Nyack, New York, June 1, 2017.

Chapter 3. Syncopation and Color

1. Michael Cooper, "At a Moment of Racial Tumult, The Little Rock Nine Inspire an Opera," *New York Times*, October 1, 2017, section C, 1.

2. Tania León, personal interview, Nyack, New York, March 17, 2018.

3. Tania León, personal interview, Nyack, New York, June 1, 2018.

4. Alex Antón and Roger E. Hernández, *Cubans in America. A Vibrant History of a People in Exile* (New York: Kensington Books, 2002), 175.

5. Tania León, personal interview, Nyack, New York, June 9, 2019.

6. Leonard Bernstein, the composer of *West Side Story*, and Aaron Copland were the only two U.S. composers León knew when she arrived in the United States.

7. For more about the urban policies and events that led to the radical transformation of the Bronx's landscape in the late 1960s and 1970s, see Nathan Glazer, "The South-Bronx Story: An Extreme Case of Neighborhood Decline," *Policy Studies* 16, no. 2 (1987): 269–276; and Jill Jonnes, *We're Still Here: The Rise, Fall, and Resurrection of the South Bronx* (Boston: Atlantic Monthly Press, 1986).

8. Sara Checa, telephone interview, May 16, 2018.

9. Peter M. Rutkoff and William B. Scott, *New School. A History of The New School for Social Research* (New York: The Free Press, 1986), 130.

10. Tania León, personal interview, Nyack, New York, March 25, 2017.

11. Ibid.

12. NYU was in the process of absorbing the NYCM at this time. It was merged with the Department of Music and Performing Arts Professions at NYU in June 1968. See Alice H. Songe, *American Universities and Colleges: A Dictionary of Name Changes* (Metuchen, NJ: Scarecrow, 1978), 137.

13. "Concerts," *New York Magazine*, April 29, 1969, 20.

14. Today's NYU's Steinhardt School of Culture, Education, and Human Development (New York City).

15. León shared this award with the Hungarian-born architect Victor Schuster.

16. Arthur Mitchell and Tania León, personal interview, New York, June 18, 2018.

17. Tania León, quoted in Jennifer Kelly, *In Her Own Words. Conversations with Composers in the United States* (Urbana: University of Illinois Press, 2013), 129.

18. William Grimes, "Dorothy Maynor, 85, Soprano and Arts School Founder, Dies," *New York Times*, February 24, 1996, section 1, 12.

19. William F. Rogers Jr., "The Establishment of the Harlem School of the Arts," *Black Music Research Journal* 8, no. 2 (1988): 225.

20. Tania León, personal interview, Nyack, New York, March 25, 2017.

21. Ibid.

22. Ibid.

23. "Arthur Mitchell," *Ballet Encyclopedia*, accessed March 9, 2019, www.the-ballet.com/mitchell.php.

24. C. Dale Gadsden, "Arthur Mitchell," in *African American Lives*, ed. by Henry Louis Gates Jr. and Evelyn Brooks Higginbotham (New York: Oxford University Press, 2004), 600.

25. Arthur Mitchell, quoted in James Haskins, *Black Dance in America. A History through Its People* (New York: T.Y. Crowell, 1990), 144.

26. Grimes, "Dorothy Maynor."

27. Arthur Mitchell, personal interview, New York, New York, June 18, 2018.

28. Tania León, personal interview, Nyack, New York, January 17, 2018.

29. Mitchell, personal interview.

30. Gadsden, "Arthur Mitchell," 600.

31. Tania León, personal interview, Nyack, New York, March 17, 2018. The first integrated classical music orchestra in the United States, The Symphony of the New World, had been founded only in 1965 as a response to the Civil Rights Act of 1964 and the Voting Rights Act of 1965. Curiously, the first truly racially integrated orchestra in the country was Machito's Afro-Cubans, which played its first concert in the United States in December 1940.

32. Virginia Johnson, personal interview, New York, New York, March 17, 2018.

33. Mitchell, personal interview.

34. Tania León, telephone conversation, April 24, 2019.

35. Tania León, personal interview, Nyack, New York, January 17, 2018.

36. Yee Sik Wong, "The Art of Accompanying Ballet Technique Classes" (DMA Thesis, University of Iowa, 2011), 24, fn. 51.

37. For a study of how these differences can aesthetically inform the relationship between music and dance, see Stephanie Jordan, "Choreomusical Conversations: Facing a Double Challenge," *Dance Research Journal* 43, no. 1 (2011): 43–64.

38. John Percival, "Classical to Exotic," *The Times*, August 15, 1974, accessed online June 5, 2020, https://archive.org/stream/NewsUK1974UKEnglish/Aug%2015%20 1974%2C%20The%20Times%2C%20%2359166%2C%20UK%20%28en%29_djvu.txt.

39. Virginia Johnson, personal interview.

40. Arthur Mitchell, personal interview.

41. Virginia Johnson, personal interview.

42. Tania León, personal interview, Nyack, New York, June 1, 2017. In our conversations, Tania León often referred to Arthur Mitchell as "Arturo." This familiarity reflects the close bond that they formed through the years.

43. Arthur Mitchell and Tania León, personal interview, New York, New York, June 18, 2018. During the interview both Mitchell and León misremembered the country where this incident took place as Germany. In fact, it happened when the company crossed the Italian-Swiss border.

44. Arthur Mitchell, personal interview.

45. Tania León, personal interview, Nyack, New York, June 9, 2019.

46. Tania León, personal interview, Nyack, New York, June 1, 2017.

47. "Dance Theatre of Harlem to Premiere New Work," *Westport News*, July 18, 1973, 15. The newspaper announced León's new ballet as *Haiku: A Dream for Brown Eyes*; the subtitle was later dropped and today this work is known simply as *Haiku*.

48. Virginia Johnson, personal interview.

49. The score specifies that the work "could be specially adapted to dance performance and theater presentation." See performance instructions in Tania León, *Haiku* (New York: Peer Music, 1974).

50. Clive Barnes, "Dance Theater of Harlem at Home on Broadway," *New York Times,* April 18, 1974, 50.

51. Tania León, personal interview, Nyack, New York, March 17, 2018.

52. Barnes, "Dance Theater of Harlem." With "atavistic brutality," Barnes may have been referring to the hypnotic repetitiveness of the drum rhythm patterns throughout the work.

53. See the documents kept in the 41st Eucharistic Congress Collection at the Catholic Historical Research Center of the Archdiocese of Philadelphia, accessed June 16, 2019, http://chrc-phila.org/faids/41stEucharisticCongress.pdf.

54. "Religion Congress Asks for Mitchell Dance Theatre," *Jet*, 20, no. 18 (1976): 16.

55. A video of the Philadelphia premiere as well as two videos of rehearsals in England are kept at the Performing Arts Research Collections of the New York Public Library. See MGZ1DVD5–1451, MGZ1DVD5–1502, and MGZ1DVD5–1509.

56. Tania León, personal interview, Nyack, New York, June 9, 2019.

57. Arthur Mitchell, personal interview.

58. Elisa de la Roche, *Teatro Hispano! Three Major New York Companies* (New York: Garland, 1995), 40.

59. Zarzuela is a Spanish or Spanish-derived lyric-dramatic genre that alternates a combination of song and speech. In Cuba, zarzuela often resorted to plots about the mulatta woman. For more information about Cuban zarzuela, see Susan Thomas, *Cuban Zarzuela. Performing Race and Gender on Havana's Lyric Stage* (Urbana: University of Illinois Press, 2008).

60. "New Operas and Premieres," *Central Opera Service Bulletin* 28, no. 4 (1988): 4.

61. Ruth Gilbert, comp., "Theater Listings," *New York Magazine* 21, no. 24, June 13, 1988, 87.

62. A recording of "La conga de Maggie Magalita" is available on flutist Néstor Torres' album *Del Caribe, soy!* Naxos, 8.579016, 2017, compact disc.

63. Julie Taymor, cited in Elysa Gardner, "Julie Taymor on the Lasting Legacy of *The Lion King.*" Broadway Direct website, November 6, 2017; accessed July 12, 2019, https://broadwaydirect.com/julie-taymor-lasting-legacy-lion-king/.

64. Tania León, personal interview, Nyack, New York, March 25, 2017.

65. Tania León, personal interview, Nyack, New York, March 17, 2018.

66. She collaborated with Ailey on several projects until his death and continued to work periodically with Judith Jamison (b. 1943), who directed the company after Ailey's passing.

67. Ibid.

68. Ibid.

69. Tania León with Jenny Raymond, Oral History of American Music Archive, Yale University Library, OHV 292 a-e.

70. Tania León, personal interview, Nyack, New York, March 17, 2018.

71. Tania León with Jenny Raymond, Oral History of American Music Archive, Yale University Library, OHV 292 a-e.

72. For more about pidgin languages in the Caribbean, see John M. Lipski, "Spanish-Based Creoles in the Caribbean," in *The Handbook of Pidgin and Creole Studies*, ed. by Silvia Kouwenberg and John Victor Singler (Hoboken, NJ: Wiley-Blackwell, 2008), 543–563; and Maria Grazia Sindoni, "Creole in the Caribbean: How Oral Discourse Creates Cultural Identities," *Journal des Africanistes* 8, nos. 1–2 (2010): 217–236.

73. Tania León with Jenny Raymond, Oral History of American Music Archive, Yale University Library, OHV 292 a-e.

74. Martha Mooke developed a score for the drummers to be able to know what to do at specific moments of the piece during rehearsal. Martha Mooke, personal interview, Nyack, New York, April 29, 2018.

75. "Arthur Mitchell: Harlem's Ballet Trailblazer," Columbia University Libraries, accessed June 19, 2019, https://exhibitions.library.columbia.edu/exhibits/show/mitchell/dance-theatre-of-harlem—compa/timeline.

76. Mitchell, personal interview.

77. Bill Keller, "Harlem Dance Theater Testing South Africa," *New York Times*, September 21, 1992, section C, 11.

78. Nelson Mandela, quoted in J. Brooks Spector, "1962–2007. The First 45 Years," *Report for The Johannesburg Civic Theatre*, September 2007, 19, accessed June 19, 2019, http://www.joburgcitytheatres.com/wp-content/uploads/2017/11/The-First-45-Years.pdf.

79. Keller, "Harlem Dance Theater Testing South Africa."

80. For a report on the discussions generated by Dance Theater of Harlem's visit to South Africa, see Keller, "Harlem Dance Theater Testing South Africa."

81. Tania León with Jenny Raymond, Oral History of American Music Archive, Yale University Library, OHV 292 f-j.

82. Tania León, quoted in Ronald De Feo, "Cross-Currents and Polyrhythms: A Conversation with Tania León," *Review: Literature and Arts of the Americas* 34, no. 63 (2001): 30.

83. Tania León with Jenny Raymond, Oral History of American Music Archive, Yale University Library, OHV 292 f-j.

84. Iva Gilbertová, "Wole Solynka: *A Scourge of Hyacinths*," *Brno Studies in English* 23 (1997): 105–106.

85. Tania León, personal interview, Nyack, New York, June 9, 2019.

86. Ibid.

87. Eulalia Piñero Gil and Cecilia Piñero Gil, "*Scourge of Hyacinths* de Tania León y Wole Solynka: La universalidad del discurso poscolonial," *Revista Canaria de Estudios Ingleses*, no. 35 (1997): 188.

88. Tania León, personal interview, Nyack, New York, March 17, 2018.

89. Tania León quoted in "Scourge of Hyacinths. Oper in zwei Akten," Münchener Biennale, Internationales Festival für neues Musiktheater, accessed June 21, 2019, http://archive.muenchener-biennale.de/en/archive/1994/programm/events/event/detail/scourge-of-hyacinths/. I would like to thank Ekaterina Pirozhenko for her transcription of this text into English.

90. Josephine R. B. Wright, "Art/Classical Music," in *African American Music: An Introduction*, ed. by Mellonee V. Burnim and Portia K. Maultsby (New York: Routledge, 2015 [2006]), 154.

91. Joel Kasow, "Been There, Done That . . ." Culturekiosque, accessed June 21, 2019, http://www.culturekiosque.com/opera/reviews/rhescourge.html.

92. Dawn Upshaw recorded it on *The World So Wide*, Nonesuch, 79245, 1998, compact disc.

93. Tania León, quoted in Anne Lundy, "Conversations with Three Symphonic Conductors: Dennis DeCoteau, Tania Leon, Jon Robinson," *Black Perspective in Music* 16, no. 2 (1988): 219, quoted in Helen Walker-Hill, *From Spirituals to Symphonies. African-American Women Composers and their Music* (Westport, CT: Greenwood Press, 2001), xiii.

94. Mary Watkins, quoted in Helen Walker-Hill, *From Spirituals to Symphonies*, 293.

95. Walker-Hill, *From Spirituals to Symphonies*, xiii.

96. The recently coined neologism "artivist," formed by the union of the words "artist" and "activist," describes the kind of activism through the arts that León was doing in the 1970s and 1980s through her work with the Brooklyn Philharmonic's Community Concert Series (see Chapter 4).

97. Tania León, personal interview, Nyack, New York, June 1, 2017.

98. Tania León, personal interview, Nyack, New York, January 13, 2019.

99. Tania León, personal interview, Nyack, New York, June 1, 2017.

100. Marian Anderson collaborated with León and Dance Theatre of Harlem as the narrator in *Spiritual Suite*. Josephine Baker and the members of the Dance Theatre of Harlem company—including León—met when they participated in the BBC's Royal Variety Show on November 18, 1974. In 1987, León composed *Elegía a Paul Robeson* for violin, cello, and piano.

101. Ibid.

102. Ibid.

103. Martha Mooke, personal interview.

104. Jason Stanyek, phone interview, May 16, 2019.

105. Carol Oja, phone interview, May 22, 2019.

106. Ibid.

107. Wiley Hitchcock, quoted by Ellie Hisama. Ellie Hisama, personal interview, Ithaca, New York, September 30, 2017.

108. Arthur Mitchell, personal interview.

Chapter 4. Direction

1. In 1970, Menotti had established a working relationship with the Juilliard Orchestra, solving a recurring problem for the festival: having to rely on second-rate orchestras formed by musicians from Italy and nearby countries. See Allen Hughes, "The Youthful Passion of Juilliard Abroad," *New York Times*, July 26, 1970, 81.

2. Tania León, personal interview, Nyack, New York, March 17, 2019.

3. Tania León with Jenny Raymond, Oral History of American Music Archive, Yale University Library, OHV 292 a-e.

4. Tania León quoted in Anne Lundy, "Conversations with Three Symphonic Conductors: Dennis DeCoteau, Tania Leon, Jon Robinson," *Black Perspective in Music* 16, no. 2 (1988): 217.

5. James Spinazzola, "Tania León (1943-)," in *Women of Influence in Contemporary Music. Nine American Composers*, ed. by Michael K. Slayton (Lanham, MD: Scarecrow, 2011), 253.

6. Margalit Fox, "Camilla Williams, Barrier-Breaking Opera Star, Dies at 92," *New York Times*, February 2, 2012, section B, 17.

7. Frank Rocca quoted in Rudolf A. Bruil, "Laszlo Halasz (1905–2001)," The Remington Site, accessed June 25, 2019, http://www.soundfountail.org/rem/remhalasz.html.

8. Tania León, personal interview, Nyack, New York, March 17, 2019.

9. The Brooklyn Philharmonic was originally called the Brooklyn Philharmonia.

10. Tania León, personal interview, Nyack, New York, June 9, 2019.

11. Tania León, personal interview, Nyack, New York, March 17, 2019.

12. Tania León, personal interview, Nyack, New York, March 25, 2017.

13. Tania León, personal interview, Nyack, New York, June 9, 2019. ASCAP is one of the leading organizations that protects its members' copyrights and collects royalties by monitoring public performances of their music.

14. Ibid.

15. Ibid.

16. Tania León with Jenny Raymond, Oral History of American Music Archive, Yale University Library, OHV 292 a-e.

17. Tania León quoted in Lundy, "Conversations with Three Symphonic Conductors," 219.

18. Ibid.

19. Tim Page, "Pierre Boulez, Conductor of Bracing Clarity, Dies at 90," *Washington Post*, January 6, 2016, accessed online June 5, 2020, https://www.washingtonpost.com/entertainment/music/pierre-boulez-conductor-of-bracing-clarity-dies-at-90/2016/01/06/b1e9a82e-b474–11e5-a842–0feb51d1d124_story.html.

20. Oleg Caetani, "Stravinsky as Pioneer of a New Conductor Style?" *Archiv für Musikwissenschaft* 73, no. 2 (2016): 83.

21. Tania León in Jennifer Kelly, *In Her Own Words: Conversations with Composers in the United States* (Urbana: University of Illinois Press, 2013), 124.

22. Maurice Edwards, *How Music Grew in Brooklyn. A Biography of the Brooklyn Philharmonic Orchestra* (Lanham, MD: Scarecrow, 2006), 98.

23. Ibid.

24. Tania León quoted in Renée Levine Packer, "Julius Eastman, a Biography," in *Gay Guerrilla: Julius Eastman and His Music*, ed. by Renée Levine Packer and Mary Jane Leach (Rochester, NY: University of Rochester Press, 2015), 48.

25. Tania León with Jenny Raymond, Oral History of American Music Archive, Yale University Library, OHV 292 a-e.

26. Including Bethlehem Lutheran Church, the Billie Holiday Theatre, I.S. (Intermediate School) 391, and P.S. (Public School) 307, among others.

27. Raoul Abdul, "New Music by Black Composers," in *Blacks in Classical Music: A Personal History* (New York: Dodd, Mead, 1977), 67. This review was originally published in the *New York Amsterdam News*.

28. Ryan Dohoney, "A Flexible Musical Identity: Julius Eastman in New York City, 1976–90," in *Gay Guerrilla*, 121–122.

29. It is unclear when and why Eastman and Hakim left or stopped actively collaborating in the programming of the Community Concert Series. Packer states that Eastman left the project voluntarily because, according to León, "he had a lack of tolerance for things he did not like" (see Packer, "Julius Eastman, a Biography," 55 and fn. 148). In a personal conversation, León told me that Hakim's death ended their collaboration. Nevertheless, Hakim died in 1988 and León's heavy hand in curating the series was already evident by the late 1970s.

30. Edwards, *How Music Grew in Brooklyn*, 106.

31. The 1977–1978 series featured three more programs besides Rivers' opera. They were presented at the Billie Holiday Theatre, the Bushwick United Methodist Church, the Harlem Performance Center, and the Hanson Place Methodist Church.

32. The season featured music by Yuji Takahashi (b. 1938), Joyce Solomon Moorman (b. 1946), Jon Gibson (b. 1940), Chou Wen-Chung (b. 1923), Angela Bofill (b. 1964), Gregory Maker (b. ca. 1950), Ulysses Kay (1917–1995), Jalalu-Kalvert Nelson (b. 1951), Dorothy Rudd Moore, Arthur Cunningham, and Talib Rasul Hakim.

33. Raymond Ericson, "Notes: A Conductor from Cuba," *New York Times*, June 22, 1980, section A, 25.

34. Edwards, *How Music Grew in Brooklyn*, 123.

35. For example, she shared the podium with Foss for the second concert of the Music + Series, conducting a program of music by Robert Cornman (1924–2008), Francisco Zumaque, Elliott Carter (1908–2012), Francis Poulenc (1899–1963), Gyorgy Ligeti (1923–2006), and Foss.

36. Maurice Edwards explains that "[w]ith the decline of subscriptions to the Family Series over the past two seasons, it made more sense to subsume [the Community and Family Concert Series] under the Community umbrella, which made them more eligible for support from foundation and government agencies than a more conventional Family Subscription Series would have been by itself"; see Edwards, *How Music Grew in Brooklyn*, 127.

37. Edward Rothstein, "Concert: 2 Theater Pieces by Noel Da Costa," *New York Times*, February 16, 1982, section C, 2.

38. Ibid.

39. The programs were presented at the Prospect Park Shell, Midtown Field, the Cadman Plaza Park, and the John Dewey and Midwood high schools. They included the premiere of *The Secret Circuit* (1982) by Judith Martin (1949–2018), conducted by Ronald Isaac. For this piece, the orchestra collaborated with Martin's own experimental group, the Sonora Ensemble—of which Julius Eastman was a founding member. The orchestra also premiered *The Frog Who Became a Prince* (1982) by Edward Barnes (b. 1958) and *The Monkey Opera* (1982) by Roger Tréfousse (n.d.), with León as conductor, as well as orchestral works by Carlos Rausch (b. 1924) and Alan Hovhaness (1911–2000); see Edwards, *How Music Grew in Brooklyn*, 126–128.

40. The concert was presented at the Freeport High School in Long Island; see Edwards, *How Music Grew in Brooklyn*, 134.

41. These concerts featured music by Carlos Surinach (1915–1997), T. J. Anderson (b. 1928), Jacques Ibert (1890–1962), Francis Schwartz (b. 1940), Scott Joplin (1868–1917), the premiere of *Rigorisms II* (1983) by Diana Greene (n.d.), a collaboration with the Alvin Ailey Repertory Theater to music by Duke Ellington (1899–1974) and Robert Ruggieri (b. 1952), and percussion works by Fay-Ellen Silverman (b. 1947), Max Lifchitz (b. 1948), Michael Udow (b. 1949), Steve Reich (b. 1936), Joel Chadabe (b. 1938), and William Albright (1944–1998); see Edwards, *How Music Grew in Brooklyn*, 140–141.

42. Ibid; the concert was given at Brooklyn's Prospect Park bandshell.

43. It included music by Roberto Sierra (b. 1953), Antonio Fernandez Ros (b. 1961), Pía Sebastiani (1925–2015), José Ardevol (1911–1981), and Heitor Villa-Lobos (1887–1959); see "Music & Dance," *New York Magazine* 18, no. 7 (February 18, 1985): 135.

44. It offered the premiere of *Calendar for Orchestra* (1985) by Taiwanese American child prodigy Wendy Fang Chen (b. 1971), who was only fourteen at the time, as well as works by Lucrecia Roces Kasilag (1918–2008), Takefusa Sasamori (b. 1928), Chou Wen-Chung (b. 1923), and Bainbridge Crist (1883–1969), and transcriptions of traditional Chinese folk tunes; see "Music & Dance," *New York Magazine* 18, no. 11 (March 18, 1985): 105.

45. The last three programs of the season included two concerts presented at the Queens Museum and the Prospect Park Picnic House, which included music by William Foster McDaniel (b. 1940), Adolphus Hailstork, and Noel Da Costa; another celebration of Martin Luther King Day at the Brooklyn Botanical Garden, featuring the Ellen Seeling Jazz Quintet; and a concert of music by women composers at the Freeport High School, including music by Sharon Kanach (b. 1957), Katherine "Tina" Hafemeister (1954–2008), and Linda Bouchard (b. 1957); see Edwards, *How Music Grew in Brooklyn*, 145.

46. Edwards, *How Music Grew in Brooklyn*, 147.

47. Besides her work as curator and conductor, León—along with the Brooklyn Philharmonic's artistic director, Maurice Edwards, and the orchestra's program coordinator, Corrine Coleman—wrote grants to support the series.

48. John Rockwell, "Concert: Five Works by Black Composers," *New York Times*, November 7, 1985, XX. The remaining Community Concerts of the season included: the traditional Martin Luther King celebration, which offered the premieres of *Sonnets on Love, Rosebuds, and Death* (1986) by Dorothy Rudd Moore and Concertino for Alto Sax and Eight Instruments (1986) by William Foster McDaniel; a concert of music by women composers from Brooklyn, featuring the premieres of works by Anna Rubin (b. 1946), Adrienne Torf (b. 1955), and Frankie Mann (b. 1955), and music by Bernadette Speech (b. 1948) and Linda Fisher (b. 1948); there were also four Family and Community concerts. The highlights of these concerts include *Frankenstein!* (1976–1977) by Heinz Karl Gruber (b. 1943), *Permutation Seven* (1981) by León, *The Lonely Loch Ness Monster* (1986) by Natasha Ghent (1933–2006) in collaboration with the Penny Jones and Company Puppets, and Ghanaian Fantasy No. 3 (1986) by Emmanuel Labi (b. 1950); see Edwards, *How Music Grew in Brooklyn*, 156–157.

49. Tania León, personal interview, Nyack, New York, June 9, 2019.

50. Tania León with Jenny Raymond, Oral History of American Music Archive, Yale University Library, OHV 292 f-j.

51. For a discussion about the development of this post–WWII trend in U.S. academia and its repercussions on contemporary "classical" music composition through the 1980s, see Leon Botstein, "Preserving Memory: Felix Galimir in Memoriam (1910–1999)," *Musical Quarterly* 83, no. 3 (1999): 295–300; Joseph N. Straus, "The Myth of Serial 'Tyranny' in the 1950s and 1960s," *Musical Quarterly* 83, no. 3 (1999): 301–343; Anne C. Schreffler, "The Myth of Empirical Historiography: A Response to Joseph N. Straus," *Musical Quarterly* 84, no. 1 (1999): 30–39; and Brian Harker, "Milton Babbitt Encounters Academia (And Vice Versa)," *American Music* 26, no. 3 (2008): 336–377. A more general discussion of these issues in the post–WWII U.S. music composition scene can be found in Chapter 11, "The Political Economy of Composition in the American University, 1965–1985," in Jann Pasler's *Writing through Music, Essays on Music, Culture, and Politics* (New York: Oxford University Press, 2008), 318–362.

52. K. Robert Schwarz, "Is There a Composer in the House? Not Always," *New York Times*, September 1, 1996, section 2, 22.

53. For a deeper look into the relationship between the New York Philharmonic, Meet the Composer, and new music in the years prior to León's selection as Revson Composer Fellow, see William Robin, "Horizon '83, Meet the Composer, and New Romanticism's New Marketplace," *Musical Quarterly* 102, no. 2–3 (2019): 158–199.

54. "New York Philharmonic Appoints Tania León to Position of Revson Composer Fellow." *New York Philharmonic News for Release*, January 21, 1993. Document preserved in Tania León's personal archive.

55. Ibid.

56. Ibid.

57. The event, which took place on May 25–26, 1994, was a success.

58. Tania León, personal interview, Nyack, New York, March 17, 2018.

59. Tania León with Jenny Raymond, Oral History of American Music Archive, Yale University Library, OHV 292 f-j.

60. Ibid. In a highly publicized trial that ran from January 25 to October 2, 1995, O. J. Simpson, a black actor and former football star, was found not guilty of the murders of two white individuals, his ex-wife, Nicole Simpson, and her friend Ron Goldman. The racially charged media affair followed the acquittal, three years earlier, of four white police officers on charges of assault and use of excessive force against Rodney Glen King, a black construction worker. The racial tensions around that verdict led to the 1992 Los Angeles riots. See David Margolick "Jury Clears Simpson in Double Murder; Spellbound Nation Divides on Verdict," *New York Times*, October 4, 1995, section A, 1; and Robert Reinhold, "Cleanup Begins in Los Angeles: Troops Enforce Surreal Calm," *New York Times*, May 3, 1992, section 1, 1.

61. Ibid.

62. Tania León, personal interview, Nyack, New York, March 17, 2018.

63. John Duffy, quoted in K. Robert Schwarz, "Is There a Composer in the House? Not Always."

64. This was despite the problems surrounding its Cuban edition in 1999, explored in detail in Chapter 2.

65. "Music & Dance," *New York Magazine* 21, no. 48 (December 5, 1988) 242. "Kabiosile" is a word of Yoruba origin usually used as a respectful salutation to Shangó, one of the main *Orishas* (deities) in the Yoruba pantheon.

66. The other two composers were Philip Glass (b. 1937) and Lou Harrison (1917–2003).

67. Léon wrote this piece for the Da Capo Chamber Players and dedicated it to her close friend, Joan Tower (b. 1938), on her fiftieth birthday. The title of León's work means "For J from T" (J stands for "Joan," T stands for "Tania"); see Daniel Cariaga, "Philip Glass and Tania Leon Open 1990 Cabrillo Festival," *Los Angeles Times*, July 21, 1990, accessed online June 5, 2020, https://www.latimes.com/archives/la-xpm-1990–07–21-ca-336-story.html.

68. Tania León, personal interview, Nyack, New York, March 17, 2018.

69. Ibid.

70. Thomas Buckner, personal interview. New York, New York, February 4, 2018.

71. Ibid.

72. Tania León, personal interview, Nyack, New York, March 17, 2018.

73. Including Yale University, Princeton University, the Juilliard School, and the State University of New York, among others. American Composers Orchestra. Sonidos de las Américas: Cuba, accessed July 3, 2019, https://www.americancomposers.org/sonidos.htm.

74. Tania León, personal interview, Nyack, New York, March 17, 2018.

75. Besides well-known works by Carlos Chávez, Silvestre Revueltas, Alberto Ginastera (1916–1983), Astor Piazzolla (1921–1992), Heitor Villa-Lobos, and Ernesto Lecuona, the festival introduced U.S. mainstream audiences to recent works, in a wide variety of musical idioms, by composers largely unknown in the country at the time, including Gabriela Ortiz (b. 1964), Ana Lara (b. 1959), Javier Álvarez (b. 1956), Marcela Rodríguez (b. 1951), Arturo Márquez (b. 1950), Beatriz Bilbao (b. 1951), Adina Izarra (b. 1959), Alfredo Rugeles (b. 1949), Diógenes Rivas (b. 1942), Loyda Camacho (b. 1960), Alicia Terzian (b. 1934), Martín Matalón (b. 1958), Mariano Etkin (1943–2016), Alejandro Iglesias-Rossi (b. 1960), María Villanueva (b. 1974), Osvaldo Golijov (b. 1960), Marta Lambertini (1937–2019), Juan Piñera, and Keyla Orozco, among others.

76. Some of the jazz, popular, and folk music performers programmed for the festival include Latin jazz flutist Dave Valentin, *batá* drummer Orlando Ríos, Los Pleneros de la 21, and tango pianist Pablo Ziegler, among others.

77. Alex Ross, "Critic's Notebook: Tuning In to Venezuelan Music and Its Rich Tradition," *New York Times*, December 6, 1994, section C, 16.

78. Michael Redmond, quoted in American Composers Orchestra, Sonidos de las Américas: Cuba, accessed July 3, 2019, https://www.americancomposers.org/sonidos.htm.

79. "Mission Statement" Composers Now, accessed July 4, 2019, https://www.composersnow.org/cn/about/mission/.

80. Tania León, personal interview, Nyack, New York, June 9, 2019.

81. Ibid.

82. Carlos Carrillo, phone interview, May 24, 2019.

83. Tania León, personal interview, Nyack, New York, March 17, 2018.

84. Carol Oja, phone interview, May 22, 2019.

85. Tania León, personal interview, Nyack, New York, March 17, 2018.
86. Carol Oja, phone interview.
87. See Chapter 3.
88. Ellie Hisama, personal interview. Ithaca, New York, September 30, 2017.
89. Jason Stanyek, phone interview, May 16, 2019.
90. Angélica Negrón, phone interview, April 12, 2019.
91. Tania León, personal interview, Nyack, New York, June 9, 2019.
92. Ibid.
93. Polina Nazaykinzkaya, phone interview, May 20, 2019.
94. Tania León, personal interview, Nyack, New York, June 9, 2019.
95. Ibid.
96. Jason Stanyek, phone interview.
97. Carlos Carrillo, phone interview.

Chapter 5. Voice

1. The montuno is the last section in a multi-sectional danzón. It is a syncopated vamp over which soloists usually improvise.
2. Alejandro L. Madrid and Robin D. Moore, *Danzón: Circum-Caribbean Dialogues in Music and Dance* (New York: Oxford University Press, 2013), 231–232.
3. Alejandro L. Madrid, *In Search of Julián Carrillo* (New York: Oxford University Press, 2015), 17.
4. John Corigliano interviewed by Zsolt Bognár in "Living the Classical Life," episode 60, accessed August 13, 2019, https://www.youtube.com/watch?v=Z3SCAlg3te8.
5. Tania León, in James Spinazzola, "Tania León (1943–)," in *Women of Influence in Contemporary Music. Nine Composers*, ed. by Michael K. Slayton (Lanham, MD: Scarecrow, 2011), 268.
6. Tania León, in Robert Raines, *Composition in the Digital World: Conversations with 21st Century American Composers* (New York: Oxford University Press, 2015), 191.
7. Tania León, in Spinazzola, "Tania León (1943–)," 268.
8. Tania León, in Robert Raines, *Composition in the Digital World*, 191.
9. Tania León, in Spinazzola, "Tania León (1943–)," 268.
10. Ibid., 269.
11. Tania León, in Robert Raines, *Composition in the Digital World*, 191.
12. *Ibid.*, 191–192.
13. Tania León, in *The Sensual Nature of Sound: 4 Composers*, directed by Michael Blackwood (New York: Michael Blackwood Productions, 2005), video documentary.
14. Tania León, telephone conversation, April 24, 2019.
15. Tania León, personal interview, Nyack, New York, March 17, 2018.
16. Tania León, electronic communication, June 11, 2019. Guajira music refers to *punto cubano*, the peasant music traditions of Andalusian and Canary origins from the Cuban countryside.
17. Quoted in Tania León, personal interview, Nyack, New York, March 25, 2017.
18. See Chapter 3.

19. Tania León and Alejandro L. Madrid, conversation, Nyack, New York, February 22, 2019.

20. There is no commercial recording of this ballet. However, a video of a performance of *Tones* at the Sadler's Wells Theatre in London on August 13, 1974, is available at the New York Public Library, *MGZIDVD 5–1458.

21. This section summarizes my electronic conversation with Sergio Cote-Barco, May 30, 2019.

22. Read more about this in the final section of Chapter 4.

23. Tania León, personal interview, Nyack, New York, March 25, 2017.

24. The main voice was that of David Gagné, a composer and pianist who also worked for Dance Theatre of Harlem at the time. He is currently a music-theory professor at Queens College.

25. Tania León and Alejandro L. Madrid, Nyack, New York, June 9, 2019.

26. This section is a summary of my conversation with Sergio Cote-Barco, Ithaca, New York, May 13, 2019.

27. Tom Johnson, "Music for Planet Earth," *The Village Voice* (January 4, 1973); reprinted in Tom Johnson, *The Voice of New Music. New York City 1972–1982. A Collection of Articles Originally Published in* The Village Voice (Eindhoven: Het Apollohuis, 1989), 35.

28. Tania León, quoted in K. Robert Schwartz, "Notes," *Tania León. Indígena*, CRI NWRCR662, 1994, compact disc.

29. See Chapter 2.

30. Tania León, quoted in K. Robert Schwartz, "Notes."

31. Spinazzola, "Tania León (1943–)," 266.

32. Kendra Preston Leonard, "Review," *Notes* 57, no. 3 (2001): 758.

33. Spinazzola, "Tania León (1943–)," 266.

34. Leonard, "Review," 758.

35. Spinazzola, "Tania León (1943–)," 266.

36. The son clave is the repeated basic timeline underlying and structuring son music, the traditional music from the highlands of Eastern Cuba.

37. Tania León and Alejandro L. Madrid, Nyack, New York, February 22, 2019.

38. Hemiola refers to a rhythmic figure in which the grouping of six beats counted in two groups momentarily changes to three groups of two. This feature is typical of many Latin American folk music styles that have a heavy Spanish influence.

39. This section is a summary of my electronic conversation with Sergio Cote-Barco, May 30, 2019.

40. Jason Stanyek, liner notes, in *Tania León, Singin' Sepia*, Bridge, 9231, 2008, compact disc.

41. Tania León, "Program Note," in *Batá* (New York: Peermusic, 1996).

42. Marc Gidal, "Latin American Composers of Art Music in the United States: Cosmopolitans Navigating Multiculturalism and Universalism," *Latin American Music Review* 31, no. 1 (2010): 53.

43. Tania León, "Program Note," in *Batá*.

44. This joke is a reference to Tania's father abandoning his family. See Chapter 1 for the details about León's relationship with her father when she was a child.

45. Tania León and Alejandro L. Madrid, Nyack, New York, June 9, 2019.

46. This section is a summary of my conversation with Sergio Cote-Barco. Ithaca, New York, May 13, 2019.

47. Tania León, quoted in Mary Ellyn Hutton, "There's No Labeling Composer and Conductor Tania Leon," *Cincinnati Post*, January 13, 1992, accessed online June 5, 2020, http://www.musicincincinnati.com/site/archives/There_s_No_Labeling_Composer_ and_Conductor_Tania_Leon.html.

48. Janelle Gelfand, "CSO Unleashes Powerful 'Carabali,'" *Cincinnati Enquirer*, January 18, 1992, section B, 4.

49. See Chapter 3.

50. Tania León and Alejandro L. Madrid, Nyack, New York, June 9, 2019.

51. This section is a summary of my electronic conversation with Sergio Cote-Barco, May 23, 2019.

52. Gidal, "Latin American Composers of Art Music," 53. Borrowing the term from cultural theorist Hohmi Bhaba, Gidal offers "vernacular cosmopolitism" as a concept to describe how the music of composers like Tania León "emphasize[s . . .] local and global affiliations, transnational mobility, and a relationship to elite culture" (53).

53. See Chapter 2.

54. Ronald De Feo, "Cross-Currents and Polyrhythms: A Conversation with Tania León," *Review: Literature and Arts of the Americas* 34, no. 63 (2001): 28.

55. The comparsa song quoted in *Indígena* is "La jardinera" ["The female gardener"].

56. Tania León and Alejandro L. Madrid, Nyack, New York, June 9, 2019.

57. This section is a summary of my conversation with Sergio Cote-Barco, Ithaca, New York, May 13, 2019.

58. James Spinazzola, "An Introduction to the Music of Tania León and a Conductor's Analysis of *Indígena*" (DMA thesis, Louisiana State University, 2006), 41.

59. Kevin Salfen, "Placing Tania León, *Indígena* of the In-Between," Sound Trove: Adventures in the Listening Library at UIW, accessed July 17, 2019, https://soundtrove. blog/2018/01/02/placing-tania-leon-indigena-of-the-in-between/.

60. De Feo, "Cross-Currents and Polyrhythms," 30.

61. Tania León, quoted in Spinazzola, "Tania León," 269.

62. Tania León and Alejandro L. Madrid, Nyack, New York, June 9, 2019.

63. See Spinazzola, "Tania León (1943-)," 269–270.

64. This section is a summary of my electronic conversation with Sergio Cote-Barco, May 23, 2019.

65. Stanyek, liner notes in *Tania León, Singin' Sepia*.

66. Will Robin, "A Composer Puts Her Life in Music, Beyond Labels," *New York Times*, February 7, 2020, section AR, 11.

67. Mari Kimura, personal interview. New York, New York, March 28, 2019.

68. Ibid.

69. Subharmonics or undertones are harmonics below the fundamental note of a given overtone series. The production of subharmonics as an extended technique on

the violin owes much to the work of Mari Kimura, who introduced them as a way to expand the violin range an octave below its open G string. See Mari Kimura, "How to Produce Subharmonics on the Violin," *Journal of New Music Research* 28, no. 2 (1999): 178–184.

70. Tania León and Alejandro L. Madrid, Nyack, New York, June 9, 2019.

71. This section is a summary of my electronic conversation with Sergio Cote-Barco, Ithaca, New York, May 13, 2019.

72. Stanyek, liner notes in *Tania León, Singin' Sepia*.

Chapter 6. Canon

1. The Dream Unfinished. An Activist Orchestra, accessed July 25, 2019, http://the dreamunfinished.org/story.

2. From the program notes of "The Dream Unfinished: Activist Orchestra," Lincoln Center's Boro-Linc 2018 with the Hostos Center for the Arts and Culture (April 18, 2018).

3. "I Am in Constant Transit!" Dream Unfinished, accessed July 25, 2019, http://thedreamunfinished.org/events/2018/4/28/i-am-in-constant-transit.

4. Eun Lee, personal interview. New York City, April 18, 2018.

5. *Notable Americans of 1976–77* (Raleigh, NC: American Biographical Institute, 1977), 383.

6. Raoul Abdul, *Blacks in Classical Music. A Personal History* (New York: Dodd, Mead, 1977), 67.

7. Anne Lundy, "Conversations with Three Symphonic Conductors: Dennis DeCoteau, Tania Leon, Jon Robinson," *Black Perspective in Music* 16, no. 2 (1988): 213.

8. Ibid., 217, 219, 225.

9. Ibid., 219.

10. Edwards mis-states León's birth year.

11. J. Michele Edwards, with contributions by Leslie Lassetter, "North America since 1920," in *Women & Music: A History*, ed. by Karin Pendle (Bloomington: Indiana University Press, 1991), 250.

12. Ibid., 372.

13. Including Florence Smith Price, Undine Smith Moore, Evelyn Pittman, Margaret Bonds, Julia Perry, Lena McLin, and Mary Rudd Moore; Anne Gray, *The Popular Guide to Classical Music* (New York: Birch Lane Press, 1993), 163–165.

14. Anne Gray, *The World of Women in Classical Music* (La Jolla, CA: WordWorld, 2007), 212.

15. James R. Briscoe, *Contemporary Anthology of Music by Women* (Bloomington: Indiana University Press, 1997), 155–163; and Orlando Jacinto García, "León, Tania (1944-)," in *Women in Music in America. An Encyclopedia*, Vol. 2, L-Z, ed. by Kristine H. Burns (Westport, CT: Greenwood Press, 2002), 374–376.

16. Joseph Kerman, *Listen*, 3rd brief edition (New York: Worth, 1996), 350–352.

17. See also Joseph Kerman and Gary Tomlinson, *Listen*, 4th brief edition (Boston: Bedford/St. Martins, 2000), 372; and Joseph Kerman and Gary Tomlinson, *Listen*, 8th edition (Boston: Bedford/St. Martins, 2015), 375–377.

18. Roger Kamien, *Music. An Appreciation*, 4th brief edition (New York: McGraw-Hill, 2002), 295. The twelfth edition of Kamien's book includes a detailed analysis of León's *Inura*; see Kamien, *Music. An Appreciation*, 12th edition (New York: McGraw-Hill, 2018), 474–475.

19. See Chapter 3 for my discussion of this book in relation to the polemic generated after León refused to be part of it; Helen Walker-Hill, *From Spirituals to Symphonies. African-American Women Composers and Their Music* (Westport, CT: Greenwood Press, 2002).

20. Adeline Mueller, "The Twentieth Century," in *From Convent to Concert Hall. A Guide to Women Composers*, ed. by Sylvia Glickman and Martha Furman Schleifer (Westport, CT: Greenwood Press, 2003), 286–287; and Pilar Ramos López, *Feminismo y música. Introducción crítica* (Madrid: Narcea, 2003), 59, 78.

21. Mark Evan Bonds, *A History of Music in Western Culture* (Upper Saddle River, NJ: Prentice Hall, 2003), 588.

22. Josephine R. B. Wright, "African-American Concert Music in the Twentieth Century," in *Music Cultures in the United States. An Introduction*, ed. by Ellen Koskoff (Routledge: New York, 2005), 318–322.

23. Adelaida Reyes, *Music in America* (New York: Oxford University Press, 2005), 26–27.

24. Josephine R. B. Wright, "Art/Classical Music: Chronological Overview," in *African American Music. An Introduction*, ed. by Mellonee V. Burnim and Portia K. Maultsby (New York: Routledge, 2006), 227.

25. James Spinazzola, "Tania León (1943-)," in *Women of Influence in Contemporary Music. Nine American Composers*, ed. by Michael K. Slayton (Lanham, MD: Scarecrow, 2011), 251–298.

26. María Elena Mendiola, "Dar vida a los sueños, que no es lo mismo que soñar," in *Afrocubanas. Historia, pensamiento y prácticas culturales*, ed. by Daisy Rubiera Castillo and Inés María Martiatu Terry (Havana: Editorial de Ciencias Sociales, 2011), 318.

27. Walter Aaron Clark, "Latin American Impact on Contemporary Classical Music," in *Musics of Latin America*, ed. by Robin Moore and Walter Clark (New York: W.W. Norton, 2012), 377.

28. Ibid., 380–382.

29. I understand that it is not Clark's intention to deal with any of these issues in his text. However, given how the framework in his chapter reverberates with issues of Latinx and Latin American identification, taking them into consideration would have enriched his text.

30. Tania León with Jenny Raymond, Oral History of American Music Archive, Yale University Library, OHV 292 a-e.

31. León's statements against labels can be found in Jennifer Kelly, *In Her Own Words. Conversations with Composers in the United States* (Urbana: University of Illinois Press, 2013); 130–131; Robert Raines, *Composition in the Digital World: Conversations with 21st Century American Composers* (New York: Oxford University Press, 2015), 198–199; Iraida Iturralde, "In Search of the Palm Tree: An Afternoon with Tania León," in *Cuba: Idea of a Nation Displaced*, ed. by Andrea O'Reilly Herrera (Albany, NY: State University of New York Press, 2007), 228, 230; Lundy, "Conversations with Three Symphonic

Conductors," 119; Spinazzola, "Tania León (1943–)," 256; and Tania León with Jenny Raymond, Oral History 292 a-e; among others.

32. León and Raymond, Oral History of American Music Archive, Yale University Library, OHV 292 a-e.

33. Ibid.

34. Alejandro L. Madrid and Robin D. Moore, *Danzón: Circum-Caribbean Dialogues in Music and Dance* (New York: Oxford University Press, 2013), 9.

35. Gidal borrows the term "vernacular cosmopolitanism" from anthropologist Pnina Werbner; see Marc Gidal, "Contemporary 'Latin American' Composers of Art Music in the United States: Cosmopolitans Navigating Multiculturalism and Universalism," *Latin American Music Review* 31, no. 1, (2010): 46.

36. Gidal, "Contemporary 'Latin American' Composers," 51–52.

37. See Chapter 2.

38. Gidal, "Contemporary 'Latin American' Composers," 53–54.

39. Paul Gilroy, *Against Race. Imagining Political Culture beyond the Color Line* (Cambridge: Harvard University Press, 2000), 125. For a reading of Gilroy's project in relation to a critique of identity politics, see Alejandro L. Madrid, "Listening from 'The Other Side': Music, Border Studies and The Limits of Identity Politics," in *Decentering the Nation. Music, Mexicanidad, and Globalization*, ed. by Jesús Ramos-Kittrell (Lanham, MD: Lexington Books, 2020).

40. Tania León quoted in Frank J. Oteri, "Tania León: What It Means to Be an American Composer," *New Music USA*, August 1, 1999, accessed August 12, 2019, https://nmbx.newmusicusa.org/tania-leon-what-it-means-to-be-an-american-composer/2/.

41. Edmund S. Morgan, "Slavery and Freedom: The American Paradox," *Journal of American History* 59, no. 1 (1972): 5–6.

42. Mendiola, "Dar vida a los sueños," 318.

43. "Legacy," Merriam-Webster Dictionary, accessed July 25, 2019, https://www.merriam-webster.com/dictionary/legacy.

44. Arthur Mitchell, personal interview. New York, New York, June 18, 2018.

45. Frantz Fanon, *The Wretched of the Earth*, trans. by Richard Philcox (New York: Grove Press: 2004 [1961]), 8.

46. Chela Sandoval defines love as hermeneutics of social change, "as a set of practices and procedures that can transit all citizens-subjects, regardless of social class, toward a differential mode of consciousness and its accompanying technologies of method and social movement. . . . This form of love is not the narrative of love as encoded in the West: it is another kind of love, a synchronic process that punctures through traditional, older narratives of love, that ruptures everyday being." See Chela Sandoval, *Methodology of the Oppressed* (Minneapolis: University of Minnesota Press, 2000), 139, 141.

47. Ibid., 139.

Epilogue

1. Tania León, words to the New York Philharmonic audience before the premiere of *Stride*, February 13, 2020.

2. William Robin, "A Composer Puts Her Life in Music, Beyond Labels," *New York Times*, February 7, 2020, section AR, 11.

3. "Tania León Talks about 'Stride' and Project 19," Peermusic Classical YouTube Channel, accessed May 22, 2020, https://www.youtube.com/watch?v=YNKyo_a5rNI.

4. "Tania León on Her Project 19 Commission, 'Stride,'" New York Philharmonic YouTube Channel, accessed May 22, 2020, https://www.youtube.com/watch?v=Eeeo5KscL_M.

5. On June 11, 2021, Tania León received the 2021 Pulitzer Prize in Music for *Stride*.

Bibliography

Abdul, Raoul. *Blacks in Classical Music. A Personal History.* New York: Dodd, Mead & Company, 1977.

Ackerman, Holly. "The Balsero Phenomenon, 1991–1994." *Cuban Studies* 26, no. (1996): 169–200.

Acosta, Iván. "La cuatro estaciones del Centro Cultural Cubano de Nueva York." *Camino Real* 9, no. 12 (2017): 201–216.

Angier, Carole. *The Double Bond: Primo Levi, A Biography.* New York: Farrar, Straus, and Giroux, 2002.

Antón, Alex, and Roger E. Hernández. *Cubans in America. A Vibrant History of a People in Exile.* New York: Kensington Books, 2002.

Ballesteros, Antonio, and Lucía Mora, eds. *Popular Texts in English: New Perspectives.* Cuenca: Ediciones de la Universidad de Castilla-La Mancha, 2001.

Benjamin, Jules R. "The Machadato and Cuban Nationalism, 1928–1932." *Hispanic American Historical Review* 55, no. 1 (1975): 66–91.

Bernal, Beatriz, ed. *Cubanos en México. Orígenes, tipologías y trayectorias migratorias (1990–2013).* Mexico City: IIJ-UNAM, 2011.

Bonds, Mark Evan. *A History of Music in Western Culture.* Upper Saddle River, NJ: Prentice Hall, 2003.

Botstein, Leon. "Preserving Memory: Felix Galimir in Memoriam (1910–1999)." *Musical Quarterly* 83, no. 3 (1999): 295–300.

Briscoe, James R. *Contemporary Anthology of Music by Women.* Bloomington: Indiana University Press, 1997.

Brismat, Nivia Marina. "La política migratoria cubana: génesis, evolución y efectos en el proceso migratorio insular," in *Cubanos en México. Orígenes, tipologías y trayectorias migratorias (1990–2013),* ed. by Beatriz Bernal, 149–179. Mexico City: IIJ-UNAM, 2011.

Brouwer, Leo. "La vanguardia en la música cubana." *Pauta. Cuadernos de Teoría y Crítica Musical* 5, no. 17 (1986): 34–38.

Brown, David H. *Santería Enthroned: Art, Ritual, and Innovation in an Afro-Cuban Religion.* Chicago: University of Chicago Press, 2003.

Burnim, Mellonee V., and Portia K. Maultsby, eds. *African American Music. An Introduction.* New York: Routledge, 2006.

Burns, Kristine H., ed. *Women in Music in America. An Encyclopedia*, Volume 2, L–Z. Westport, CT: Greenwood Press, 2002.

Caetani, Oleg. "Stravinsky as Pioneer of a New Conductor Style?" *Archiv für Musikwissenschaft* 73, no. 2 (2016): 82–90.

Clark, Walter Aaron. "Latin American Impact on Contemporary Classical Music," in *Musics of Latin America*, ed. by Robin Moore and Walter Aaron Clark, 371–396. New York: W. W. Norton, 2012.

Cornelius, Steven. "The Convergence of Power: Meaning and Taxonomy of the Musical Instruments of Santería in New York." PhD Dissertation, University of California at Los Angeles (1989).

Correa, Armando. "El teatro cubano de los 80: creación versus oficialidad." *Latin American Theatre Review* 25, no. 2 (1992): 67–77.

Croft, Clare. *Dancers as Diplomats. American Choreography in Cultural Exchange.* New York: Oxford University Press, 2015.

De Feo, Ronald. "Cross-Currents and Polyrhythms: A Conversation with Tania León." *Review: Literature and Arts of the Americas* 34, no. 63 (2001): 23–30.

de la Cuesta, Leonel Antonio. "Perfil biográfico," en *Itinerario ideológico. Antología de Lourdes Casal*, ed. by María Cristina Herrera and Leonel Antonio de la Cuesta, 3–8. Miami: Instituto de Estudios Cubanos, 1982.

de la Fuente, Alejandro. *A Nation for All. Race, Inequality, and Politics in Twentieth-Century Cuba.* Chapel Hill: The University of North Carolina Press, 2001.

de la Roche, Elisa. *Teatro Hispano! Three Major New York Companies.* New York: Garland, 1995.

Dohoney, Ryan. "A Flexible Musical Identity: Julius Eastman in New York City, 1976–90," in *Gay Guerrilla: Julius Eastman and His Music*, ed. by Renée Levine Packer and Mary Jane Leach, 116–130. Rochester, NY: University of Rochester Press, 2015.

D'Rivera, Paquito. *My Sax Life. A Memoir.* Evanston, IL: Northwestern University Press, 2005.

Edwards, J. Michele, with contributions by Leslie Lassetter. "North America since 1920," in *Women & Music. A History*, ed. by Karin Pendle, 211–257. Bloomington: Indiana University Press, 1991.

Edwards, J. Michele, with contributions by Leslie Lassetter, "North America since 1920," in *Women & Music: A History*, 2nd edition, ed. by Karin Pendle, 314–386. Bloomington: Indiana University Press, 2001.

Edwards, Maurice. *How Music Grew in Brooklyn. Biography of the Brooklyn Philharmonic Orchestra.* Lanham, MD: Scarecrow Press, 2006.

Eli Rodríguez, Victoria, and Elena Torres Clemente, eds. *Música y construcción de identidades: poéticas, diálogos y utopias en Latinoamérica y España.* Madrid: Sociedad Española de Musicología, 2018.

English, T. J. *Havana Nocturne: How the Mob Owned Cuba and Then Lost It to the Revolution.* New York: Harper, 2008.

Fanon, Frantz. *The Wretched of the Earth*, trans. by Richard Philcox. New York: Grove Press, 2004 [1961].

Fornet, Jorge. *El 71. Anatomía de una crisis.* Havana: Letras Cubanas, 2013.

Gadsden, C. Dale. "Arthur Mitchell," in *African American Lives*, ed. by Henry Louis Gates Jr. and Evelyn Brooks Higginbotham, 599–600. New York: Oxford University Press, 2004.

Galloway, Janice. *Clara: A Novel.* New York: Simon and Schuster, 2002.

Garcia, Maria Cristina. *Havana, USA: Cuban Exiles and Cuban Americans in South Florida, 1959–1994.* Berkeley: University of California Press, 1997.

García, Orlando Jacinto. "León, Tania (1944-)," in *Women in Music in America. An Encyclopedia*, Volume 2, L-Z, ed. by Kristine H. Burns, 374–376. Westport, CT: Greenwood Press, 2002.

Gates Jr., Henry Louis, and Evelyn Brooks Higginbotham, eds. *African American Lives.* New York: Oxford University Press, 2004.

Gidal, Marc. "Contemporary 'Latin American' Composers of Art Music in the United States: Cosmopolitans Navigating Multiculturalism and Universalism." *Latin American Music Review* 31, no. 1 (2010): 40–78.

Gilbertová, Iva. "Wole Solynka: *A Scourge of Hyacinths.*" *Brno Studies in English* 23 (1997): 105–114.

Gilroy, Paul. *Against Race. Imagining Political Culture beyond the Color Line.* Cambridge: Harvard University Press, 2000.

Glazer, Nathan. "The South-Bronx Story: An Extreme Case of Neighborhood Decline." *Policy Studies Journal* 16, no. 2 (1987): 269–276.

Glickman, Sylvia, and Martha Furman Schleifer, eds. *From Convent to Concert Hall. A Guide to Women Composers.* Westport, CT: Greenwood Press, 2003.

Gómez Sotolongo, Antonio. "Tientos y diferencias de la *Guantanamera* compuesta por Julián Orbón. Política cultural de la revolución cubana de 1959." *Cuadernos de Música, Artes Visuales y Artes Escénicas* 2, no. 2 (2006): 146–175.

Gorusch, Anne E., and Diane P. Kroenker, eds. *The Socialist Sixties: Crossing Borders in the Second World.* Bloomington: Indiana University Press, 2013.

Gray, Anne. *The Popular Guide to Classical Music.* New York: Birch Lane Press, 1993.

Gray, Anne K. *The World of Women in Classical Music.* La Jolla, CA: WordWorld, 2007.

Guevara, Ernesto "Ché." "Crear dos, tres . . . muchos Vietnam: Mensaje a los pueblos del mundo a través de la *Tricontinental*," April 16, 1967. https://www.marxists.org/espanol/guevara/04_67.htm.

Guilbault, Jocelyne, and Roy Cape, *Roy Cape. A Life on the Calypso and Soca Bandstand.* Durham, NC: Duke University Press, 2014.

Hagedorn, Katherine. *Divine Utterances: The Performance of Afro-Cuban Santería.* Washington, DC: Smithsonian Institution Press, 2001.

Harker, Brian. "Milton Babbitt Encounters Academia (And Vice Versa)." *American Music* 26, no. 3 (2008): 336–377.

Haskins, James. *Black Dance in America. A History through Its People.* New York: T. Y. Crowell, 1990.

Hernandez-Reguant, Adriana. "Writing the Special Period: An Introduction," in *Cuba in the Special Period: Culture and Ideology in the 1990s*, ed. by Adriana Hernandez-Reguant, 1–20. New York: Palgrave Macmillan, 2009.

Hernandez-Reguant, Adriana, ed. *Cuba in the Special Period: Culture and Ideology in the 1990s*. New York: Palgrave Macmillan, 2009.

Herrera, María Cristina, and Leonel Antonio de la Cuesta, eds. *Itinerario ideológico. Antología de Lourdes Casal*. Miami: Instituto de Estudios Cubanos, 1982.

Hess, Carol A. *Experiencing Latin American Music*. Oakland: University of California Press, 2018.

Iturralde, Iraida. "In Search of the Palm Tree: An Afternoon with Tania León," in *Cuba. Idea of a Nation Displaced*, ed. by Andrea O'Reilly Herrera, 223–234. Albany: State University of New York Press, 2007.

Jatar-Hausmann, Ana Julia. *The Cuban Way: Capitalism, Communism, and Confrontation*. West Hartford, CT: Kumarian Press, 1999.

John, Suki. *Contemporary Dance in Cuba*. Técnica Cubana *as Revolutionary Movement*. Jefferson, NC: McFarland and Company, 2012.

Johnson, Tom. *The Voice of New Music. New York City 1972–1982. A Collection of Articles Originally Published in* The Village Voice. Eindhoven, The Netherlands: Het Apollohuis, 1989.

Jonnes, Jill. *We're Still Here: The Rise, Fall, and Resurrection of the South Bronx*. Boston: Atlantic Monthly Press, 1986.

Jordan, Stephanie. "Choreomusical Conversations: Facing a Double Challenge." *Dance Research Journal* 43, no. 1 (2011): 43–64.

Kamien, Roger. *Music. An Appreciation*, fourth brief edition. New York: McGraw-Hill, 2002.

Kamien, Roger. *Music. An Appreciation*, twelfth edition. New York: McGraw-Hill, 2019.

Kelly, Jennifer. *In Her Own Words. Conversations with Composers in the United States*. Urbana: University of Illinois Press, 2013.

Kerman, Joseph. *Listen*, third brief edition. New York: Worth Publishers, 1996.

Kerman, Joseph, and Gary Tomlinson. *Listen*, fourth brief edition. Boston: Bedford/ St. Martins, 2000.

Kerman, Joseph, and Gary Tomlinson. *Listen*, eighth edition. Boston: Bedford/St. Martins, 2015.

Kimura, Mari. "How to Produce Subharmonics on the Violin." *Journal of New Music Research* 28, no. 2 (1999): 178–184.

Koskoff, Ellen, ed. *Music Cultures in the United States. An Introduction*.New York: Routledge, 2005.

Kouwenberg, Silvia, and John Victor Singler, eds. *The Handbook of Pidgin and Creole Studies*, ed. by Silvia Kouwenberg and John Victor Singler. Hoboken, NJ: Wiley-Blackwell, 2008.

León, Tania. "Polyrhythmia in the Music of Cuba." *Diagonal: An Ibero-American Music Review* 1, no. 2 (2016): 82–99.

Leonard, Kendra Preston. "Review." *Notes* 57, no. 3 (2001): 757–759.

Lieblich, Amia. *Conversations with Dvora: An Experimental Biography of the First Modern Hebrew Writer*. Berkeley: University of California Press, 1997.

Lipski, John M. "Spanish-Based Creoles in the Caribbean," in *The Handbook of Pidgin and Creole Studies*, ed. by Silvia Kouwenberg and John Victor Singler, 543–563. Hoboken, NJ: Wiley-Blackwell, 2008.

López, Antonio. *Unbecoming Blackness. The Diaspora Cultures of Afro-Cuban America*. New York: New York University Press, 2012.

López, Kathleen. *Chinese Cubans: A Transnational History*. Chapel Hill: The University of North Carolina Press, 2013.

Loss, Jaqueline. *Dreaming in Russian. The Cuban-Soviet Imaginary*. Austin: University of Texas Press, 2013.

Luke, Anne. "Listening to *los Beatles*. Being Young in 1960s Cuba," in *The Socialist Sixties: Crossing Borders in the Second World*, ed. by Anne E. Gorusch and Diane P. Kroenker, 287–302. Bloomington: Indiana University Press, 2013.

Lundy, Anne. "Conversations with Three Symphonic Conductors: Dennis DeCoteau, Tania Leon, Jon Robinson." *Black Perspective in Music* 16. no. 2 (1988): 213–226.

Madrid, Alejandro L. *In Search of Julián Carrillo and Sonido 13*. New York: Oxford University Press, 2015.

Madrid, Alejandro L. "Listening from 'The Other Side': Music, Border Studies and The Limits of Identity Politics," in *Decentering the Nation. Music, Mexicanidad, and Globalization*, ed. by Jesús Ramos-Kittrell. Lanham, MD: Lexington Books, 2020.

Madrid, Alejandro L., and Robin D. Moore. *Danzón: Circum-Caribbean Dialogues in Music and Dance*. New York: Oxford University Press, 2013.

Martínez, Joaquín Rafael. *Del verde de las palmas al rojo de la traición. Memorias de la revolución de Fidel Castro en Cuba*. Bloomington, IN: Palibro, 2013.

McNamee, Gregory. "León, Tania (May 14, 1943)," in *Latin Music: Musicians, Genres, and Themes*, ed. by Ilan Stavans, 417–418. Santa Barbara, CA: Greenwood, 2014.

Mendiola, María Elena. "Dar vida a los sueños, que no es lo mismo que soñar," in *Afrocubanas. Historia, pensamiento y prácticas culturales*, ed, by Daisy Rubiera Castillo and Inés María Martiatu Terry, 318–323. Havana: Editorial de Ciencias Sociales, 2011.

Montejo Arrachea, Carmen V. *Sociedades negras en Cuba, 1878–1960*. Havana: Editorial de Ciencias Sociales, 2004.

Moore, Robin D. *Music and Revolution. Cultural Change in Socialist Cuba*. Berkeley: University of California Press, 2006.

Moore, Robin, and Walter Aaron Clark, eds. *Musics of Latin America*. New York: W. W. Norton, 2012.

Morales Flores, Iván César. *Identidades en proceso. Cinco compositores cubanos de la diaspora (1990–2013)*. Havana: Casa de las Américas, 2018.

Morgan, Edmund S. "Slavery and Freedom: The American Paradox." *Journal of American History* 59, no. 1 (1972): 5–29.

Mueller, Adeline. "The Twentieth Century," in *From Convent to Concert Hall. A Guide to Women Composers*, ed. by Sylvia Glickman and Martha Furman Schleifer, 217–303. Westport, CT: Greenwood Press, 2003.

Muguercia, Magaly. *El teatro cubano en vísperas de la Revolución*. Havana: Letras Cubanas, 1988.

Narvaez, Benjamin Nicolas. "Chinese Coolies in Cuba and Peru: Race, Labor, and Immigration, 1839–1886." PhD Dissertation, University of Texas at Austin (2010).

Navarro Vega, Armando. *Cuba, el socialismo y sus éxodos*. Bloomington, IN: Palibrio, 2013.

Notable Americans of 1976–77. Raleigh, NC: American Biographical Institute, 1977.

Obama, Michelle. *Becoming*. New York: Crown, 2018.

O'Reilly Herrera, Andrea. *Cuba. Idea of a Nation Displaced*. Albany: State University of New York Press, 2007.

Orovio, Helio. *Cuban Music from A to Z*. Durham, NC: Duke University Press, 2004.

Orovio, Helio. *Diccionario de la música cubana*. Havana: Letras Cubanas, 1981.

Packer, Renée Levine. "Julius Eastman, a Biography," in *Gay Guerrilla: Julius Eastman and His Music*, ed. by Renée Levine Packer and Mary Jane Leach, 9–74. Rochester, NY: University of Rochester Press, 2015.

Packer, Renée Levine, and Mary Jane Leach, *Gay Guerrilla: Julius Eastman and His Music*. Rochester, NY: University of Rochester Press, 2015.

Pasler, Jann. *Writing through Music. Essays on Music, Culture, and Politics*. New York: Oxford University Press, 2008.

Pedraza, Silvia. *Political Disaffection in Cuba's Revolution and Exodus*. Cambridge: Cambridge University Press, 2007.

Pedraza-Bailey, Silvia. "Cuba's Exiles: Portrait of a Refugee Migration." *International Migration Review* 19, no. 1 (1985): 4–34.

Pendle, Karin, ed. *Women & Music. A History*. Bloomington: Indiana University Press, 1991.

Pendle, Karin, ed. *Women & Music. A History*, 2nd edition. Bloomington: Indiana University Press, 2001.

Pérez Jr., Louis A. *On Becoming Cuban: Identity, Nationality, and Culture*. Chapel Hill: University of North Carolina Press, 1999.

Peyser, Joan. *To Boulez and Beyond*. Lanham, MD: Scarecrow, 2008.

Pignot, Elsa. "El asociacionismo negro en Cuba: una vía de integración en la sociedad republicana (1920–1960)." *Revista de Indias* 70, no. 250 (2010): 837–862.

Piñero, Cecilia. "El eco popular en la escritura culta de Tania León," in *Popular Texts in English: New Perspectives*, ed. by Antonio Ballesteros and Lucía Mora, 255–264. Cuenca: Ediciones de la Universidad de Castilla-La Mancha, 2001.

Piñero, Cecilia. "La riqueza multicultural en la composición de Tania León." *Pauta. Cuadernos de Teoría y Crítica Musical* 28, no. 110 (2009): 20–37.

Piñero Gil, Carmen Cecilia. "Tania León: diálogo con la vida y el arte desde la deconstrucción de las categorías," in *Música y construcción de identidades: poéticas, diálogos y utopias en Latinoamérica y España*, ed. by Victoria Eli Rodríguez and Elena Torres Clemente, 385–397. Madrid: Sociedad Española de Musicología, 2018.

Piñero Gil, Carmen Cecilia, and Eulalia Piñero Gil. "*Scourge of Hyacinths* de Tania León y Wole Soyinka: la universalidad del discurso poscolonial." *Revista Canaria de Estudios Ingleses*, no. 35 (1997): 185–193.

Raines, Robert. *Composition in the Digital World: Conversations with 21st Century American Composers.* New York: Oxford University Press, 2015.

Ramos-Kittrell, Jesús, ed. *Decentering the Nation. Music, Mexicanidad, and Globalization.* Lanham, MD: Lexington Books, 2020.

Ramos López, Pilar. *Feminismo y música. Introducción crítica.* Madrid: Narcea, 2003.

Redmond, Shana. *Everything Man: The Form and Function of Paul Robeson.* Durham, NC: Duke University Press, 2020.

Reyes, Adelaida. *Music in America.* New York: Oxford University Press, 2005.

Reyes Fortún, José. *Biobibliografía de Odilio Urfé.* Havana: Ediciones Museo de la Música, 2007.

Robin, William. "Horizon '83, Meet the Composer, and New Romanticism's New Marketplace," *Musical Quarterly* 102, no. 3–2 (2019): 158–199.

Robinson, Dylan. *Hungry Listening. Resonant Theory for Indigenous Sound Studies.* Minneapolis: University of Minnesota Press, 2020.

Rodríguez Duverger, Nairin. "La Orquesta Sinfónica Nacional de Cuba. Trayectoria artística durante el periodo 1980–2010." Bachelor Thesis, Instituto Superior de Arte (2017).

Rodríguez Rivera, Guillermo. *Decirlo todo. Políticas culturales (en la Revolución cubana).* Havana: Ojalá, 2017.

Rodríguez Rivera, Guillermo. "La fiesta cubana, 1959–1972," en *La canción en Cuba a cinco voces,* ed. by María Elena Vinueza and Carmen Souto Anido, 250–331. Havana: Ojalá, 2017.

Rogers Jr., William F. "The Establishment of the Harlem School of the Arts." *Black Music Research Journal* 8, no. 2 (1988): 223–236.

Roucek, Joseph S. "Changes in Cuban Education since Castro." *Phi Delta Kappan* 45, no. 4 (1964): 193–197.

Rubiera Castillo, Daisy, and Inés María Martiatu Terry, eds. *Afrocubanas. Historia, pensamiento y prácticas culturales.* Havana: Editorial de Ciencias Sociales, 2011.

Rutkoff, Peter M., and William B. Scott. *New School. A History of The New School for Social Research.* New York: The Free Press, 1986.

Sandoval, Chela. *Methodology of the Oppressed.* Minneapolis: University of Minnesota Press, 2000.

Schreffler, Anne C. "The Myth of Empirical Historiography: A Response to Joseph N. Straus." *Musical Quarterly* 84, no. 1 (1999): 30–39.

Sexton, Jared. "People-of-Color-Blindness. Notes on the Afterlife of Slavery." *Social Text* 28, no. 2 (2010): 31–56.

Sindoni, Maria Grazia. "Creole in the Caribbean: How Oral Discourse Creates Cultural Identities." *Journal des Africanistes* 8, nos. 1–2 (2010): 217–236.

Slayton, Michael K., ed. *Women of Influence in Contemporary Music. Nine American Composers.* Lanham, MD: Scarecrow, 2011.

Songe, Alice H. *American Universities and Colleges: A Dictionary of Name Changes.* Metuchen, NJ: Scarecrow, 1978.

Spinazzola, James. "An Introduction to the Music of Tania León and a Conductor's Analysis of *Indígena*." DMA Thesis, Louisiana State University (2006).

Spinazzola, James. "Tania León (1943-)," in *Women of Influence in Contemporary Music. Nine American Composers*, ed. by Michael K. Slayton, 251–298. Lanham, MD: Scarecrow, 2011.

Stavans, Ilan, ed. *Latin Music: Musicians, Genres, and Themes*. Santa Barbara, CA: Greenwood, 2014.

Storhoff, Timothy P. "Beyond the Blockade: An Ethnomusicological Study of the Policies and Aspirations for U.S.-Cuban Musical Interactions." PhD Dissertation, Florida State University (2014).

Straus, Joseph N. "The Myth of Serial 'Tyrany' in the 1950s and 1960s." *Musical Quarterly* 83, no. 3 (1999): 301–343.

Thomas, Susan. *Cuban Zarzuela. Performing Race and Gender on Havana's Lyric Stage*. Urbana: University of Illinois Press, 2008.

Torres, María de los Angeles. "*Donde los Fantasmas Bailan Guaguancó*: Where the Ghosts Dance *el Guaguancó*," in *By Heart/De Memoria. Cuban Women's Journeys In and Out of Exile*, ed. by María de los Angeles Torres, 23–56. Philadelphia: Temple University Press, 2003.

Torres, María de los Angeles. "*El Exilio*: National Security Interests and the Origins of the Cuban Exile Enclave," in *Latino/a Thought: Culture, Politics, and Society*, ed. by Francisco H. Vázquez, 305–326. Lanham, MD: Rowman and Littlefield, 2009.

Torres, María de los Angeles, ed. *By Heart/De Memoria. Cuban Women's Journeys In and Out of Exile*. Philadelphia, PA: Temple University Press, 2003.

Valdés, Alicia. *Diccionario de mujeres notables en la música cubana*. Santiago de Cuba: Editorial Oriente, 2011 [2005].

Vázquez, Francisco H., ed. *Latino/a Thought: Culture, Politics, and Society*. Lanham, MD: Rowman and Littlefield, 2009.

Vinueza, María Elena, and Carmen Souto Anido, eds. *La canción en Cuba a cinco voces*. Havana: Ojalá, 2017.

Walker-Hill, Helen. *From Spirituals to Symphonies. African-American Women Composers and Their Music*. Westport, CT: Greenwood Press, 2002.

Whitney, Robert. "The Architect of the Cuban State: Fulgencio Batista and Populism in Cuba, 1937–1940." *Journal of Latin American Studies* 32, no. 2 (2000): 435–459.

Whitney, Robert. *State and Revolution in Cuba: Mass Mobilization and Political Change, 1920–1940*. Chapel Hill: University of North Carolina Press, 2001.

Wong, Yee Sik. "The Art of Accompanying Ballet Technique Classes." DMA Thesis, University of Iowa (2011).

Wright, Josephine R. B. "African-American Concert Music in the Twentieth Century," in *Music Cultures in the United States. An Introduction*, ed. by Ellen Koskoff, 318–322. New York: Routledge, 2005.

Wright, Josephine R. B. "Art/Classical Music: Chronological Overview," in *African American Music. An Introduction*, ed. by Mellonee V. Burnim and Portia K. Maultsby, 211–244. New York: Routledge, 2006.

Periodicals

Cincinnati Enquirer
Cincinnati Post
Clarion-Ledger
Evening Sun
Granma
Hoy
Independent Press-Telegram
Juventud Rebelde
Los Angeles Times
New York Magazine
New York Times
New York Times Magazine
Progress Bulletin
Statesville Record & Landmark
Theatre Australia
Times
Wall Street Journal
Washington Post
Westport News

Personal Interviews

Amoros, Juan Gabriel
Brouwer, Leo
Buckner, Thomas
Carrero, Sullen
Carrillo, Carlos
Checa, Sara
Diez Nieto, Alfredo
D'Rivera, Paquito
Feliciano, Brenda
González, Niurka
Gonzalo Saura, Yolanda
Herman, Nadine
Hernández, Isabelle
Herrera, Huberal
Hisama, Ellie
Johnson, Virginia
Kent, Adam
Kimura, Mari
Lee, Eun
León, Alain
León, Oscar
León, Tania
León, Yordanka
López Gavilán, Guido
Loyola, José
Mitchell, Arthur
Mooke, Martha
Moulton, Stephanie Jensen
Nazaykinskaya, Polina
Negrón, Angélica
Oja, Carol
Ordieres, Josefina "Fifi"
Pérez Mesa, Enrique
Piñera, Juan
Rodríguez, Caridad "Cachita"
Rosen, Jesse
Singleton, Alvin
Stanyek, Jason
Starobin, David
Valdés, Marta
Vunderink, Todd

Videography

Blackwood, Michael. *The Sensual Nature of Sound: 4 Composers.* New York: Michael Blackwood Productions, 2005.

Discography

40 Most Beautiful Folk Classics. Warner Classics. 825646585663. 2012. (Includes "El manisero," arr. by Tania León).
An AIDS Quilt Songbook: Sing for Hope. GPR Records. 12014. 2014. (Includes *Zero plus Anything* [2014]).
Peggy Benkeser and Laura Gordy, *A City Called Heaven.* ACA Digital Recordings. CM20064. 2003. (Includes *A la par* [1986]).

Thomas Buckner, *New Music for Baritone & Chamber Ensemble*. Mutable Music. 17528–2. 12007. (Includes *Canto* [2001]).

Chanticleer, *Wondrous Love. A World Folk Song Collection*. Teldec. 706301667668. 2006. (Includes "El manisero," arr. by Tania León).

Anthony De Mare, *Liaisons: Re-Imagining Sondheim from the Piano*. ECM. 00028948117819. 2015. (Includes *going . . . gone* [2012]).

Paquito D'Rivera, *La Habana Rio Conexión*. Messidor. 15820–2. 1992. (Includes "Ciego reto" [ca. 1965]).

Foundation Philharmonic Orchestra, *Women Write Music*. ATMA. ACD 2 2199. 1999. (Includes *Batá* [1985, rev. 1988]).

Jubal Trio, *Jubal Songs*. CRI. CD 738. 1997. (Includes *Journey* [1990]).

Adam Kent, *Piano Music by Tania León*. Albany Records. 2021. (Includes *Homenatge* [2011], *Tumbao* [2005], *Momentum* [1984], *Rondó a la criolla* [ca. 1965], *Ritual* [1987], *Homenaje a Prokfiev* [ca. 1965], *Mística* [2003], Prelude No. 1 "Sorpresa" [ca. 1965], Prelude No. 2 "Pecera" [ca. 1965], *going . . . gone* [2012], and *Variación* [2004]).

Mari Kimura, *Polytopia. Music for Violin & Electronics*. Bridge Records. 9236. 2007. (Includes *Axon* [2002]).

Tania León, *Indígena*. CRI eXchanges. CD 662. 1994. (Includes *Indígena* [1991], *Parajota delaté* [1988], *Ritual* [1987], *A la par* [1986], and *Batéy* [1989]).

Tania León, *In Motion*. Albany Records. TROY 1284. 2011 (Includes *Haiku* [1973] and *Inura* [2009]).

Tania León, *Singin' Sepia*. Bridge Records. 9231. 2008. (Includes *Bailarín* [1998], *Singin' Sepia* [1996], *Axon* [2002], *Arenas d'un tiempo* [1992], *Satiné* [2000], and *Horizons* [1999]).

Louisville Orchestra, *Augusta Read Thomas/Tania León*. First Edition Recordings. LCD 010. 1995. (Includes *Batá* [1985, rev. 1988] and *Carabalí* [1991]).

Martha Marchena, *Sonoric Rituals*. Albany Records. TROY 242. 1997. (Includes *Rituál* [1987]).

Marya Martin and Colette Valentine, *Eight Visions. A New Anthology for Flute and Piano*. Naxos. 8.559629. 2009. (Includes *Alma* [2007]).

Meridian Arts Ensemble, *Timbrando*. Channel Classics. CCS SA 25508. 2008. (Includes *Saoko* [1997]).

Mexico City Woodwind Quintet, *Visiones Panamericanas*. Urtext. JBCC051. 2001. (Includes *De memorias* [2000]).

Nodus Ensemble, *Sonidos Cubanos*. Innova. 322. 2010. (Includes *To and Fro* [1990]).

Of Love of You. A Tribute to Emery W. Harper. MSR Classics. MS 1611. 2016. (Includes *Mi amor es* [2015]).

Kane Richeson and Kathleen Murray, *A la Par*. CRI. CD 738. 1997. (Includes *A la par* [1986]).

Elena Riu, *Salsa Nueva*. Somm Recordings. 237. 2005. (Includes *Tumbao* [2005]).

Ana María Rosado, *We've Got (Poly)Rhythm*. Albany Records. TROY 087. 1992. (Includes *Paisanos semos!* [1984]).

Edith Salmen, *Percussion*. Castigo. 02419. 2004. (Includes *A la par* [1986]).

Schanzer/Spear Duo, *Dualities*. Mode Avant. O2. 1991. (Includes *Ajiaco* [1992]).

Sequitur, *To Have and to Hold*. Koch. KIC-CD-7593. 2007. (Includes *Ivo, Ivo* [2000]).

Nanette Kaplan Solomon, *Character Sketches. Solo Piano Music by 7 American Women*. Leonarda. LE 334. 1994. (Includes *Momentum* [1984]).

David Starobin, *Family Album (New Music with Guitar 7)*. Bridge Records. 9239. 2007. (Includes *Bailarín* [1998]).

Eileen Strempel and Sylvie Beaudette, *(In)Habitation. Musical Settings of Margaret Atwood Poetry by American Women Composers*. Centaur. CRC 3002. 2009. (Includes *Atwood Songs* [2007]).

Néstor Torres, *Del Caribe, soy!* Naxos. 8.579016. 2017. (Includes "La conga de Maggie Magalita" [1980]).

Trio Neos, *Mujeres de las Américas. Music of Women of the Americas*. Quindecim. QP 043. 2000. (Includes *Entre nos* [1998]).

Dawn Upshaw, *The World So Wide*. Nonesuch. 79458–2. 1998. (Includes "Oh Yemanja (Mother's Prayer)" [1994]).

Voices of Change, *Voces Americanas*. CRI eXchanges. CD 773. 1998. (Includes *Pueblo mulato* [1987]).

Karen Walwyn, *Dark Fires*. Albany Records. TROY 266. 1997. (Includes *Rituál* [1987]).

Western Wind, *Blessings and Batéy*. Wester Wind. WW 2001. 1993. (Includes *Batéy* [1989]).

Western Wind, *Satires, Ballads, & Bop*. Newport Classics. NPD 85507. 1991. (Includes *De Orishas* [1982]).

Airi Yoshioka, *Stolen Gold*. Albany Records. TROY 1305. 2011. (Includes *Abanico* [2007]).

Index

Abdul, Raoul, 101, 169

Acción Católica (Catholic Action), 36–37

Adams, Diana, 64

Adams, John, 59

African American Music: An Introduction (Burnim and Maultsby), 173

African diaspora: aesthetics of the, 74–92, 145–152, 176–177; historiographic representations of the, 87–92, 173–177. *See also* Dance Theatre of Harlem; León, Tania; migration; race/racism

Afro-Cuban: as label, 176–177. *See also* African diaspora; identity politics; labels; race/racism

Afrocubanas: Historia, pensamiento y prácticas culturales (Rubiera Castillo & Martiatu Terry), 174

Ailey, Alvin, 76, 81–82

Alejandro García Caturla Conservatory, 28–29, 104

Alvin Ailey American Dance Theater Company, 76, 81–82

American Composers Orchestra. *See* Sonidos de las Américas events

American Council for Emigres in the Professions, 61–62

American music. *See* historiography of U.S. Music; León, Tania

American Society of Composers, Authors and Publishers (ASCAP), 97, 113, 217n13

Amoros, Juan Gabriel, 19, 205n13 (TL's second brother). *See also TL's family members*

Anderson, Marian, 77–78, 90, 216n100

Annabella Gonzalez Dance Theater, 104

Año del Vietnam Heróico (Year of Heroic Vietnam), 35–37. *See also* Cuban politics

Anthony, Susan B., 6, 181–182

Arango, Marcelino, "El Gallego," 21, 22

Arcaño y sus Maravillas, 28

Ardévol, José, 29, 131

Armstrong-Jones, Anthony, 123

Artizi, Cecilia, 170

ASCAP. *See* American Society of Composers, Authors and Publishers (ASCAP)

Ashkenazy, Vladimir, 97

avant-garde musical techniques, 137–141. *See also* Cuban contemporary music; León, Tania

Babbitt, Milton, 145

Bacall, Lauren, 98

Badillo, Herman, 62

Baker, Josephine, 90

Balanchine, George, 64–65, 69, 84

ballet. *See* Dance Theatre of Harlem; León, Tania; Mitchell, Arthur

Barrueco, Manuel, 95–96
Bartók, Béla, 22, 117, 134, 137
Batista, Fulgencio, 19–20, 25
Belafonte, Harry, 123
Bernstein, Leonard, 1, 97–98, 121, 212n6
biography: and the author/León's relationship, 2–6, 204n6; and "contrapuntal" methodology, 3–10; theory, genre, and writing of, 1–10. *See also* counterpoint
Bizet, Georges, 79
blackness. *See* African diaspora; race/racism
Blacks in Classical Music: A Personal History (Abdul), 169
Blanco, Juan, 48, 209–210n30
Bland, Ed, 103
Bonds, Mark Evan, 172–173
Borda, Deborah, 181
Borge, Victor, 98
Boulez, Pierre, 99
Brant, Henry, 107
Bravo Academy, 20, 22–23, 120
Brecht, Bertolt, 30
Brigada Hermanos Saíz, 29, 130, 207n46
Brisco, Antonia, 170
Brisco, James R., 171
Brooklyn College, 52, 91–93, 106, 115–116. *See also* León, Tania (as teacher and mentor)
Brooklyn Philharmonia (original name of Brooklyn Philharmonic). *See* Brooklyn Philharmonic
Brooklyn Philharmonic, 78, 85, 95, 100–105, 109–115, 169
Brouwer, Leo, 27, 29, 50–53, 174, 209–210n30
Brown, Minnijean, 60
Brown v. Board of Education (court case), 59. *See also* civil rights movement
Buckner, Thomas, 111–112
Burke, Elena, 29
Burnim, Mellonee V., 173
Burns, Kristine H., 171
Bush, Margaret, 62

Cabrillo Festival of Contemporary Music, 110
Cage, John, 107
Camilo, Michel, 82, 173
canonization, 2, 10, 165–168, 175–176

Carlos Alfredo Peyrellade Conservatory, 20–22, 27–28
Carnegie Hall, 46, 49, 110, 112
Carrillo, Carlos, 115, 118–119
Carrillo, Julián, 10
Carter, Betty, 103, 105
Casal Valdés, Lourdes, 39–40, 42
Castro, Fidel, 20, 26, 31, 34, 57. *See also* Cuban politics
Castro, Raúl, 34, 53. *See also* Cuban politics
Caturla, Alejandro García. *See* Alejandro García Caturla Conservatory
Cervantes, Ignacio, 28
Chagas, Paulo, 175
Chappel, Wallace, 80
Chávez, Carlos, 110
Checa, Fernando, 61, 63
Checa, Sara "Sarita," 61, 63
Chen Yi, 91
Chopin, Frédéric, 26, 28, 62, 117
choreography. *See* Dance Theatre of Harlem; León, Tania; Mitchell, Arthur
City University of New York, Graduate Center, 52
civil rights movement, 2, 59–61, 64–65, 74–77, 90, 213n31. *See also* race/racism
Clark, Aaron, 173–174
Clay, Omar, 101
Clinton, Bill, 46
CMBF, Radio Universal, 23
colonialism. *See also* migration
Comissiona, Sergiu, 97
Community Concert Series. *See* Brooklyn Philharmonic
Companhia Brasileira de Ballet, 64
Composers Now, 1, 113–115, 206n32
Concert Orchestra and Choir of Long Island, 95–96
conducting: as critical concept, 8, 93–94, 115; as a form of teaching and mentoring, 115–119; of music, 11–12, 33–34, 55, 94–99, 115; as transmission of ideas, 93–94, 99–100, 115. *See also* León, Tania
Con Edison, 101
Conservatorio Municipal de Música, 27
Contemporary Anthology of Music by Women (Briscoe), 171–172
Copland, Aaron, 131

Corigliano, John, 8, 124, 128, 165

Cornell University, 126–127

cosmopolitanism. *See* vernacular cosmopolitanism

Cote-Barco, Sergio, 9, 127

counterpoint: as communal/"polyphonic" analysis of works, 9–10, 127–128, 164–165; as scholarly methodology, 3–10. *See also* biography; León, Tania

Cowell, Henry, 107

Creshevsky, Noah, 162

Cuban contemporary music, 27, 34, 51–53, 130–131, 174–175, 208n2. *See also* avant-garde techniques; León, Tania

Cubanos de adentro (Cubans residing on the island) versus *cubanos de afuera* (Cubans living abroad), 7–8, 34, 50–58, 61. *See also* migration

Cuban politics: of gender, 51–53; and the revolution, 2–3, 19–20, 25–27, 31–42, 90; during the Special Period (1990s), 44–46, 208n2, 210n38; Stalinization of (1960–70s), 31–32, 35–42; and the USA, 31, 35–36, 40, 44–46, 52–54. *See also* León, Tania; migration; race/racism

Cubela, Rolando, 25

Cunningham, Arthur, 101–102

Da Costa, Noel, 101–104

dance. *See* Dance Theatre of Harlem; León, Tania; Mitchell, Arthur

Dance Theatre of Harlem: lecture demonstrations/open rehearsals by the, 67–68, 84; social bonds within the, 70, 72–73, 119, 213n42; TL's collaborations with the, 1–2, 65–79, 83–84, 90–92, 132–133; tours by the, 69–72, 78, 83–84, 94–95. *See also* León, Tania; Mitchell, Arthur

Danza Nacional de Cuba, 42–43, 209n30

danzón, 14, 20, 28, 126, 150–152

Davidovsky, Mario, 175

Davies, Dennis Russell, 46, 96, 110–111

Davis, Anthony, 60

de Blanck, Olga, 170

Debussy, Claude, 98, 137

DeCocteau, Dennis, 169

de Falla, Manuel, 108

de Jager, Felicity, 84

de la Vega, Aurelio, 46, 48–49

de los Mederos, Rosa Julia ("Mamota," TL's grandmother): biographical background on, 15–18; passing of, 37, 72; and Santería, 18, 24, 76, 82, 85–86; support of TL and her music, 20–21, 89–90, 119, 182; on TL's romantic life, 30–31. *See also* TL's family members

del Tredici, David, 107

de Paz López-Novoa, Xavier, 109

de Pérez-Goñi, Juana Valles, 20–21

diaspora. *See* African diaspora; migration

Diez Nieto, Alfredo, 13, 28, 47–48, 130–131

Dinizulu and his African Dancers, Drummers and Singers, 104

Domingo, Miguel, 85–86

Dove, Rita, 124

D'Rivera, Paquito, 29, 38–39, 42, 49–50, 104, 211n54

Duffy, John, 105–106, 110

Dunham, Katherine, 82

Eastman, Julius, 81, 101–102, 218n25, 218n29, 218n39

Eckford, Elizabeth, 59

Edwards, J. Michele, 170–171

Edwards, Maurice, 95–96, 219n47

EGREM (record label), 31

Eisenhower, Dwight, 60

Eitler, Esteban, 29

Elliott, Cynthia, 114

Embil, Pepita, 95, 120

Escuela Elemental de Música Manuel Saumell, 45

Escuela Nacional de Instructores de Arte, 45

Escuela Profesional de Comercio de Marianao, 27

Estes, Simon, 108

Experiencing Latin American Music (Hess), 174–175

Fajardo y sus Estrellas, 26

Fanon, Frantz, 179

Fariñas, Carlos, 47

Faubus, Orval, 59

Feble, Ajay, 9

Feminismo y música. Introducción crítica (Ramos López), 172

Fernández, Nohema, 48
Ferneyhough, Brian, 117
Ferrá, Max, 40, 79
Ferrán, Dora ("Mima," TL's mother): bio-
  graphical background on, 14–15, 18; pass-
  ing of, 53; presence in TL's music, 51–52,
  86–87; on the revolution in Cuba, 25–26;
  support of TL and her music, 20–21, 23,
  89–90, 119; on TL's romantic life, 30–31.
  See also *TL's family members*
Festival de Música de Cámara Leo Brouwer.
  See Brouwer, Leo
Ford Foundation, 49, 66, 013
Foss, Lukas, 78, 96, 100, 104–105
Frank, Gabriela Lena, 175
From Convent to Concert Hall (Glickman &
  Furman Schleifer), 172
From Spirituals to Symphonies (Walker-Hill),
  172
Furman Schleifer, Martha, 172

García, Orlando Jacinto, 48–49, 54, 171
Gates Jr., Henry Louis, 60, 85–86,
gender: and Cuban identity, 54–57; dynamics
  at Brooklyn College, 91–92, 116; historio-
  graphic representations of, 87–92, 169–175.
  See also identity politics; León, Tania;
  race/racism
Gewandhausorchester, 108
Gidal, Marc, 152, 177–178
Gilroy, Paul, 178
Glass, Philip, 91
Glickman, Sylvia, 172
González, Niurka, 52
González Moreno, Liliana, 56–57
Gramatges, Harold, 27–28, 46, 48–49, 130–131
Gray, Anne, 171
Green, Ernest, 60
Grupo Teatro Estudio, 30, 207n51
Guerra Suárez, Ramiro, 42–43, 209–210n30
Guevara, Ernesto "Che," 25, 35. *See also* Cu-
  ban politics

Hailstorck, Adolphus, 103
Hakim, Talib Rasul, 101–102, 218n29
Halasz, Laszlo, 95
Hamilton, Judith, 74

Hammoniale Festival der Frauen, 156
Harlem, New York. *See* Dance Theatre of
  Harlem; Harlem School of the Art; León,
  Tania; Mitchell, Arthur; *and other artists
  in Harlem*
Harlem School of the Arts, 63, 65, 103
Havana Festival of Contemporary Music
  (XXIX), 53–57. *See also* National Sym-
  phony Orchestra of Cuba
Henze, Hans Werner, 85–86
Herrera, Huberal, 48
Hess, Carol, 174–175
Hisama, Ellie, 92, 116
historiography of U.S. Music, 168–178. *See
  also* identity politics; labels; León, Tania;
  migration; race/racism
History of Music in Western Culture, A
  (Bonds), 172
Hitchcock, Wiley, 92
Holder, Geoffrey, 8, 75–76, 83–84
Horton, Lester, 74
Hostos Center for the Arts and Culture,
  167–168, 176
Huber, Nicholas, 110
Hughes, Langston, 108

identity politics, 1–3, 75–76, 87–92, 108–9,
  168–183. *See also* gender; labels; León,
  Tania; race/racism
improvisation, 24, 64–65, 117–118, 128–130,
  135–138. *See also* León, Tania
Instituto Cubano de la Música, 47
Instituto de la Pesca, 27
Instituto Hermanos Gómez, 27
INTAR, 8, 40, 79–80
intersectionality. *See* gender; identity politics;
  race/racism
ISCM World Music Days, 161
Ives, Charles, 107, 150, 152

jazz. *See* León, Tania
Jenkins, Leroy, 85
Johnson, Lyndon B., 35
Johnson, Virginia, 68–70, 74–75
Jones, Quincy, 98
Jordan, James, 114
Juilliard School, 94–95

Kamien, Roger, 172

Kaminsky, Laura, 114

Kerman, Joseph, 172

Kesselman, Wendy, 80

Kimura, Mari, 161–162, 225n69

King, Martin Luther, Jr., 64, 77–78, 90, 104

Klotzman, Dorothy, 91, 115

Koch, Ed, 105

Koskoff, Ellen, 173

Koussevitzky, Serge, 97

Krein, Mikhail, 29

labels: Dance Theatre of Harlem's rejection
of, 70, 74–75; and identity, 1–3, 87–92,
167–169, 173–178. *See also* gender; identity
politics; León, Tania; race/racism

Lake, Oliver, 101–102, 122

Lamos, Mark, 87

Lang, David, 91

La Selva, Vincent, 95

Latin American musical identity. *See* historiography of U.S. Music; identity politics;
León, Tania; *and entries about Cuba*

Latinx: as label, 174–175. *See also* identity
politics

League of American Orchestras, 1, 3

Lecuona, Ernesto, 12, 28, 46

Lee, Eun, 166–167

Leginska, Ethel, 170

León, Alain (TL's nephew), 22, 41–44, 53, 55,
153. See also *TL's family members*

León, José (TL's grandfather), 15–16, 21. See
also *TL's family members*

León, Oscar (TL's father): biographical background on, 14–16, 18, 22, 205n13; presence
in TL's music, 141–146; relationship with
TL, 41–44, 58. See also *TL's family members*

León, Oscar José (TL's brother): biographical background on, 12, 18–19; on childhood, 22; on family tension, 38; musical
activities of, 12, 20–23, 27; on the revolution in Cuba, 25–27. See also *TL's family
members*

León, Tania: as advocate for underrepresented
artists and composers of color, 93–94,
100–105, 108–115, 167–168, 179–180; with

the Alvin Ailey Dance Theater Company,
81–82, 214n66; on "American" identity,
178–179; avant-garde techniques of, 137–141;
at the Brooklyn Philharmonic, 95–96,
100–105; and canonization, 2, 10, 165–168,
175–176; at the Carlos Alfredo Peyrellade
Conservatory, 20–22; childhood of, 19–25;
and the civil rights movement, 2, 8, 59–61,
90; at Composers Now, 1, 113–115, 206n32;
compositional process of, 128–130; as conductor of music, 11–12, 33–34, 55, 94–99,
115; on Cuban musical diversity, 176–178;
on Cuban musical influences, 42–44, 52,
80, 131–132, 141–156; and dance counts in
music, 68, 132–133; at the Dance Theatre of
Harlem, 1–2, 65–79, 83–84, 90–92, 132–133;
early conservatory and professional life of,
27–30; early family history of, 14–19, 32;
early neoclassical compositions of, 130–131,
134–137, 142; electronics in the work of,
161–164; emigration from Cuba to the U.S.,
2–5, 35–39, 59–63, 71–73, 88–90, 160–161;
on equality, diversity, and inclusion, 1–3,
108–109, 113–115, 182; on gender in Cuba,
56–57; historiographic representations of,
10, 41, 87–92, 167–175; on identity labels and
politics, 1–3, 8–10, 87–88, 167–168, 175–176;
and improvisation, 24, 64–65, 117–118,
128–130, 135–138; interest in Paris, 2, 24–27,
31–32, 35–36, 60; and jazz, 102–103, 105, 151,
153–154; legacy of, 10, 178–180; marriage
to Eduardo Viera, 30–31, 38; and musical
theater, 78–82, 96; at the New York Philharmonic, 8, 97, 105–110, 113, 181–183; as organizer and cultural broker, 8, 94, 100–115,
219n47; as pianist, 21–22, 27–30, 62–64, 95,
137; popular music interests of, 12, 23–24,
28–30, 80–82, 148–156; as programmer of
Latin American composers, 110–113; and
the revolution in Cuba, 6–7, 25–28, 35–37;
and the Sonidos de las Américas events,
39, 46–50, 110–113; as teacher and mentor,
115–119; technique, style, and voice of, 9–12,
33–34, 42–44, 75–78, 126–165 (*passim*); trips
back to Cuba, 39–44, 50–58; universalism
versus locality in the works of, 176–178; as
vernacular cosmopolitan, 152, 177–178

León, Tania, works, arrangements, and/ or directorship: *Abanico,* 162; *A la par,* 161–162; *Alma,* 51–52; *Arenas d'un tiempo,* 51; *Axon,* 10, 161–164; *Batá,* 10, 44, 127, 145–148, 161; *Batéy,* 82, 161, 163, 173; *Belé,* 83; *The Beloved,* 74; *Carabalí,* 10, 148, 160; *Carmencita,* 79–80; "Ciego reto," 130; *Crisp,* 79; *Death, Destruction, & Detroit,* 81; *Desde,* 152; *Dougla,* 75–78, 84, 141; *Drummin',* 82–83; *Edison,* 81; *Four Pieces for Violoncello,* 10, 44, 141–145, 148, 160–161; *The Golden Windows,* 81; *Haiku,* 74–75, 137–141, 156, 162; *Homenaje a Prokofiev,* 130–131; *Horizons,* 10, 152, 156–161, 174; *The Human Comedy,* 80; *Indígena,* 12, 33, 44, 54–55, 152–156, 160–161; *Kabiosile,* 110, 172, 221n65; *The Lion King,* 81; *Maggie Magalita,* 80; *The Magic of Katherine Dunham,* 82; *Mística,* 51; *Momentum,* 171; *Parajota delaté,* 110; *Permutations Seven,* 125, 219n48; *La ramera de la cueva,* 79; *Rice and Beans,* 79; *Rita and Bessie,* 79–80; *Rituál,* 172; *Rondó a la criolla* (Creole Rondo), 29, 130–132; *Scourge of Hyacinths,* 81, 85–87; *Seven Spirituals,* 108; *Spiritual Suite,* 75–76, 101, 141, 169; *Stride,* 6, 181–183; *Swallows,* 79; *Tones,* 10, 68–70, 78, 132–137, 223n20; *Toque,* 126, 150, 152; *Two Preludes,* 29, 130–131; *The Wiz,* 78–79, 81, 96
León, Yordanka (TL's niece), 22, 38, 45, 150, 152–153. See also *TL's family members*
Ligeti, György, 117
Lincoln Center, 62, 73, 103, 166, 182
Listen (Kerman), 172
listening: as collaborative process. *See* biography; counterpoint; voice
Little Rock Nine, 59. *See also* civil rights movement
López, Edmundo, 22, 24–25, 28–29, 130
López, Jesús, 28
López Gavilán, Guido, 39, 48, 53
López Marín, Jorge
Loyola, José, 29, 39, 47–49

MacDermot, Galt, 80
Machado, Gerardo, 19, 205n14
Malcolm, Carlos, 29
Mamlok, Ursula, 137–138

"Mamota" (TL's grandmother). *See* de los Mederos, Rosa Julia
Mandela, Nelson, 83–84
Manfugás, Zenaida, 28–29, 49, 120, 211n51
Mariatu Terry, Inés María, 174
Martín, Edgardo, 48
Martín, Manuel, 79–80
Masur, Kurt, 105–110. *See also* New York Philharmonic
Maultsby, Portia K., 173
Maynor, Dorothy, 63–65
Meet the Composer program, 105–107, 111, 113. *See also* New York Philharmonic
Mehta, Zubin, 97, 107
Mendiola, María Elena, 174
Mendive, Manuel, 53
Menotti, Gian Carlo, 94–95, 216n1
Messiaen, Olivier, 12
Midori, 98
migration: and colonialism in the Americas, 178–179; and Cuban identity, 7–8, 31–45, 50–58, 87–92, 152, 156, 176–177; Cuban policy toward, 35–37, 44–45, 57, 208n5, 210n38; historiographic representations of, 170–171, 174–175; in pre-revolutionary Cuba, 14–16, 204–205n7. *See also* African diaspora; Cuban politics; León, Tania
"Mima" (TL's mother). *See* Ferrán, Dora
Mitchell, Arthur: on African American art (and his rejection of the label), 70, 74–75, 77–78, 92; author's interview with, 204n6; on counting systems for dancers, 68, 132–133; at the Dance Theatre of Harlem, 2, 64–74, 83–84, 132–137; friendship and affinity with TL, 72–73, 92, 94, 179, 213n42; and neoclassicism, 134. *See also* Dance Theatre of Harlem; León, Tania
modernism. *See* avant-garde techniques; Cuban contemporary music
Modugno, Domenico, 25
Montaner, Rita, 80
Mooke, Martha (TL's partner), 4, 38, 44, 91, 215n74. See also *TL's family members*
Moore, Carman, 101–102
Moore, Dorothy Rudd, 101–102, 109
Moore, Kermit, 104
Moore, Robin, 126, 174, 177
Moravia, Alberto, 85

Morgan, Edmund, 179
Morris, Philip, 101
Mueller, Adeline, 172
Münchener Biennale, 85
Music: An Appreciation (Kamien), 172
Music Cultures in the United States (Koskoff), 173
Music Cultures in the United States (Wright), 173
Music in America (Reyes), 173
Musics of Latin America (Clark & Moore), 174

Nancarrow, Conlon, 107–108
nationality/nationalism. *See* historiography of U.S. music; identity politics; labels
National Symphony Orchestra of Cuba, 5, 12, 33–34, 53–57, 174, 179
Nazaykinzkaya, Polina, 117–118
neoclassicism, 130–131, 134–137, 142
Negrón, Angélica, 117
Neves, Ignacio, 104
New York City. *See* León, Tania; *all individuals and organizations within New York City*
New York City Ballet, 64, 70
New York City Opera, 95
New York College of Music. *See* New York University (NYU)
New York Philharmonic, 8, 97, 105–110, 113, 181–183
New York University (NYU), 62–63, 137, 212n12, 212n14
Nobre, Marlos, 69
Nunez-Medrano, Ivory, 166–167

Obama, Barack, 52–53
Obama, Michelle, 6
Oja, Carol, 92–93, 116
Oliveros, Pauline, 91
Oppens, Ursula, 51, 110
Ordieres, Josefina ("Fifi," TL's friend), 22. *See also TL's family members*
Orozco, Keyla, 48–49, 51
Oteri, Frank J., 178
Ozawa, Seiji, 97–98

Palacio de Bellas Artes, 29, 87
Palmateer Pennee, Donna, 9

Pardo, Enrique, 29
Perea, Alicia, 46–47
Periodo Especial (Special Period). *See* Special Period
Peña, Mario, 40
Pendle, Karen, 170
Pérez Prado, Dámaso, 25
Pérez-Velázquez, Ileana, 48–49
Pickett, Georgiana, 114
Piñera, Juan, 13, 47–50, 53
"polyrhythmic life," 6–7, 178–180, 183. *See also* biography; counterpoint
Popular Guide to Classical Music (Gray), 171
popular music. *See* León, Tania
Prida, Dolores, 79
Prokofiev, Sergei, 131, 134, 137
Puente, Tito, 105, 123

Queen Elizabeth The Queen Mother, *123*
Quinquenio gris (Gray Period), 31, 41. *See also* Cuban politics
Quintero, Héctor, 79

race/racism: and African American arts and identity, 14, 64–65, 70, 74–79, 87–92; and Afro-diasporic arts and identity, 2, 14, 74–92, 145–152, 170–171; at Brooklyn College, 91–92, 116; in Cuba versus the USA, 88–90; as eurocentrism, 175–178; gender and, 60, 87–92; historiographic representations of, 82–92, 168–178. *See also* African diaspora; civil rights movement; and identity politics
Radio Cramer, 23
Raines, Walter, 73–74, 137–138
Raizan, Konishi, 139
Ramos López, Pilar, 172
Ravel, Maurice, 131
religion: in TL's family and childhood, 18, 24–25; in TL's music, 78, 82, 85–86, 146, 153–154. *See also* Santería
revolutionary Cuba. *See* Cuban politics
Revuelta de los sargentos (Sergeant's Revolt), 19. *See also* Cuban politics
Revueltas, Silvestre, 110
Reyes, Adelaida, 173
Riegger, Wallingford, 107
Riley, Terry, 107

Rivers, Sam, 102, 218n31
Robbins, Jerome, 61
Robeson, Paul, 90, 216n100
Robin, Will, 161
Robinson, Dylan, 9
Robinson, Janice, 104
Robinson, Jon, 169
Rockefeller, Nelson, 84
Rodrigo, Joaquín, 95–96
Rodríguez, Santiago, 48
Roldán, Amadeo, 131
Rostropovich, Mstislav, 98
Rubiera, Castillo, 174
Ruggles, Carl, 107

Salfen, Kevin, 156
Salud Street (TL's childhood home), 11, 19–25,
    32, 41–42, 89–90. See also *TL's family
    members*
Santaolalla, Gustavo, 175
Santería: in TL's family and personal life, 18,
    24–25, 76, 206n32; in TL's music, 76–78,
    82–83, 146, 153–154, 210n32
Schleier, Irmgard, 156
Schnüre, Market, 72, 74
Schoenberg, Arnold, 152
Schulyer, Philippa, 156
Schumann, Robert, 62
Schwartz, Francis, 104
Seminario de Música Popular (Cuban Popu-
    lar Music Seminar), 20, 28–30, 130. See
    also *entries on the Urfé family*
Shook, Karel, 65, 73, 77, 123
Simpson, O. J., 108, 220n53
Slayton, Michael K., 173–174
Smith, Bessie, 80
Smith, Federico, 29
Smith, Hale, 101–102
Smith Moore, Undine, 104
Society of Black Composers, 101–102. See
    also Brooklyn Philharmonic
Sonidos de las Américas events, 39, 46–50,
    110–113
Soyinka, Wole, 85–86
Special Period, 44–46, 210n38, 210n41
Spinazzola, James, 155, 157, 173–174
Spohr, Louis, 29

Stanyek, Jason, 91, 116, 118, 145, 161, 164
Staudinger, Else, 61
St. George, Chevalier de, 104
Stravinsky, Igor, 12, 64, 99
stride: as concept, 6–7, 183. *See also* León,
    Tania, works, arrangements, and/or di-
    rectorship
Struthers, J. R., 9
Swanson, Howard, 101–102
Symphony Space, 114

Tan Dun, 91
Tanglewood Festival, 1, 97–98, 131
Taymor, Julie, 81
Teatro Duo, 80
Thorne, Francis, 111
tokenism. *See* identity politics; labels; León,
    Tania
Tower, Joan, 122, 171, 221n67

Urfé, José, 20
Urfé, Joseíto, 20
Urfé, Odilio, 20, 28, 30, 42
Urfé, Orestes, 20, 22, 28, 97

Valdés, Abelardo, 126, 150–152
Valdés, Marta, 13, 30, 207n49
Valera, Roberto, 29, 55
Valle, Rosa, 22
van Haeerden, Augustus, 84
vernacular cosmopolitanism, 152, 177–178
Viera, Eduardo (TL's husband), 30, 38. See
    also *TL's family members*
Viera, Tania (TL's married name). See León,
    Tania
Vuelos de la Libertad (Freedom Flights),
    34–35, 208n5. *See also* Cuban politics;
    migration
voice: as basis for communal/"polyphonic"
    analysis of works, 127–128, 164–165; as sign
    of identity, 41–42, 153; as style and idea,
    8–9, 126–28, 164–165. *See also* biography;
    León, Tania; "polyrhythmic life"

Wagenaar, Bernard, 131
Walker-Hill, Helen, 87–88, 90, 92, 172
Warsaw Autumn Festival, 27

Watkins, Mary, 88, 90
White, José, 104
Williams, Camilla, 95
Wilson, Ransom, 153
Wilson, Robert, 81, 87
Wise, Robert, 61
Women & Music: A History (Pendle), 170
Women and Music in America since 1900: An Encyclopedia (Burns), 171
women in classical music. *See* gender
Women of Influence in Contemporary Music (Slayton), 173

The World of Women in Classical Music (Gray), 171
Wright, Josephine R. B., 173

Yo-Yo Ma, 98

Zafra de los Diez Millones (10-Million Ton Sugar Harvest), 44
zarzuela, 80, 214n59
Zumaque, Francisco, 103
Zweden, Jaap van, 181

ALEJANDRO L. MADRID is a professor of musicology at Cornell University. He is the author of the award-winning *In Search of Julián Carrillo and Sonido 13* and coauthor of *Danzón: Circum-Caribbean Dialogues in Music and Dance.*

Music in American Life

Only a Miner: Studies in Recorded Coal-Mining Songs   *Archie Green*
Great Day Coming: Folk Music and the American Left   *R. Serge Denisoff*
John Philip Sousa: A Descriptive Catalog of His Works   *Paul E. Bierley*
The Hell-Bound Train: A Cowboy Songbook   *Glenn Ohrlin*
Oh, Didn't He Ramble: The Life Story of Lee Collins, as Told to Mary Collins
    Edited by Frank J. Gillis and John W. Miner
American Labor Songs of the Nineteenth Century   *Philip S. Foner*
Stars of Country Music: Uncle Dave Macon to Johnny Rodriguez
    Edited by Bill C. Malone and Judith McCulloh
Git Along, Little Dogies: Songs and Songmakers of the American West   *John I. White*
A Texas-Mexican *Cancionero*: Folksongs of the Lower Border   *Américo Paredes*
San Antonio Rose: The Life and Music of Bob Wills   *Charles R. Townsend*
Early Downhome Blues: A Musical and Cultural Analysis   *Jeff Todd Titon*
An Ives Celebration: Papers and Panels of the Charles Ives Centennial Festival-
    Conference   *Edited by H. Wiley Hitchcock and Vivian Perlis*
Sinful Tunes and Spirituals: Black Folk Music to the Civil War   *Dena J. Epstein*
Joe Scott, the Woodsman-Songmaker   *Edward D. Ives*
Jimmie Rodgers: The Life and Times of America's Blue Yodeler   *Nolan Porterfield*
Early American Music Engraving and Printing: A History of Music Publishing
    in America from 1787 to 1825, with Commentary on Earlier and Later Practices
    Richard J. Wolfe
Sing a Sad Song: The Life of Hank Williams   *Roger M. Williams*
Long Steel Rail: The Railroad in American Folksong   *Norm Cohen*
Resources of American Music History: A Directory of Source Materials from Colonial
    Times to World War II   *D. W. Krummel, Jean Geil, Doris J. Dyen, and Deane L. Root*
Tenement Songs: The Popular Music of the Jewish Immigrants   *Mark Slobin*
Ozark Folksongs   *Vance Randolph; edited and abridged by Norm Cohen*
Oscar Sonneck and American Music   *Edited by William Lichtenwanger*
Bluegrass Breakdown: The Making of the Old Southern Sound   *Robert Cantwell*
Bluegrass: A History   *Neil V. Rosenberg*
Music at the White House: A History of the American Spirit   *Elise K. Kirk*
Red River Blues: The Blues Tradition in the Southeast   *Bruce Bastin*
Good Friends and Bad Enemies: Robert Winslow Gordon and the Study of American
    Folksong   *Debora Kodish*
Fiddlin' Georgia Crazy: Fiddlin' John Carson, His Real World, and the World of His
    Songs   *Gene Wiggins*
America's Music: From the Pilgrims to the Present (rev. 3d ed.)   *Gilbert Chase*
Secular Music in Colonial Annapolis: The Tuesday Club, 1745–56   *John Barry Talley*
Bibliographical Handbook of American Music   *D. W. Krummel*
Goin' to Kansas City   *Nathan W. Pearson Jr.*
"Susanna," "Jeanie," and "The Old Folks at Home": The Songs of Stephen C. Foster from
    His Time to Ours (2d ed.)   *William W. Austin*
Songprints: The Musical Experience of Five Shoshone Women   *Judith Vander*

"Happy in the Service of the Lord": Afro-American Gospel Quartets in Memphis
    Kip Lornell
Paul Hindemith in the United States   *Luther Noss*
"My Song Is My Weapon": People's Songs, American Communism, and the Politics of
    Culture, 1930–50   *Robbie Lieberman*
Chosen Voices: The Story of the American Cantorate   *Mark Slobin*
Theodore Thomas: America's Conductor and Builder of Orchestras, 1835–1905
    Ezra Schabas
"The Whorehouse Bells Were Ringing" and Other Songs Cowboys Sing
    Collected and Edited by Guy Logsdon
Crazeology: The Autobiography of a Chicago Jazzman   *Bud Freeman,
    as Told to Robert Wolf*
Discoursing Sweet Music: Brass Bands and Community Life in Turn-of-the-Century
    Pennsylvania   *Kenneth Kreitner*
Mormonism and Music: A History   *Michael Hicks*
Voices of the Jazz Age: Profiles of Eight Vintage Jazzmen   *Chip Deffaa*
Pickin' on Peachtree: A History of Country Music in Atlanta, Georgia
    Wayne W. Daniel
Bitter Music: Collected Journals, Essays, Introductions, and Librettos   *Harry Partch;
    edited by Thomas McGeary*
Ethnic Music on Records: A Discography of Ethnic Recordings Produced in the United
    States, 1893 to 1942   *Richard K. Spottswood*
Downhome Blues Lyrics: An Anthology from the Post–World War II Era
    Jeff Todd Titon
Ellington: The Early Years   *Mark Tucker*
Chicago Soul   *Robert Pruter*
That Half-Barbaric Twang: The Banjo in American Popular Culture   *Karen Linn*
Hot Man: The Life of Art Hodes   *Art Hodes and Chadwick Hansen*
The Erotic Muse: American Bawdy Songs (2d ed.)   *Ed Cray*
Barrio Rhythm: Mexican American Music in Los Angeles   *Steven Loza*
The Creation of Jazz: Music, Race, and Culture in Urban America   *Burton W. Peretti*
Charles Martin Loeffler: A Life Apart in Music   *Ellen Knight*
Club Date Musicians: Playing the New York Party Circuit   *Bruce A. MacLeod*
Opera on the Road: Traveling Opera Troupes in the United States, 1825–60
    Katherine K. Preston
The Stonemans: An Appalachian Family and the Music That Shaped Their Lives
    Ivan M. Tribe
Transforming Tradition: Folk Music Revivals Examined   *Edited by Neil V. Rosenberg*
The Crooked Stovepipe: Athapaskan Fiddle Music and Square Dancing in Northeast
    Alaska and Northwest Canada   *Craig Mishler*
Traveling the High Way Home: Ralph Stanley and the World of Traditional Bluegrass
    Music   *John Wright*
Carl Ruggles: Composer, Painter, and Storyteller   *Marilyn Ziffrin*
Never without a Song: The Years and Songs of Jennie Devlin, 1865–1952
    Katharine D. Newman

The Hank Snow Story   *Hank Snow, with Jack Ownbey and Bob Burris*
Milton Brown and the Founding of Western Swing   *Cary Ginell,*
    with special assistance from Roy Lee Brown
Santiago de Murcia's "Códice Saldívar No. 4": A Treasury of Secular Guitar Music from
    Baroque Mexico   *Craig H. Russell*
The Sound of the Dove: Singing in Appalachian Primitive Baptist Churches
    Beverly Bush Patterson
Heartland Excursions: Ethnomusicological Reflections on Schools of Music
    Bruno Nettl
Doowop: The Chicago Scene   *Robert Pruter*
Blue Rhythms: Six Lives in Rhythm and Blues   *Chip Deffaa*
Shoshone Ghost Dance Religion: Poetry Songs and Great Basin Context   *Judith Vander*
Go Cat Go! Rockabilly Music and Its Makers   *Craig Morrison*
'Twas Only an Irishman's Dream: The Image of Ireland and the Irish in American
    Popular Song Lyrics, 1800–1920   *William H. A. Williams*
Democracy at the Opera: Music, Theater, and Culture in New York City, 1815–60
    Karen Ahlquist
Fred Waring and the Pennsylvanians   *Virginia Waring*
Woody, Cisco, and Me: Seamen Three in the Merchant Marine   *Jim Longhi*
Behind the Burnt Cork Mask: Early Blackface Minstrelsy and Antebellum American
    Popular Culture   *William J. Mahar*
Going to Cincinnati: A History of the Blues in the Queen City   *Steven C. Tracy*
Pistol Packin' Mama: Aunt Molly Jackson and the Politics of Folksong   *Shelly Romalis*
Sixties Rock: Garage, Psychedelic, and Other Satisfactions   *Michael Hicks*
The Late Great Johnny Ace and the Transition from R&B to Rock 'n' Roll
    James M. Salem
Tito Puente and the Making of Latin Music   *Steven Loza*
Juilliard: A History   *Andrea Olmstead*
Understanding Charles Seeger, Pioneer in American Musicology   *Edited by Bell Yung*
    and Helen Rees
Mountains of Music: West Virginia Traditional Music from Goldenseal
    Edited by John Lilly
Alice Tully: An Intimate Portrait   *Albert Fuller*
A Blues Life   *Henry Townsend, as told to Bill Greensmith*
Long Steel Rail: The Railroad in American Folksong (2d ed.)   *Norm Cohen*
The Golden Age of Gospel   *Text by Horace Clarence Boyer;*
    photography by Lloyd Yearwood
Aaron Copland: The Life and Work of an Uncommon Man   *Howard Pollack*
Louis Moreau Gottschalk   *S. Frederick Starr*
Race, Rock, and Elvis   *Michael T. Bertrand*
Theremin: Ether Music and Espionage   *Albert Glinsky*
Poetry and Violence: The Ballad Tradition of Mexico's Costa Chica   *John H. McDowell*
The Bill Monroe Reader   *Edited by Tom Ewing*
Music in Lubavitcher Life   *Ellen Koskoff*
Zarzuela: Spanish Operetta, American Stage   *Janet L. Sturman*

Bluegrass Odyssey: A Documentary in Pictures and Words, 1966–86   *Carl Fleischhauer and Neil V. Rosenberg*
That Old-Time Rock & Roll: A Chronicle of an Era, 1954–63   *Richard Aquila*
Labor's Troubadour   *Joe Glazer*
American Opera   *Elise K. Kirk*
Don't Get above Your Raisin': Country Music and the Southern Working Class
   Bill C. Malone
John Alden Carpenter: A Chicago Composer   *Howard Pollack*
Heartbeat of the People: Music and Dance of the Northern Pow-wow   *Tara Browner*
My Lord, What a Morning: An Autobiography   *Marian Anderson*
Marian Anderson: A Singer's Journey   *Allan Keiler*
Charles Ives Remembered: An Oral History   *Vivian Perlis*
Henry Cowell, Bohemian   *Michael Hicks*
Rap Music and Street Consciousness   *Cheryl L. Keyes*
Louis Prima   *Garry Boulard*
Marian McPartland's Jazz World: All in Good Time   *Marian McPartland*
Robert Johnson: Lost and Found   *Barry Lee Pearson and Bill McCulloch*
Bound for America: Three British Composers   *Nicholas Temperley*
Lost Sounds: Blacks and the Birth of the Recording Industry, 1890–1919   *Tim Brooks*
Burn, Baby! BURN! The Autobiography of Magnificent Montague   *Magnificent Montague with Bob Baker*
Way Up North in Dixie: A Black Family's Claim to the Confederate Anthem
   Howard L. Sacks and Judith Rose Sacks
The Bluegrass Reader   *Edited by Thomas Goldsmith*
Colin McPhee: Composer in Two Worlds   *Carol J. Oja*
Robert Johnson, Mythmaking, and Contemporary American Culture
   Patricia R. Schroeder
Composing a World: Lou Harrison, Musical Wayfarer   *Leta E. Miller and Fredric Lieberman*
Fritz Reiner, Maestro and Martinet   *Kenneth Morgan*
That Toddlin' Town: Chicago's White Dance Bands and Orchestras, 1900–1950
   Charles A. Sengstock Jr.
Dewey and Elvis: The Life and Times of a Rock 'n' Roll Deejay   *Louis Cantor*
Come Hither to Go Yonder: Playing Bluegrass with Bill Monroe   *Bob Black*
Chicago Blues: Portraits and Stories   *David Whiteis*
The Incredible Band of John Philip Sousa   *Paul E. Bierley*
"Maximum Clarity" and Other Writings on Music   *Ben Johnston, edited by Bob Gilmore*
Staging Tradition: John Lair and Sarah Gertrude Knott   *Michael Ann Williams*
Homegrown Music: Discovering Bluegrass   *Stephanie P. Ledgin*
Tales of a Theatrical Guru   *Danny Newman*
The Music of Bill Monroe   *Neil V. Rosenberg and Charles K. Wolfe*
Pressing On: The Roni Stoneman Story   *Roni Stoneman, as told to Ellen Wright*
Together Let Us Sweetly Live   *Jonathan C. David, with photographs by Richard Holloway*
Live Fast, Love Hard: The Faron Young Story   *Diane Diekman*
Air Castle of the South: WSM Radio and the Making of Music City   *Craig P. Havighurst*

Traveling Home: Sacred Harp Singing and American Pluralism   *Kiri Miller*
Where Did Our Love Go? The Rise and Fall of the Motown Sound   *Nelson George*
Lonesome Cowgirls and Honky-Tonk Angels: The Women of Barn Dance
     Radio   *Kristine M. McCusker*
California Polyphony: Ethnic Voices, Musical Crossroads   *Mina Yang*
The Never-Ending Revival: Rounder Records and the Folk Alliance   *Michael F. Scully*
Sing It Pretty: A Memoir   *Bess Lomax Hawes*
Working Girl Blues: The Life and Music of Hazel Dickens   *Hazel Dickens
     and Bill C. Malone*
Charles Ives Reconsidered   *Gayle Sherwood Magee*
The Hayloft Gang: The Story of the National Barn Dance   *Edited by Chad Berry*
Country Music Humorists and Comedians   *Loyal Jones*
Record Makers and Breakers: Voices of the Independent Rock 'n' Roll Pioneers
     John Broven
Music of the First Nations: Tradition and Innovation in Native North America
     Edited by Tara Browner
Cafe Society: The Wrong Place for the Right People   *Barney Josephson,
     with Terry Trilling-Josephson*
George Gershwin: An Intimate Portrait   *Walter Rimler*
Life Flows On in Endless Song: Folk Songs and American History   *Robert V. Wells*
I Feel a Song Coming On: The Life of Jimmy McHugh   *Alyn Shipton*
King of the Queen City: The Story of King Records   *Jon Hartley Fox*
Long Lost Blues: Popular Blues in America, 1850–1920   *Peter C. Muir*
Hard Luck Blues: Roots Music Photographs from the Great Depression   *Rich Remsberg*
Restless Giant: The Life and Times of Jean Aberbach and Hill and Range Songs
     Bar Biszick-Lockwood
Champagne Charlie and Pretty Jemima: Variety Theater in the Nineteenth
     Century   *Gillian M. Rodger*
Sacred Steel: Inside an African American Steel Guitar Tradition   *Robert L. Stone*
Gone to the Country: The New Lost City Ramblers and the Folk Music Revival
     Ray Allen
The Makers of the Sacred Harp   *David Warren Steel with Richard H. Hulan*
Woody Guthrie, American Radical   *Will Kaufman*
George Szell: A Life of Music   *Michael Charry*
Bean Blossom: The Brown County Jamboree and Bill Monroe's Bluegrass
     Festivals   *Thomas A. Adler*
Crowe on the Banjo: The Music Life of J. D. Crowe   *Marty Godbey*
Twentieth Century Drifter: The Life of Marty Robbins   *Diane Diekman*
Henry Mancini: Reinventing Film Music   *John Caps*
The Beautiful Music All Around Us: Field Recordings and the American
     Experience   *Stephen Wade*
Then Sings My Soul: The Culture of Southern Gospel Music   *Douglas Harrison*
The Accordion in the Americas: Klezmer, Polka, Tango, Zydeco, and More!
     Edited by Helena Simonett
Bluegrass Bluesman: A Memoir   *Josh Graves, edited by Fred Bartenstein*

One Woman in a Hundred: Edna Phillips and the Philadelphia Orchestra
  Mary Sue Welsh
The Great Orchestrator: Arthur Judson and American Arts Management
  James M. Doering
Charles Ives in the Mirror: American Histories of an Iconic Composer   *David C. Paul*
Southern Soul-Blues   *David Whiteis*
Sweet Air: Modernism, Regionalism, and American Popular Song
  Edward P. Comentale
Pretty Good for a Girl: Women in Bluegrass   *Murphy Hicks Henry*
Sweet Dreams: The World of Patsy Cline   *Warren R. Hofstra*
William Sidney Mount and the Creolization of American Culture   *Christopher J. Smith*
Bird: The Life and Music of Charlie Parker   *Chuck Haddix*
Making the March King: John Philip Sousa's Washington Years, 1854–1893
  Patrick Warfield
In It for the Long Run   *Jim Rooney*
Pioneers of the Blues Revival   *Steve Cushing*
Roots of the Revival: American and British Folk Music in the 1950s   *Ronald D. Cohen
  and Rachel Clare Donaldson*
Blues All Day Long: The Jimmy Rogers Story   *Wayne Everett Goins*
Yankee Twang: Country and Western Music in New England   *Clifford R. Murphy*
The Music of the Stanley Brothers   *Gary B. Reid*
Hawaiian Music in Motion: Mariners, Missionaries, and Minstrels   *James Revell Carr*
Sounds of the New Deal: The Federal Music Project in the West   *Peter Gough*
The Mormon Tabernacle Choir: A Biography   *Michael Hicks*
The Man That Got Away: The Life and Songs of Harold Arlen   *Walter Rimler*
A City Called Heaven: Chicago and the Birth of Gospel Music   *Robert M. Marovich*
Blues Unlimited: Essential Interviews from the Original Blues Magazine
  Edited by Bill Greensmith, Mike Rowe, and Mark Camarigg
Hoedowns, Reels, and Frolics: Roots and Branches of Southern Appalachian
  Dance   *Phil Jamison*
Fannie Bloomfield-Zeisler: The Life and Times of a Piano Virtuoso
  Beth Abelson Macleod
Cybersonic Arts: Adventures in American New Music   *Gordon Mumma,
  edited with commentary by Michelle Fillion*
The Magic of Beverly Sills   *Nancy Guy*
Waiting for Buddy Guy   *Alan Harper*
Harry T. Burleigh: From the Spiritual to the Harlem Renaissance   *Jean E. Snyder*
Music in the Age of Anxiety: American Music in the Fifties   *James Wierzbicki*
Jazzing: New York City's Unseen Scene   *Thomas H. Greenland*
A Cole Porter Companion   *Edited by Don M. Randel, Matthew Shaftel,
  and Susan Forscher Weiss*
Foggy Mountain Troubadour: The Life and Music of Curly Seckler   *Penny Parsons*
Blue Rhythm Fantasy: Big Band Jazz Arranging in the Swing Era   *John Wriggle*
Bill Clifton: America's Bluegrass Ambassador to the World   *Bill C. Malone*
Chinatown Opera Theater in North America   *Nancy Yunhwa Rao*

The Elocutionists: Women, Music, and the Spoken Word   *Marian Wilson Kimber*
May Irwin: Singing, Shouting, and the Shadow of Minstrelsy   *Sharon Ammen*
Peggy Seeger: A Life of Music, Love, and Politics   *Jean R. Freedman*
Charles Ives's *Concord*: Essays after a Sonata   *Kyle Gann*
Don't Give Your Heart to a Rambler: My Life with Jimmy Martin, the King of
    Bluegrass   *Barbara Martin Stephens*
Libby Larsen: Composing an American Life   *Denise Von Glahn*
George Szell's Reign: Behind the Scenes with the Cleveland Orchestra
    Marcia Hansen Kraus
Just One of the Boys: Female-to-Male Cross-Dressing on the American Variety
    Stage   *Gillian M. Rodger*
Spirituals and the Birth of a Black Entertainment Industry   *Sandra Jean Graham*
Right to the Juke Joint: A Personal History of American Music   *Patrick B. Mullen*
Bluegrass Generation: A Memoir   *Neil V. Rosenberg*
Pioneers of the Blues Revival, Expanded Second Edition   *Steve Cushing*
Banjo Roots and Branches   *Edited by Robert Winans*
Bill Monroe: The Life and Music of the Blue Grass Man   *Tom Ewing*
Dixie Dewdrop: The Uncle Dave Macon Story   *Michael D. Doubler*
Los Romeros: Royal Family of the Spanish Guitar   *Walter Aaron Clark*
Transforming Women's Education: Liberal Arts and Music in Female Seminaries
    Jewel A. Smith
Rethinking American Music   *Edited by Tara Browner and Thomas L. Riis*
Leonard Bernstein and the Language of Jazz   *Katherine Baber*
Dancing Revolution: Bodies, Space, and Sound in American Cultural
    History   *Christopher J. Smith*
Peggy Glanville-Hicks: Composer and Critic   *Suzanne Robinson*
Mormons, Musical Theater, and Belonging in America   *Jake Johnson*
Blues Legacy: Tradition and Innovation in Chicago   *David Whiteis*
Blues Before Sunrise 2: Interviews from the Chicago Scene   *Steve Cushing*
The Cashaway Psalmody: Transatlantic Religion and Music in Colonial
    Carolina   *Stephen A. Marini*
Earl Scruggs and Foggy Mountain Breakdown: The Making of an American
    Classic   *Thomas Goldsmith*
A Guru's Journey: Pandit Chitresh Das and Indian Classical Dance in Diaspora
    Sarah Morelli
Unsettled Scores: Politics, Hollywood, and the Film Music of Aaron Copland
    and Hanns Eisler   *Sally Bick*
Hillbilly Maidens, Okies, and Cowgirls: Women's Country Music, 1930–1960
    Stephanie Vander Wel
Always the Queen: The Denise LaSalle Story   *Denise LaSalle with David Whiteis*
Artful Noise: Percussion Literature in the Twentieth Century   *Thomas Siwe*
The Heart of a Woman: The Life and Music of Florence B. Price   *Rae Linda Brown,
    edited by Guthrie P. Ramsey Jr.*
When Sunday Comes: Gospel Music in the Soul and Hip-Hop Eras
    Claudrena N. Harold
The Lady Swings: Memoirs of a Jazz Drummer   *Dottie Dodgion and Wayne Enstice*

Industrial Strength Bluegrass: Southwestern Ohio's Musical Legacy
    Edited by Fred Bartenstein and Curtis W. Ellison
Soul on Soul: The Life and Music of Mary Lou Williams   *Tammy L. Kernodle*
Unbinding Gentility: Women Making Music in the Nineteenth-Century
    South   *Candace Bailey*
Punks in Peoria: Making a Scene in the American Heartland   *Jonathan Wright
    and Dawson Barrett*
Homer Rodeheaver and the Rise of the Gospel Music Industry   *Kevin Mungons
    and Douglas Yeo*
Americanaland: Where Country & Western Met Rock 'n' Roll   *John Milward,
    with Portraits by Margie Greve*
Listening to Bob Dylan   *Larry Starr*
Lying in the Middle: Musical Theater and Belief at the Heart of America   *Jake Johnson*
The Sounds of Place: Music and the American Cultural Landscape   *Denise Von Glahn*
Peace Be Still: How James Cleveland and the Angelic Choir Created a Gospel
    Classic   *Robert M. Marovich*
Politics as Sound: The Washington, DC, Hardcore Scene, 1978–1983   *Shayna Maskell*
Tania León's Stride: A Polyrhythmic Life   *Alejandro L. Madrid*

The University of Illinois Press
is a founding member of the
Association of University Presses.

Composed in 10.25/14 Minion Pro
with Proxima Nova Alt Ext and De Driekleur display
by Lisa Connery
at the University of Illinois Press
Manufactured by Sheridan Books, Inc.

University of Illinois Press
1325 South Oak Street
Champaign, IL 61820-6903
www.press.uillinois.edu